The Counselor

THE COUNSELOR
...as if soul and spirit matter
INSPIRATIONS FROM ANTHROPOSOPHY

by

WILLIAM BENTO, PH.D.

EDMUND KNIGHTON, PH.D.

ROBERTA NELSON, PH.D.

DAVID TRESEMER, PH.D. (editor)

SteinerBooks | 2015

Published by STEINERBOOKS
An imprint of Anthroposophic Press, Inc.
610 Main Street
Great Barrington, MA 01230
www.steinerbooks.org

Print ISBN: 978-1-62148-127-0
eBook ISBN: 978-1-62148-128-7

CONTENTS

A Note on the Structure of this Book

This book comes from presentations at seminars on anthroposophic psychology, transcribed, edited, and amended. As such, it does not include all the footnotes and references that professional papers might have. This deficit is remedied somewhat by the many references included in the appendix. We chose this approach as it makes the material much more accessible to the counselor who may be asking "What do I believe about counseling, and where am I going?"

The presenters and authors of this book have a wide variety of experience in anthroposophy, psychology, mental health, and counseling. In a seminar setting, we emphasize the balance between thinking, feeling, and willing. By its nature, a printed book emphasizes thinking, though it can hint at feeling and willing. We invite you to find the feeling realm in relation to anthroposophy and anthroposophic psychology, and to bring these ideas and exercises into your will—into your deeds.

The book has four main sections:

- Two introductory chapters, the first by the editor, and another by William Bento, director of the programs in anthroposophic psychology in the United States of America.
- Fundamental Principles, introduced briefly in that section.
- Reformulating Contemporary Clinical Issues, wherein four major areas of dysfunction and suffering—personality disorders, depression, addiction, and trauma—are approached from the perspective of anthroposophic psychology.
- Inner Development of the Counselor, wherein we address the oft-forgotten member of the team—the counselor—and her or his needs for health and growing.

More about anthroposophic psychology, its worldwide spread, and trainings in this approach can be found on the web at: www.APANA-services.org.

INTRODUCTION

CHAPTER I

The Counselor Inspired by Anthroposophic Psychology

by David Tresemer, Ph.D.

A counselor can be found in many places. A counselor sits with a client who is trying to decide whether or not to take a job offer. A counselor facilitates a group meeting of trauma survivors. A "life coach," a kind of counselor, helps a client make priorities in his or her life. A psychotherapist listens to a client describe dreams of glory from the night before, and guides the client to distinguish the personal associations from the timeless myths activated in the dream. A lawyer, often called a counselor, discusses a pre-nuptial agreement with a client. A medical doctor ponders different choices for surgery with a patient. Friends walk together poring over the feelings of one of them struggling through a painful divorce. Lawyers, policemen, funeral directors, school teachers, eco-tourism guides, human resources departments in every company, the military (when in the "winning hearts and minds" mode), financial planners, social workers, nurses and doctors, wedding planners: All of these involve counseling, some professional, some personal.

An uncle can give warm and wise counsel to a niece or nephew. A "licensed professional clinical counselor" (LPCC) can wear a white lab coat and move through a hospital-like institution for treatment of drug addicts. A counselor can be everything in between. There are thousands of such counselors—some say fifty thousand "life coaches" in the United States alone, in addition to the more thoroughly trained licensed counseling psychologists. If you add in everyone who mentors another, or who listens, counseling includes everybody.

Each form of counseling involves the encounter between someone in need—the client, the friend—and someone who has more life experience, someone who can guide the one in need with recommendations, advice, plans for action ... or simply through listening. Counsel comes from the ancient Proto-Indo-European roots *kom-* (together) and *kele-* (call, speak), sharing these same roots with conciliate, council, and consult.

In any encounter between two human beings, especially where one is asking and the other is giving, there are assumptions—about who are you and who am I, about what it means to be a human being, about where life comes from and where it's going. Assumptions underlie the definition of a "problem," whether it's only a passing bad experience, or an indication of an inherently deficient person, or an opportunity with positive future value. There are assumptions about what is the appropriate exchange for me to engage in your "problem"—money, or you listening to me too, or some other exchange. Many factors determine the quality and outcomes of the encounter. Counselors vary widely in their philosophies and methods. Given the wide variety of human conundrums, there is room for many different forms of counseling.

A recent trend is to treat the human being as a bag of chemicals that can be adjusted by the right psychotropic drugs. In that view, all that matters is physical matter. *The Counselor* asks if soul and spirit matter; the play on the word "matter" is intentional. What *matters*? Is it only something that can be defined by number, weight, and measure? Or can you touch the substantiality of soul and spirit? Can you feel the truth of these phenomena? *The Counselor* speaks about counseling, its content and process, in the many settings in which it occurs; *The Counselor* asks about the counselor as a human being with soul and spirit.

In this book we introduce a way of understanding counseling and the counselor, based on the philosophy of "anthroposophy"—"Anthropos"—Greek for the possible and becoming human being—"Sophia"—the feminine principle of creation from divine thought into living matter. Though I will examine these terms in greater depth below, we can notice a first impression of a cooperation between a cosmic act of creation and the destiny of humanity.

Originally developed by the Austrian philosopher Rudolf Steiner in the early 1900s, and elaborated by others since then, anthroposophy emphasizes the preciousness of each and every human being, because of the workings of soul and spirit. A word should be said about Rudolf Steiner, the historical and continuing source of the intimate understanding of Anthropos in relation to Sophia. Though others have brought his concepts into modern language and applications, there are many ideas and concepts that he shared—amazing conceptions often shared only once in his six thousand lectures, never to be revisited—that help us formulate an entirely new approach to psychology, to the human being, to counseling. He lived from 1861 to 1925. In addition to his many lectures, sometimes four a day on different topics, he wrote a dozen books. He inspired a wide range of initiatives, from Waldorf schools and their special curricula, to biodynamic farming, to anthroposophic medicine, to a comprehensive art of movement named eurythmy, and others. The Anthroposophical Society exists in many countries; the international headquarters are in Dornach, Switzerland.

Though we will reveal many of the principles of anthroposophic psychology in this chapter and in this book, anthroposophy cannot be grasped only with the intellect. An experienced counselor already knows the limits of thinking: The intellect is helpful, but inadequate to the tasks that face a counselor. We need other tools to receive the guidance that anthroposophic psychology has to offer.

The Diverse Needs for Counseling: Response to Pathos

Counselors need to be aware of the full spectrum of needs, even if they can't serve every situation. We can picture the wide range of human problems, concerns, and ailments along a dimension of pathology—from -*ology*, or logos (pattern), of *pathos* (passion, suffering, the human drama): pattern of suffering. We are all entangled in the pathos of life to some extent or another. Too much pathos makes us dysfunctional; too little means we are not prodded to grow. A counselor joins in another's pathos through em-pathy.

Antipathy means that the counselor feels revulsion for the client's pathos—thus *anti* (against) *pathy* (pathos); a reaction of rejection has been triggered in the counselor that the counselor should explore. Sympathy means that the counselor identifies with the pathos of the client; the counselor loses his or her Self. Empathy means that the counselor understands through resonance what the client is going through, as on a parallel track, yet does not drown in it along with the client. In every case, the counselor observes and feels the client's pathos, with empathy the most healthy approach.

The pathos of human experience can range from little to large, creating a kind of Pathos Scale:

The popular *Diagnostic and Statistical Manual* (DSM, version IV, Axis V) features a parallel scale that it calls the GAF, for Global Assessment of Functioning: High on the Pathos Scale means low functioning. The DSM-5 uses the World Health Organization (WHO) Disability Assessment Schedule 2.0. These continua are bumpy and not smooth, just like pathos, just like life.

The writhing knots of pathos grind their constrained and painful cycles over and over in our lives. We respond to pathos with maturity, with pathology, or with both. For counseling, we can observe a series of situations escalating along the continuum of a Pathos Scale, understood by the way the human being responds to pathos:

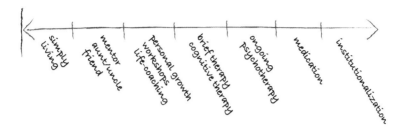

This is obviously simplified, yet helps us understand the continuum of pathos. At the left end, at little pathos, people have no problems, and do not seek counseling; they simply live their lives. Those who have simple problems seek mentoring from friends and relatives: an aunt or uncle becomes a helpful mentor, a helpful piece of advice keeps them going for a long time. Those who have more problems (higher on the Pathos Scale) seek to work with those nagging issues through personal growth, motivational workshops, trainings of all sorts, ropes-courses, self-help books, and life-coaching. These problems can appear as large obstacles in the road of life, but amenable to change: one life-coach training site advertises a course, "How to Change Your Life in Forty-Five Minutes." At this lower level of pathos, such a claim may not be ridiculous. Rhonda Byrne's book and movie, *The Secret,* sold many millions of copies; its formula of positive thinking, in the tradition of Emile Coué and Ernest Holmes, can be very helpful at this level of pathos. At this end of the Pathos Scale, simple fix-its can sometimes work large changes.

Further to the right, "The Top 3 Ways to Fix your Love Life" ceases to be adequate. One finds more serious problems that require better trained counselors who can use methods such as Solution Focused Brief Therapy (SFBT), or Cognitive Behavioral Therapy (CBT), or Dialectical Behavioral Therapy (DBT). It makes a difference if the counselor is thumbing through a manual (in their minds or, as has been occasionally reported, in the session), or is meeting a human soul present in the room. Though Albert Ellis's Rational Emotional Behavior Therapy (father to the three methods just mentioned) can sometimes seem reductionist in its application—"All you've been saying is merely Irrational Belief #5"—Ellis in person was dynamic, funny, intuitive, and confronting. Indeed, he was able to make the "irrational beliefs" come alive, and accomplish great transformations in just a few sessions. Therapists with a formulaic approach can be effective with those with less pathos. Greater pathos demands a more mature counselor.

The person with more pathos—more serious problems— seeks ongoing psychotherapy, suggesting issues more deeply imbedded in the psyche. Even Martin Seligman suggested that learned helplessness took many retrainings, in his studies with traumatized dogs up to sixty, to undo.

As pathos becomes more severe, medications may be brought in. One of the issues of our time is that drugs are brought in far too early, at a level of pathos where the problem could simply be endured, rather than drugged. As Robert Whitaker has documented, the drugs drive people more deeply into pathos when they needn't have gone there. Whitaker calls this an epidemic of iatrogenic (doctor-caused) mental illness, a monumental failure of medicine whose impacts will increase over the coming years. In the terms of this continuum, powerful drugs may push the user up the Pathos Scale. There may be appropriate times when medication must be used, as in intractable schizophrenia, or to help stabilize a person in order to allow for their personal development through therapy. With that said, there is a rampant overuse through prescriptions and self-medication in the world due to the influence of pharmaceutical corporations. There is also the cultural push toward immediate gratification and numbing from any pain. In the coming years, we must ready ourselves to care for the many thousands of people impaired through overuse of medications.

For the most serious levels of pathos, the human being has to be contained and held much more strongly. Increased suffering can lead to outbreaks of violence against self and others. Institutions, from psychiatric hospitals to prisons, have been set up by society to deal with those suffering high pathos.

Each of these levels of pathos requires a different kind of

counseling. Many counselors advertise that they can meet any human being and address any problem, but in truth they cannot. Each of these levels on a Pathos Scale requires a different understanding of the human being and different techniques.

A common assumption in counseling psychology is that we must move the client's Pathos-meter from right to left, from high pathos to less pathos, from suffering to comfort. We assume that our duty is to enable the pursuit of happiness—stated as a right, along with life and liberty, in the Declaration of Independence of the United States of America—Indeed, to maximize happiness! But is this the best goal?

Spiritus and Pathos

To understand anthroposophic psychology in relation to a Pathos Scale, another dimension becomes very helpful, that of Spiritus—low on the scale meaning less developed capacities of soul and spirit, and higher on the scale meaning more highly developed capacities of soul and spirit. Moving vertically accomplishes the various steps of human development—not only to what Erik Erikson called intimacy and generativity, or what Lawrence Kohlberg called post-conventional moral development, or what Sri Aurobindo called self-realization—but further up to what Aurobindo called God-realization, and anthroposophy calls manas, buddhi, and atma. The point here is that there are states of development of Spiritus that are known and described. (Chapters 4 and 5 give other criteria for understanding the development of the human being vertically.)

What happens when we consider a dimension of Spiritus in relation to a dimension of Pathos? In the following, the central horizontal line of the Pathos Scale is exactly as we framed it above. What happens above and below that line, however, differs.

One could easily argue that these shapes should be adjusted this way or that. And certainly there are overlaps and shadings of each approach. However, the essential picture of this diagram yields several realizations.

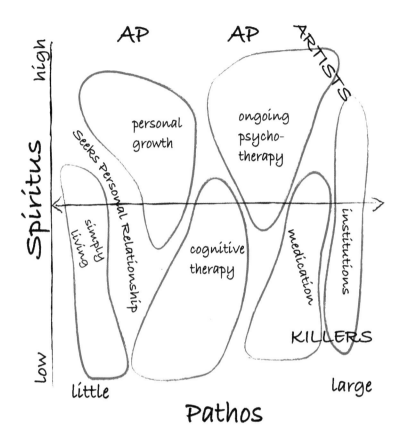

First, the gradations between types of Pathos along the horizontal middle line, and thus the appropriate types of counseling, do not hold true at all levels of development of Spiritus. Any one technique claimed to be good for every person and every condition yields only a partial solution to symptoms and to the course of maturation.

We don't have a GAF or WHO Assessment Scale for Spiritus. In truth, you don't go up and down in Spiritus the same way that you go right and left with your level of suffering. Psychologists can create stress scales to measure right and left. In Spiritus, we often sample many different states all in the same day. This picture depicts the journey of the main mass of one's individuality, the essential progress of one's personal development.

Lifting your Spiritus through soul development does not ensure freedom from pathology. Artists, for example, can often have the challenge of high Pathos; because of high development of soul capacities, this Pathos can be brought into constructive expression (documented in Kay Jamison's amazing book, *Touched with Fire*). In that top right area—large Pathos and high Spiritus—can be found the lives of heroes and heroines who have braved extreme difficulties and then gone on to motivate others to overcome great adversity (as in David Menasche's and Janine Shepherd's stories); while seemingly stories of overcoming pathos, the real stories are a growth in Spiritus.

This upper right corner includes the work of the Spiritual Emergence Network, pioneered by Christina Grof and Emma Bragdon. Their observation has been that people with high Spiritus, and undergoing high Pathos, whether temporary or long-term, can become severely dysfunctional. Because their crisis involves maturation of Spiritus, they should not be drugged but rather cared for in a special way to support that development.

For a long time, people have been seeking these high-Spiritus experiences, and expect that they come with a higher level of pathos (that is hopefully temporary). Here's part of a poem from Rumi, writing in the 13th century: "I want that kind of grace from God that, when it hits, I won't get off the floor for days. And when I finally do stagger into a semblance of poise, I will still need a cane and a shoulder to help me walk, and I will need great patience from any who try to decipher my slurred speech."[1] Rumi expects the high-Spiritus "peak experience" to bring him high-Pathos. Today these symptoms would warrant medication; for Rumi, that would undermine the thoroughness of the foray into high-Spiritus.

The studies from the pre-drug era (prior to the entry of Thorazine in 1954) showed that the great majority of people who experienced depression or anxiety (or any of the other common debilitating diagnoses, including schizophrenia) self-regulated and rejoined their lives after three to twelve months (this re-

---

[1] From Daniel Ladinsky (2002). *Love Poems from God*. New York: Penguin Compass, p. 83.

search from Whitaker). These were episodes of higher Pathos on a rough journey to work out a lift in Spiritus.

Anthroposophic psychology has a unique ability to assist those who have attained high development of Spiritus. Every point in this map of Pathos and Spiritus requires a different quality and content of whole-soul conversation to meet the individual along his or her unique path of development. Understanding the journey in terms of the dynamics of soul and spirit assists one to find the appropriate counseling response.

Exclusively cognitive approaches to therapy are more successful with people who have developed their soul capacities to some extent. Those who have developed more in Spiritus veer away from mechanistic models; they become more interested in approaches that recognize soul and spirit in action. A good cognitive psychologist adapts to these differences in development of Spiritus.

Over the millennia, levels of pathos have always ranged from little to large, though some say that times are getting harder. Anthroposophy asserts that Spiritus for the mass of humanity moves upward over the centuries. Though there have always been those advanced in spiritual development, as well as those very little developed, anthroposophy posits that the bulk of humanity is slowly advancing in spiritual development. This has great importance for a counselor's task in relating to a person in need.

Perhaps the most important revelation of this picture is this: Anthroposophic psychology does not measure success as how far a client moves to the left—diminishing pathos, solving problems, reducing suffering, finding more happiness, adapting more readily to the client's surroundings. Rather, progress is seen when one lifts in the dimension of Spiritus, the strengthening and realization of soul and spirit, moving upward in this diagram. The world is seen as a school for soul growth, rather than as a vehicle for pleasure. Each moves toward the realization that life is not only about individual happiness, but about a task for each and all (more in chapter 6). Progress is thus seen when soul/spirit realities are integrated into awareness, in this picture when one moves vertically. Horizontal movement becomes less important. Of course, crippling pathos has to be dealt with, in service of the increasing ability to develop oneself through stages of sophistication of soul and spirit. The counselor helps the client draw nearer the purpose of a single human life, and all human life—and one finds this through the warmth and interaction of love.

Bringing Soul and Spirit to Mind: What am I?

Despite a common, if vague, understanding of soul and spirit amongst human beings, the profession of counseling psychology often ignores these levels. The word psychology comes from pattern (*logos*) of soul (*psyche*), yet the profession of psychology in the last several decades has turned toward measurable behavior, in other words, what can be seen on the outside.

It's helpful to contemplate different levels of human experience, from large to small. I can define myself in many ways:

1. I am Spirit, in constant play with the stars of the cosmos, and interpenetrated by other spirit beings.
2. I am an individuality, an "I AM," my most true Self, with a continuity spanning lifetimes.
3. I am a Soul, a dynamic interplay of capacities, in constant play with the planetary spheres.
4. I am my Karma, the specific relationships from the past to which this life leads me back again—knots that I have to figure out and untie.
5. I am a character, emphasizing the qualities and eccentricities that I express.
6. I am a personality, a synthetic whole of my heredity (nature) and learning (nurture).
7. I am a gathering of large patterns of conditioned behavior—my complexes.
8. I am a collection of small patterns of conditioned behavior—fixed action patterns, habits, instincts, and every pattern of learned operant-conditioned behavior. I can point to the locations in my physical brain where my behavior is determined.

9. I am my DNA and chemicals that express my unique-
    ness. I am determined by heredity. I believe as true, "I am
    chemicals interacting, determined by the DNA sequenc-
    es gained from my parents—that is the whole of me."
10. I am an immense gathering of sub-atomic particles,
    quarks, gluons, and others.

In this line-up, one can see the roots of psychology from the
Greeks coming from the top of the list. Sigmund Freud focused
further down the list, emphasizing the psychosexual basis of
behavior (in the zone of #5 and #6). Carl Jung expanded back
up the scale to grand visions of mysterious and powerful "archetypes" working from spirit into people's lives. B. F. Skinner
took the focus further down to #8. Many forms of counseling are
quite satisfied if a maladaptive behavior changes after a counseling session that emphasizes changing the way the client thinks
about things.

Medical science based on neo-Darwinism has been pressing
the explanation for "human being" further down. Level #8 includes the rise of neuroscience to explain all thought and behavior—MRI images of the locations in the brain that light up when
you behave in a certain way. The romance with neurology is in
full swing, increasingly sophisticated equipment focusing on ex-
citation of very small areas of the physical brain as the locus,
cause, and consequence of experience and behavior.

Receiving increasing attention is level #9. Francis Crick, co-
discoverer of the structure of DNA, has represented this well:
"'You,' your joys and your sorrows, your memories and your am-
bitions, your sense of personal identity and free will, are in fact
no more than the behavior of a vast assembly of nerve cells and
their associated molecules."[2]

In *Science Set Free*, Rupert Sheldrake, who studied with Crick,
tells the story of how Crick confidently announced that he
would demonstrate that consciousness was entirely determined
by chemistry and, of course, by genetics. The deadline he set for
himself to accomplish this came and passed, and then he met

2 From Francis Crick (1995). *The Astonishing Hypothesis*. New York:
Scribner.

his own dead-line. His contribution to science was immense. Perhaps his concentration on level #9 was necessary to focus his attention toward his discoveries. However, as van der Kolk says in *The Body Keeps the Score*, studies have shown that our behavior and life experience is more determined by our zip code rather than by our genetic code—a clever sound-bite that nonetheless summarizes millions of dollars of research.

So far, no theory of human behavior has gone to #10, which I include to show the folly of insistence on getting to the simplest explanation—reductionism. Some scientists invoke Occam's razor (after the fourteenth century William of Ockham), that is, the principle of parsimony, to explain reality, a goal restated in the terms of the table above as—"Go as far down the list as possible for origins, and don't look up." Such an approach ignores the true complexities of life, evidenced in the wide variety of outcomes from the same input—in every field of inquiry. Reductionism and simplification cross a line somewhere in the middle of these ten steps between I-Thou to I-It, meaning the counselor moves from seeing the other human being as a mystery of aliveness to seeing the other human being as an object whose mechanism may need adjustment. When one moves to I-It, as in the application of therapeutic techniques from a printed manual, the "I" of the other becomes an "It." Just as important, the "I" of the counselor also becomes an "It." One "It" interacts with another "It" according to learned patterns: They begin to look like robots, what we can find in some versions of levels #8 and #9.

Anthroposophic psychology embraces aspects of all of these levels as true. That's important to emphasize—all of these approaches have merit. They serve as appropriate guides at different times. Anthroposophic psychology reminds the counselor, client, and others that levels #1 through #4 are ever present, even if ignored by the materialists concentrating on levels #8 and #9. When you perceive the human being who comes to you in need as soul, as "I AM," and as spirit, this affects the way in which conversation occurs, and in which treatment is planned and evaluated. You have a different frame of reference: "Living your life small" versus "living to your full potential" takes on a much expanded meaning. This larger embrace of human experience makes the job of counseling far more interesting. Too often, a more mechanical approach—at level #8, the systematic reprogramming of stimulus-response mechanisms—makes the counselor into a positive-negative reinforcement automaton. Materialism simply demands efficiency-managers, as in that view there isn't anything else. Not only does this miss the soul content of the client; it degrades the soul experience of the counselor. And, to repeat, some attention to techniques at level #8 may be necessary as well.

An anthroposophic psychology can also assist with the desire of many to jump past the levels further down on the scale in order to seek after the magical secret teachings in the higher levels that will make everything right—a phenomenon we call "spiritual bypass." For some clients, attention has to be turned away from esoteric alchemical formulas for transcendence to what they're eating and how they're sleeping.

Generally speaking, the aim of mainstream psychology as used in clinics and hospitals is to assist the suffering client to adapt to the world; adequate functioning means a manageable level of suffering—a pathos level just less than dysfunction—so that the tasks of daily life can be performed. The troubles are smoothed over; the troublemaker is calmed; the squeaky wheel is oiled; the sufferer moves down the Pathos Scale; the client goes back to work. Labeled a success, the counselor moves on. No attention is given to Spiritus.

Conversely, the apotheosis of a psychology of what some call "creative normals," that is, people lower on the Pathos scale than those suffering debilitating troubles, those who emphasize personal growth and the management of the normal range of crises, dramas, and neurotic styles, is an independent self-realized individuated human being. Individuation is the goal and measure of success—the individual standing as sovereign and apart from others. Where do these goals leave relationship with others? What relation do these successes have to the task of humanity as a whole, the task of Anthropos? Where does this kind of success leave the destiny of the earth, of Sophia?

The Syllables of "Anthroposophic Counseling Psychology"

Twelve syllables is a lot to speak every time you invoke this guidance for a counselor. However, all of these syllables have importance. Here are the roots of those syllables:

Psychology: The story or pattern (*logos*) of soul (*psyche*) and its characteristic patterns. Mainstream psychology has lost sight of the soul and continues to rely more and more on identifying the source and patterns of behavior in neurons and chemicals within the complex of the human body. Transpersonal psychology reclaims the soul, and ventures beyond the personal, including family, country, humanity as a whole (the "anthropos" of anthroposophy), and further out into realms of cosmic mystery.[3]

Anthroposophic psychology: A sophisticated understanding of the genesis of the individual human being from spiritual realms, including ongoing connections with those realms on a daily basis. Distinctive to this approach is a cosmology that elucidates the origin, nature, and destination of the human "I," and perceives the whole of the human soul in action in the world. (The meanings of Anthropos and Sophia are detailed further on in this chapter, in chapter 3, and in chapter 6.)

Anthroposophic counseling psychology: Engaging with another: The "I" of the therapist and the "I" of the client engage in "whole-soul conversation," which includes movement and artistic expression, as well as words. The recently popular counseling technique of Ho'oponopono, an approach portrayed in a book, television show, and other media by Joe Vitale, can best be understood in terms of anthroposophic psychology as interaction at the whole-soul level with another.

An Anthroposophic Counseling Psychologist must learn to speak the languages of conventional psychology, as well as transpersonal and anthroposophic psychology, thereby becoming capable of translating between those languages and articulating the nature and care of the soul. A recent gathering in Dor-

---

3 Rudolf Steiner sometimes used the term Psychosophy—Psyche-Sophia—personal soul and world soul. We use this term on occasion as well. However, as others have used this term in ways not consonant with anthroposophy, we have shied away from using it very much.

nach, Switzerland, of anthroposophic psychologists brought hundreds of people together from all over the world. Training programs now exist in many countries, and recently also in the English-speaking world. An International Federation of Anthroposophic Psychology Associations (IFAPA) links the associations of anthroposophic psychologists in many countries. The Anthroposophic Psychology Associates of North America (APANA), sponsor of this book, is the organization for North America.

What are the Fundamental Principles of Anthroposophic Psychology?

A full explication of anthroposophic psychology would take volumes. This volume moves in that direction. It is not comprehensive; it can't be. Learning about matters of such importance requires a balance, on the one hand, between words and concepts, and on the other hand, learning in the body, learning through the heart, and learning in relation to a mentor.

Anthroposophic psychology understands human existence in ways not found in mainstream psychology. I have found it useful to define anthroposophic psychology by a short list of points of uniqueness. These are *spirit, spirits, bodies, soul, the arts as portals, destiny, stars,* and *humor.* There are more, but this is a good beginning. We can recognize each of these to a degree. As the tip of an iceberg, so to speak, the greater part is submerged below our normal sensory capacity, though we can find out more if we investigate more carefully.

Spirit

Human experience is determined by far more than genes and chemicals. All of creation is permeated with an animated and animating consciousness that we can call spirit. The phenomenon of life—the ability of a plant to rise to the sun and open a blossom, the ability of a human being to start off at nine pounds and end up twenty times that weight—is barely described by modern science, and seldom appreciated for the immensity of the transformation. Life sparks matter to organize; life moves; life has awareness. Life-power is a mystery far beyond matter as stuff.

Rupert Sheldrake's *Science Set Free* is a very valuable resource to answer those who insist on mechanism working on matter as the only truth of existence. Sheldrake demonstrates that mind is not bound by the physical brain, that intuition exists beyond the communication channels of the physical world, etc.—in ways that are meant to assist those who claim that "what you see is what you get" to comprehend a larger picture.

Indeed, mainstream culture (and mainstream psychology) has not kept up with ongoing scientific discoveries—from quantum physics to demonstrations of non-locality (communications traveling instantaneously across distance) to the miraculous healings of self and other in the human body. In my work with the elements fire (warmth), air, water, and earth (with the Sophia Elements Meditations), I have come to realize how little we know of the elements in which we live. Though things generally seem stable and obedient to so-called physical "laws," there are many instances where one can feel spirit moving in oneself, the world, and the cosmos. Indeed, Steiner charged philosophers of the west to establish a new spiritualized cosmogony or story of the origin of this beauteous existence. (More at chapter 6.) Spirit summarizes the mysteries of life and consciousness, the full glory of creation. Spiritus denotes a developmental path toward greater experience and understanding of spirit.

A general sense for "spirit" can be found in the value of myth and dream, often emphasized in Jungian psychology, whose practitioners can point to an immense volume of rich research from Jungian analysts and scholars. However, Steiner had already developed a deep understanding of the power of myths and dreams as pathways of communication with realms of spirit. His contributions simply haven't been codified as yet for the profession of psychology.[4]

Spirits

Anthroposophy posits that spirit works through a host of

---

4 The comprehensive review of counseling psychology by Howard Rosenthal (*Vital Information for Counseling Exams* and *Encyclopedia of Counseling*) states: "Milton Erickson pioneered the story-telling technique." Again, Steiner was there prior to Erickson, though unrecognized.

beings who, unseen by most, though felt by many, are active in the world. Different spirits are identifiable, self-energizing, self-organizing, conscious in their own way, and active in different frequencies of life. Anthroposophy posits spirits ranging from each human being's personal angel to those that govern the orderly orbiting of the planets, and beyond. The full cast of beings is complicated and, since any claim of anthroposophy has to be verified by personal experience, that kind of specific training is beyond the scope of this book.

Anthroposophy identifies both facilitating spirits as well as hindering spirits. Awareness of these forces can bring great assistance to a counselor grounded in anthroposophy, and we recommend that you find the means whereby you can learn more about spirits, both the strengthening ones and the destructive ones.

A psychologist once responded with raised voice to something I said about anthroposophic psychology: "Beings! What do you mean *beings*!? Why add complexity when we can explain everything in a simpler way?" I heard this as, "Why not continue to see the world as dead substance, interacting automatically and chemically in obedience to our commonly accepted physical laws? Why not see people's problems as chemical imbalances or, at best, patterns inherited from parents' genes, or learned from childhood traumas?" The best response to this question is: "Look around you; observe, and observe more. Can you become the true scientist, that is, open in mind and senses?" If you are suspicious of what you view as backward superstitious thinking about "spirits," then I will not be able to sway you through the printed word. I have found that this kind of resistance (and attachment to levels #9 and #10 of the numbered list above) is worthy of acknowledgement, and perhaps can lead to a scientific investigation through careful observation of all of one's senses (note in chapter 6 the invitation to expand those senses). Anthroposophy believes that materialism has valuable contributions, but is not the only way to experience the world.

The general public understands spirits. A recent anti-tobacco advertisement reads: "I am Tobacco. I will waste away your money. Ruin your health. And attack anyone who gets near." But professional psychology doesn't recognize spirits, and semi-professional psychology has only vague references to spirits. An anthroposophic psychology has to be specific about what and who we are dealing with, in those levels #1 through #4.

Anthroposophy understands conscience as the influence of other spirits, either positive spirits helping you make a moral decision, or hindering spirits when you beat yourself up for something that you thought or did. Yes, there are times when conscience is merely the operation of rules and regulations that you learned when young—the superego. Anthroposophy invites you to consider other times when there is truly a voice whispering to you to care for your soul.

Bodies

Let's be honest. To begin with, I don't know who or what I am, nor where I begin and end, nor who's speaking. The common notion that "I" equal my physical body is easily disproven:

1. The clarity of consciousness that I know as "I" does not penetrate my entire body. Many zones remain strange and unfamiliar to my "I," impenetrable.
2. My sense of my "I"—what I know as alive-awake-aware-enthusiastic, my feelings and thoughts—extends far beyond my physical boundaries.
3. In sleep, the disengaged resting physical body does not hold my "I," which roams here and there.
4. Many of my most potently intimate moments delving into creation with completely awake insight have no physicality, indeed no sense of objects, are sometimes non-sensory, and sometimes without orientation or dimension.

Anthroposophy tries to help by identifying several bodies for each individuality. Bodies, plural, generally overlapping, generally agreeing—but not always. We are used to seeing objects whose boundaries we can easily define—a tea cup, an automobile, an umbrella—but not so with the bodies that provide me with the qualities of energy that I value. You might object, "Form follows function, so to the extent that these bodies have function, they must have form."[5] They do not. It's as if we stand together peering into a fog: I point toward subtle qualities of vaguely boundaried shimmerings in that fog. These bodies cannot be defined by out-lines, but rather by in-feeling.

Understanding different bodies working together can be very helpful to a counselor. Anthroposophy proposes four bodies: physical, etheric, astral, and the "I-organization." To these are added further differentiations, though we keep coming back to the basic four. "My inner child," "the puer archetype," "the pain body," "sub-personalities"—these and other formulations are ways of speaking about the multiplicity within. We begin with the basic four.

What we usually identify as the physical body is actually the substance—oxygen, nitrogen, carbon, and others—that manifests the true physical body's brilliant design that organizes the substances.

Animating the physical body is the etheric body (or vital body or life body). Its field of influence extends usually an inch or so outside of the physical body, though it can extend further. You can experience the vitality with a charismatic presenter whose etheric body can extend far beyond the confines of his or her physical body. He or she electrifies the audience with the force of a power that you recognize as it relates to your etheric body. You can experience your own sensing through the etheric body when you "know" where things are in a dark room. You can experience the palpable buzz from a lover, whose touch has life-force in it.

Extending further out than the etheric body, yet interpenetrating to the core, we can find in every human being the astral body. What we experience as emotions are the expressions mostly of the astral body, though the more basic urges and instincts have also a seat in the etheric body. The etheric buzz from beholding a lover also has pictures, associations, poetry, and Love—activity in the astral body. Anthroposophy and other

---

5 From the American architect, Louis Sullivan, "Form ever follows function, and this is the law," and quoted as "law" by many since 1896 when Sullivan wrote these words.

traditions differentiate between parts of the astral body that are more refined and mature—the higher astral—and parts that are less refined and less mature—the lower astral. (As the soul has its seat in the higher astral body, we will revisit qualities of the astral in the section on soul.)

In consonance with oriental medicine, anthroposophy understands each organ system as having its own body. For example, the physical liver is part of a liver system that works independently and collaboratively with other systems. (Chapter 3 relates the organ systems to the four basic bodies.) Fortunately, the many organ systems work together most of the time. When the systems energetically separate, as they do at death and occasionally before death, pathos can increase—and, when embraced consciously, Spiritus can increase as well.

In anthroposophy the physical body is the eldest and most sophisticated of all the bodies. This is very important, as one can often find in mainstream psychology and the culture at large an attitude that the mind is more important than the body. Thomas Edison summarized this: "My body is merely a bucket for my brains." The common approach seems to say: Just calm the pesky physical body with drugs, and then the mind can enjoy its chosen entertainments. The "transcendent man" cyborg predicted by Ray Kurzweil and others elevates the mind and leaves the body behind. Anthroposophy emphasizes the wisdom that can be found in the physical body.

The "I-organization" means the part of me that can speak these words: "I am; I exist; I feel; I know;" and "I feel awake and aware that I am speaking." While we can point at the physical body, and determine its boundaries by the skin, the other bodies are increasingly difficult to locate. Rudolf Steiner wrote of the sense of I as *Ich*, German for I. Translators of the early lectures, influenced by the rising popularity of Freudian theory, felt they had to translate Ich differently from I, and instead wrote "ego," Latin for "I" and used by psychoanalysts since Freud.

How can the "I" be the same in all of these situations—"I can't stop eating chocolate," "I love you," "I hate homework," "I am one with all creation"? Back to not knowing myself, not knowing my "I." There's confusion between "I," I (without quotes), The I (sometimes used in anthroposophic writing), i (a computer has difficulty not capitalizing this letter—why is that?), "I AM" (as in the seven sayings of Christ such as "The I-AM is the way, the truth, and the life"), the I-becoming (as in what Moses heard in the burning bush, ehyeh-asher-ehyeh), me, myself, ego, Ego (we can't do away with these terms because they are so embedded in our language: ego-strength, superego, egoism), self, Self, Higher Self, individuality (meaning not-divisible, a unity), personality (that which sounds or speaks—*son*—through—*per*—a human being, from the term for a mask used in Greek theatre), soul, spirit...

This confusion—this inability to define the edges of containers of soul and spirit—is unavoidable. It comes with the territory of soul and spirit. To communicate with each other, we try to define these, and yet we have to accept the life-infused shifting and changing of all of these vessels for spirit as it comes into manifestation. One can find a variety of references to these bodies in anthroposophical writing and presentations, as well as in this book.

Steiner was clearer when he spoke "I-organization," clumsy yet clearer: Though not boundaried, the I is not diffuse. The I has organization; it has continuity over great spans of time, across lifetimes; the I learns and matures, and (as developed in chapter 6) relates to divine origins for humanity and all creation.

We often field the question, "Can you please define these bodies and soul functions exactly?" This seems a fair question. The answer is, "You have to experience these different bodies and qualities of soul. They do not have clear boundaries that we expect of objects in the world. And you can't hold them outside of you to examine them—they are more inside of you than outside. It takes time to learn about these bodies and kinds of soul. As living aspects of your own being, in relation to living beings around and within you, they are always changing." The questioner sometimes rolls the eyes and insists on accurate definitions, even to the extent of ignoring everything that can not be defined as a tea cup, an automobile, or an umbrella.

Anthroposophy can define the four bodies, and the soul, but cannot guarantee that the listener can understand. The science of consciousness has in some places devolved to a focus on the lowest common denominator, which by its nature makes more refined and subtle capacities difficult to describe and comprehend.

From an understanding of the different bodies, anthroposophic psychology has developed special antennae for "spiritual bypass," when a person would like to "zone out," "get high," and bypass his or her problems in the physical and emotional bodies. Bypassing means going for bliss in the "I-AM," skipping over the hard lessons learned in the bodies of physical, etheric, and astral that mature the individual, that lead to wisdom, insight, and joy, and that form a firmer foundation for experiencing the bliss of the "I-AM" whenever it calls.

Working with several bodies and functions, anthroposophic psychology can also better understand the phenomena of "splitting" and "projection" as dysfunctions of cooperation of the bodies.

A Note on Spiritual Science

Anthroposophy is not opposed to accuracy, and recommends the development of one's capacities for objective observation and critical thinking; indeed, anthroposophy calls this process spiritual science. This kind of science demands that you know yourself—to some greater extent than the norm. Compared to the enormity of the task of knowing yourself, symptoms of pathos look easy. More important, from chapter 13, symptoms can be comprehended as steps along the path to wholeness and full realization of Self. You feel crippled by symptoms? Then give a good look at how crippled you are for want of knowing your soul.

To continue the response to criticisms against the verification of "soul" or "spirit," let's look at mainstream science. Is the mind in the brain inside the cranium, as conventional science assumes? There are examples of people missing parts of their brains yet functioning well. Researchers have recently discovered large nerve plexus centers in the region of the heart, as well as in the gut, leading them to speak about a "second brain" and "third brain," and wondering if there are other locations. One must also examine careful demonstrations of premonition and non-local perception.

Taking a different tack, examine the studies that report on clinical trials of a particular drug. The mode of action of the drug is far from being "accurately defined." The researchers often don't know how it works, and sometimes admit it doesn't always work. Far from it: a drug is deemed successful if it can outperform a placebo sugar pill by a few percent. The developers then give a long list of side effects that often predominate over the intended effect, through unknown pathways. Mainstream science can't be too critical of a psychology oriented to "soul" when it has so loosely mastered the chemical explanation for things.

Soul

In anthroposophy, from its home in the higher astral body, the soul connects the "I" and the world. It has different "qualities" and different "functions." It is the great translator of the spiritual power of the "I-organization" to your sensory organization.

Sometimes in anthroposophy and anthroposophic psychology, the words that I have listed, from "I" to ego to spirit, are used interchangeably. Often they are summarized by the word "soul." It's sloppy yet you must forgive it, as you can only figure out what is intended when you have some experience yourself of these realms, and can begin to make differentiations based on a foundation of your own knowing.

The soul connects, on the one hand, the spirit streaming in glory through the "I," the individuality, with, on the other hand, the demands of the physical world. In anthroposophy, there are different forms and qualities of soul, from sentient soul (enhanced powers of feeling, relating to sensory and sensual stimulation, intense awareness of likes and dislikes) to intellectual soul (also called mind soul, enhanced powers of thinking, rationality and cleverness) to spiritual soul (also called consciousness soul, enhanced powers of will, increased sense of one's "I" ranging from narcissistic individuality to the ability to sense another's "I," thus the route to opening to spirit interpenetrating creation).

The main soul functions are thinking, feeling, and willing, a triumvirate found since ancient times, also termed cognitive, affective, and volitional, or head, heart and hand—or, in the traditions of indigenous cultures, eagle (for soaring thinking), lion (for warmth of heart, in South America the puma), and serpent (for pure doing, the will, dark and silent, sometimes also depicted as an earthy bull). Each realm has to be understood in its own terms. However, some people claim the whole theatre for one of the three. Albert Ellis, founder of Rational Emotive Behavioral Therapy (the precursor of Cognitive Behavioral Therapy, CBT) once said, "There are no feelings. There are only thoughts, and then arousal that you label with your thoughts." CBT has to do with re-orientation of thoughts. The measurable results or "evidence-based" research that the insurance companies rely upon to show the effectiveness of techniques rely on questionnaires to determine a person's thoughts. Anthroposophy, however, finds equal importance in the domains of feeling and will (deeds).

An orientation to soul means that we are not merely dealing with symptoms of dysfunctional behavior and trying to make them go away. We are always feeling the healthy wholeness of the person. Then the symptoms become not the center of the person's life but a flavoring or coloring. Anthroposophy emphasizes artistic expression (and you will see some of that in this book), though we can only hint at some of the movement work that we demonstrate in our seminars, or the work with color and clay, or singing, or drama. The anthroposophic counselor has many more methods available than are usually offered in counseling settings, methods that open avenues for the soul to be present and express its story. For that is the center, the part that we wish to woo back into prominence in the life.

The Arts as Portals

An artistic approach is not a frivolous luxury lagging behind the intellect. Each of the arts provides a portal to different aspects of the human being—to the different bodies. You can come to know the physical on its own through anatomy. You can come to know the etheric body through sculptural-plastic activities with wax, clay, plaster, and other materials. From this you come to know the forces of expansion and contraction, and their combination through invagination, that is, the turning in upon itself of material to create cavitation, that is, space.

You can come to know the astral body through music—rhythm harmony, and melody—which give you a sense of time, playing upon the nerves as upon the strings of a lyre.

You can come to know the "I-organization" through the arts of speech, drama, and poetry, the true value of sounds in how they originate and are continuously empowered from the cosmos, from realms of spirit. You understand the creative power of the Word fully embraced—"In the beginning was the Word"—as vehicle for the "I." The other arts function also as gateways to these insights. They all interlink one human being with another in unique ways.

Destiny

Mainstream psychology emphasizes adaptation to the circumstances of one's present life, and getting through life's stages as best as possible. Anthroposophy understands the present life as one in a series, where the "I" develops through the different circumstances of different lives. Except in rare circumstances, we forget those other lives, as they would otherwise overwhelm our attention for tasks in this one; highly developed people can access those memories. Thus an anthroposophic counselor does not emphasize comfort (low on the Pathos Scale) as the goal of life, rather the development of one's capacities (Spiritus). The notion of karma enters here. Each of us connects with other human beings through deeds and thoughts. We can transform karmic patterns through improved quality of relationship.

Anthroposophic psychology posits that there is a destiny to a human being, and a destiny to humanity, and a destiny to the earth. Consciousness develops in individuals and in humanity as a whole. Anthroposophy can say that Spiritus for all of humanity has evolved over time, that we're in the "Consciousness Soul Age" now, that a large percent of humanity moved into that age in 1413. This is an example of how anthroposophy can be specific. To understand where that date came from requires study. Most important in this context is to say that the quality of life, indeed the quality of matter, was different some thousands of years ago, and will be different in the future, according to grand patterns of development. Thus the counselor and client are part of an evolving structure guided by and infused by spirit and spirits, including a spirit of the times.

Orientation to destiny makes the goal of psychology different. One moves beyond adaptation to suffering, beyond adaptation to a dysfunctional world; one moves beyond individuation as the apotheosis of development. One moves, rather to the importance of relationships, both to solve one's personal karma, as well as to develop the qualities necessary to engage with Anthropos and Sophia.

Anthroposophy has ideas that are difficult to verify only intellectually. One has to develop capacities of soul to understand soul! I would like to give one example, chosen from many possible examples, something Steiner spoke directly about on one occasion. Don't expect to understand the picture from the next three paragraphs, nor to verify it quickly. Do expect to be stimulated to observe your interactions with other human beings more fully. Steiner gave this guidance in relation to teacher and student. However, it pertains exactly to the task of counselor. It goes like this: A counselor often offers herself as a model to the client, hoping that the client will imitate her: "If you become more like me, you'll get better." Far from being flattery, however, imitation misses the opportunity of the encounter and fails at the level of soul. The counselor may be a model human being, yet the life-task of the client may be quite different. Imitation could thus be a wrong turn in the client's life-path. To integrate this view fully would already be a big step for many.

The example gains power by explaining why this is so: The successful encounter of counselor and client involves soul-substance streaming from the next incarnation of the counselor's "I" in interaction with what streams into the encounter from the client's previous incarnation. You may need to read that again, and experience how the understanding of the encounter between counselor and client has suddenly expanded enormously. Time has opened up in both directions. Your thirty-minute sessions suddenly seem more important. "Evidence-based" research seems superficial, unable to contemplate such vistas. You wonder in a new way what brought you into the role of counselor in the first place.

Steiner's suggestion goes further by giving some advice: The encounter works best when the counselor experiences the process musically (that is, through the astral body, feeling inspirations from the future), and the client experiences it sculpturally, as the shaping of stuff (that is, through the etheric body, working with material from the past as with clay or wax). The counselor creates music; the client shapes and re-shapes a palpable life-reality. Such an encounter cannot be defined nor led by a diagnostic nor a technique manual. The encounter involves destiny, something I often find missing in a counselor's understanding of who comes into your office, or sits down with you at the coffee shop. Perhaps this example in more technical anthroposophic language will interest you more deeply in your relationships, as well as in learning more about anthroposophic psychology. Perhaps you will find some way to verify or dispute what was just said.

Stars

Human beings live primarily in a horizontal world, looking neither up to the stars nor down into the earth. Our senses are geared to the horizontal. Anthroposophy understands the great importance of the relation between Earth, Sun, Moon, planets, and stars. Astrology is often mocked for its sloppy thinking, a reputation unfortunately often deserved. However, the references made to astrology in anthroposophy are much more careful and helpful. A counselor can benefit greatly from knowing something about star wisdom, in relation to the counselor's own constitution, in relation to the birth and unfolding life of the client, and even in relation to the day and hour in which the consultation occurs.

Humor

This may seem like a step back from the starry heavens. It is perhaps one of the larger cosmic features. Humor can mean the humors, as in the soul temperaments used in anthroposophy (melancholic, phlegmatic, sanguine, and choleric). It can mean an encounter with paradox, humility, and a great big laugh about all of it—Pathos, Spiritus—so that we don't take these serious matters too seriously. I find this a refreshing insistence from anthroposophy often missing in other disciplines. If we don't treat our foibles with levity, then heaviness will take over and crush us down.

What's Yet to Be Presented

What we give in this book is a foundation for understanding anthroposophic counseling psychology. It begins the process of infusion, a process of living with these concepts and applying them practically, leading to a more fulfilling practice as counselor, for oneself and for one's clients—or patients, or nieces and nephews....

I find it useful to name and briefly speak to some of the topics not covered here, and which will be articulated and discussed in future seminars and publications.

○ *Perception and Memory and other pure psychological phenomena.* Anthroposophy has unique and important views of basic phenomena in the functioning of mind. One must understand how percepts lead to concepts to know how memory functions. One must comprehend the degree to which our picture of Self is a patchwork of perceptions, memories, concepts, and fantasies, joined by bits of psychic thread and glue. One must understand why memories transform over time, under the influence of active soul forces.

○ *The Twelve Senses.* One of great contributions of anthroposophy is the delineation of not five but twelve major senses, the human being's means for assessing the outer environment, as well as the inner environment. Though touched on in this book, the senses deserve a fuller treatment.

○ *Sleep and Dreams.* When asked what is the most important thing to teach young people, the anthroposophic counseling psychologist Karl König replied, "Teach them how to sleep!" Sleep is not simply time-out, undeserving of our attention; it is critical for all of our bodies. Dreams can be greeted as messengers of the work of the soul at night. We must also understand how Ambien, Lunesta, Xanax, and other drugs affect the spiritual work undergone in sleep.

o *Death and birth.* Learning what occurs before birth and after death has a great impact on one's approach to life. What is our relationship to those who have crossed the threshold of death? What is our relationship to those who have yet to be born? How do prenatal and perinatal experiences influence our lives? How can we understand the notion of pre-earthly intentions for this life?

o *Grief and strong emotions.* How does anthroposophic psychology deal with strong emotions? In modern culture, grief is often viewed as disruptive, and therapies have been designed to minimize or remove it. When you understand that relationships often involve long-term connections and struggles between souls—what has traditionally been understood as karma, though anthroposophy has refined the traditional Hindu understanding of karma—then a kind of grief is an appropriate response as the relationship is continued in very different form. With this understanding, a person stuck in the wallows of grief (Pathos) can then be led out more successfully via Spiritus. Other emotions: How is anger understood? Joy?

o *Psychological measurement.* A counselor needs to know about all the tools available to the mainstream, and how to interpret them from an anthroposophic point of view. Anthroposophic psychology uses an apparently old system of the temperaments (melancholic, phlegmatic, sanguine, choleric) in relation to the four bodies (physical, etheric, astral, and I-organization) in a very modern way that reveals the imbalances between the bodies, with clear indications about how to rebalance. In anthroposophy also there is reference to systems of energy—ethers—that science at one time embraced, and then rejected, and may embrace yet again: warmth ether, light ether, sound ether, life ether.... Understanding these has great power to assist those in need.

o *Technique.* We have given some indications of technique

in this book, some from anthroposophic psychology and some adapted from the mainstream. Any existing modality or technique, including Solution-Focused Brief Therapy, and even CBT and DBT, can be enriched when understood within the context of anthroposophic psychology. These techniques deserve further explanation.

o *Artistic expression through color, sound, and movement.* We hint in this book at the use of painting, clay, singing, toning, forms of movement... In an anthroposophic counseling setting, these activities are not relegated to the edges, "if we have time." Often they are more direct lines of communication to the realm of soul than spoken words, or in conjunction with spoken words. It can help to understand one kind of struggle with Pathos and Spiritus as a major-7th and another as a perfect-5th.

o *Drama.* As I have a love of drama, I have always been drawn to Moreno's Psychodrama work, and its many offshoots, also admiring Hellinger's Family Constellation work as drama. How does the connection of anthroposophy with mythic structures (from the medieval story of Parzival to fairy tales to personal dreams), enhance the work of the counselor? Even the games that people play, from the work of Eric Berne, Fritz Perls, and R.D. Laing, can be dramatized to good effect.

o *Supervision and mentoring.* No counselor or therapist, no matter how mature, should be without a mentor or supervisor. What are the guidelines for this relationship?

o *History of psychology and other theories of the human being.* Despite any fashions dominating the current scene, great contributions have been made by our predecessors, whom we should seek to understand. The contributions of others expands when put into an anthroposophic psychological context. Carl Rogers's person-centered therapy becomes much more rich. Sigmund Freud's discoveries become much more meaningful. Shamanism finds its place, as well as neurology.

o *Spiritual beings, a complete guide, including relations to arche-*

types. What are the different spiritual beings with whom a counselor works, with or without awareness of these living powers?

o *Shadow, double, hindering and retarding spirits.* Anthroposophical psychology has a particularly helpful approach when dealing with the negative and repressed sides of human experience, as well as the phenomena of possession. A study of delusions and phantasms can be very helpful for understanding the counselor's role in relation to the client. Anthroposophy has a good grasp of the difference between hindering spirits, in the group affiliated with Lucifer (The Illusionist) or those affiliated with Ahriman (The Hardener), in relation to personal psychological obstacles. This discernment requires a much more careful description.

o *Suicide.* What is the view of anthroposophic psychology on suicide and its ripples on the one who has ceased to function in the body, and on all those affected by such a deed? Would the spiritual understanding of the consequences of suicide impact its rising frequency?

o *Projection versus intuition.* A client doesn't show up at your office—or a nephew doesn't show up at the coffee shop. After fifteen minutes, you call, no answer. You leave a message of concern. A story arises within you of why he didn't show. Later you hear from him and find out that your story was ... true, or not true. If true, was your story clairvoyance and intuition—or was it projection of your own psychodynamics? How do you tell the difference?

o *Transference, counter-transference, projection, clairvoyance, object-relations, transmission, possession....* These dynamics that take place between people (not only between counselors and clients) have a special understanding in anthroposophic psychology.

o *An understanding of the rise of the psychopathic/sociopathic personality, the rise of Asperger's syndrome, extreme sports, and fundamentalism, the fall of empathy, the rapid and vast expansion of incarceration, the fall in the facility of feeling in general, mob phenomena, and more.* These all relate to changes in our collective consciousness, and to the advent of the Consciousness Soul Age, with its unique opportunities and challenges. What do these cultural shifts mean for the individual client? Are the human psyche and the world hardening over time, or loosening, or staying the same?

o *Multi-Cultural.* Interest in this branch of counseling psychology is increasing. Anthroposophy has a very important contribution through the understanding of how folk souls (archangels connected to geography and cultural differences) work through individuals. Whether etic or emic, when you feel the folk souls at work through individuals, you have a much better grasp of the human being before you.

o *Christ.* How can we work with the Christic principle and the life of Christ Jesus in a constructive way that does not end up in clashes of beliefs? How can we avoid the hijacked Christs, the ones set up by zealots either for or against Christianity, and yet find the true zeal of a living principle?

o *Sacred vocation.* An understanding of the soul assists the counselor and client to seek not just a job but a sacred vocation. The profession of counseling psychology began as guidance toward a right use of will, going beyond the commodification of oneself in a "job" to something more related to one's calling and destiny. How does anthroposophy work with and beyond StrengthsFinder?

o *Sexuality, "love," and relationships.* "Love makes the world go round," and anthroposophy offers special approaches for counselors to sexuality, relationship, marriage, and the multi-faceted experiences of love. We differentiate between forms of love—between philia, eros, and agape. We realize the great importance of physical and emotional touch between human beings, as a mode of intimacy that everyone can share. Confusion around the meaning of touch has led to laws prohibiting touch, and thus leading to a kind of starvation amongst the young who need to be touched—in respect, and with nurturance. In a world where pornography is responsible for a significant percentage of internet content how can we find what's healthy in sex?

o *Parenting and education.* Anthroposophy has led to the Waldorf School movement, which has a thousand schools around the world. What are the guidelines that come from anthroposophic psychology for children, for parenting those children, and for leading out (the literal translation of the word education) what lives in seed form in those children?

o *Freedom.* The greatest strength of anthroposophy, and can be its greatest confusion. What guidelines can anthroposophic psychology offer to a counselor in relation to the freedom or constraint-of-freedom of self and client?

o *Gerontology and other life stage issues.* Emphasis on longevity that emphasizes physical survival can actually impede soul growth unless we change the ways that we understand the tasks of advanced years. Why does anthroposophy recommend strongly against parking the elderly in front of a television? What is the task of the elderly? I give a course at Mountain Seas on "Preparing for Longevity" to coach people on what to do with themselves in later years, in essence how to embrace a change of careers and express the wisdom that comes after decades of experience. How can we assist the increasing numbers of the elderly to approach the greatest transition of their lives—through the door of death into realms of spirit? How does anthroposophy address degeneration towards the end of a life?

o *Psychology for the gifted.* Those who come in with extraordinary capacities—how can they be met? How can they deal with the inevitable imbalances between thinking, feeling, and willing?

o *Psychology for those labeled challenged, with developmental or learning disabilities, or differently abled.* Those who cannot do what others do have been institutionalized, tortured, even killed, and also cared for lovingly. The latter approach stands at the center of the Camphill Movement centers begun by anthroposophist Karl König, where the importance of Spiritus is recognized in all human beings.

o *Pharmacology.* How do psychoactive substances—from

Ayahuasca to coffee to benzodiazepines—relate to soul and spirit? What is the impact of the Selective Serotonin Reuptake Inhibitors (SSRIs) on the etheric and astral bodies? Do the popular medicines, such as the most prescribed drug, hydrocodone, chain the soul or liberate it? Prescribed drugs and recreational drugs, as well as dietary choices, require an understanding in terms of the spiritual beings activated, and the organ systems and bodies of the human being most affected. This extends also to an anthroposophic understanding of the rising incidence of chemotherapy, radiation therapy, and electro-convulsive therapy. When are diseases iatrogenic (doctor-caused)?

o *Medicine, nutrition.* Psychology has struggled a hundred years to be seen as separate but equal to medicine. They are, however, not parallel but interwoven. Steiner predicted that nutrition in modern times would be insufficient to support psychological health and spiritual growth. Can we assess this? A medical and nutritional understanding of a client's situation complements insights from anthroposophic psychology. "Stress" is often blamed as the causative agent for both psychological and physical pathos; anthroposophy understands stress not only as pathos, but perhaps as Spiritus-moving, involving turbulence and growth in soul and spirit. Anthroposophic medicine utilizes many herbs and homeopathic preparations, which are more energetic and subtle than mainstream medicines, thus emphasizing the soul and spirit in interaction with the physical and etheric. The present fashion is to find "explanations" for every behavior, feeling, and thinking by identifying specific locations in the brain (neurology) or in genes or in chemicals— what I spoke about above as #9 in the scale of materialism-versus-spirit. We must stand up to this reductionism with complementary facts in realms of soul and spirit.

o *Microbes.* From the point of view of anthroposophy, the rise of destructive microbes can be traced to fear, alarm, and hatred in a nation or culture, an approach touched upon by the field of psychoneuroimmunology, and yet going much further. The symbiosis between the nine trillion microbes now estimated to inhabit each human body and the psyche is little touched by mainstream medicine, nutritional science, or psychology, yet becomes important when we consider microbes as expressions of the life ether and of deep emotional states in the collective of humanity.

o *Statistics.* Though often the dreaded subject in any professional training, and a topic assumed that heart-based anthroposophists would ignore, statistics as a basis for knowing what's true in research is important to understand. We need to examine the ways in which we come to know something as true. We need to look at the underlying assumptions, the tricks of statistical manipulation, the dissonance between experimental designs and claimed results—not only from a technical point of view, but also from an anthroposophic point of view.

o *Star Wisdom.* Cosmogony, cosmology, astrosophy. We have a role in understanding the heavens in relation to individual and world events. We have a role in speaking to the stars. Knowing where you came from has great power in assisting you to awaken to where you are going. Anthroposophy has a brilliant creation story that repeats every moment—immense ages of time with names such as Old Saturn, Old Sun, and Old Moon, culminating in the Earth stage can be experienced daily.

o *Technocracy.* Increasingly, the task of the counselor will be to assist human beings to survive and thrive under the pressure (and domination) of technological influences. Technology can no longer be considered as an incidental aspect of our daily lives, but must be seen in terms of the qualities of spirit forces moving through it. Marshall McLuhan gave prescient warnings. It helps a great deal to understand the media as aspects of the will sphere, delivering an apparent message in the thinking sphere. McLuhan said, "the medium is the message"—not the thought, but rather the way in which we stare at screens. His observations were preceded by Rudolf Steiner's predictions for our time. Practically speaking, how can a "digital native" find a way to soul and spirit? How can we understand "cyber-bullying"? How can we embrace the efflorescence of available knowledge along with the rapid reduction in social and manual skills?

o *Ecology.* As ecological destruction has left wounds to the earth, ecological restoration has increased as a vocation. Ecological restoration has as a prerequisite psychological restoration, in relation to the earth as a whole. Anthroposophy is particularly well suited to describe and encourage a view beyond the improvement of the individual to embrace the whole earth (Sophia—see chapter 6).

o *Space, time, and geometry.* Mainstream psychology accepts the consensual definition of these foundations of reality. Transpersonal, Jungian, Diamond Heart (from Almaas), and anthroposophical psychologies press at the edges of these phenomena. Anthroposophy has a powerful grasp of time flowing both from the past (powers of thinking) and future (powers of will), with feeling in the present moment. Are prescience and prophecy possible, and what are their nature?

o *Other.* There are other topics, of course, that a counseling psychology inspired by anthroposophy would address. This is a growing and changing movement and may it ever be so!

Recommended Resources for Further Study

The main resources for an anthroposophic psychology are at the end of this book. Here are other resources that relate to points made in this chapter:

Bento, William, Robert Schiappacasse, and David Tresemer (2001). *Signs in the Heavens: A Message for Our Time.* Boulder, CO: TheStar-House.org. This study relates social and psychological phenomena of our time to celestial events occurring in 1996 and 1997, in relation to Greek myths, utilizing anthroposophic principles. From the anthroposophic point of view, the so-called laws of the material world, and the "laws" in the worlds of energy and psyche, have not always been the same for millions of years. Indeed, they are changing. This book relates some of these changes to celestial phenomena.

Bragdon, Emma (2013). *The Call of Spiritual Emergency*, eBookIt.com.

Spiritual emergency identifies those in the upper right of the Pathos-Spiritus diagram. The Network helps them move on their way. The American Center for the Integration of Spiritually Transformative Experiences (Aciste.org) also works in this field. Stan and Christina Grof have also been key people in this arena.

Byrne, Rhonda (2006, 2010). *The Secret.* Atria/Beyond Words. It's important to recognize the books that attract people, this one selling over 19 million copies and translated into 46 languages. This approach extends the insights of CBT—the active working with the sphere of repeated pronouncement-thoughts to the exclusion of feeling and willing—to create solutions to material problems. People desperately seek guidance to reduce their pathos, especially if there is a patina of Spiritus behind it. The popularity of books such as this (with its accompanying movie) demonstrates the yearning in people to grow, even though their emphasis appears to be on physical comfort. Without a sense of the aims of soul and spirit, people latch on to material goals.

Drucker, Ernest (2013). *A Plague of Prisons: The Epidemiology of Mass Incarceration in America*. New Press. This paints a picture of the rapid increase in pathos in our society, much of it caused by the American state that imprisons far more people than other countries. That induced pathos makes the journey up through Spiritus more difficult.

Edelstein, Emma J., and Ludwig Edelstein (1998). *Asclepius: Collection and Interpretation of the Testimonials.* Baltimore: Johns Hopkins. I include this to remind us that psychological diagnosis and treatment have been with us for a long time. These hundreds of pages include transcripts and translations of the testimonials made by those who were healed at the psycho-physical healing centers of ancient Greece, the aesclepions, after the Greek god of healing Asclepius, two thousand four hundred years ago. In their gratitude for the healing, the clients hired stone-masons to carve their stories in stone.

Ellis, Albert, and Robert Harper (1997). *A Guide to Rational Living.* Chatsworth, CA: Melvin Powers Wilshire Book Co. This is a fully revised version of the original 1961 book that laid out the principles of Rational Emotive Behavior Therapy which gave the foundation for Cognitive Behavioral Therapy (CBT). We can see it as the manifesto of the intellectual or mind soul. The ten Irrational Beliefs and their antidote are a potent guide to thinking your way through problems, though, from the point of view of anthroposophic psychology, not the full picture of the human being.

Greenblatt, Stephen (2011). *The Swerve: How the World Became Modern*. New York: Norton. In this chapter, I mentioned the year 1413 as a teaser. The anthroposophic origin of that year as the transition to the

Consciousness Soul Age can be found in numerous references in *The Counselor's* appendix. *The Swerve* gives you one perspective on how it happened culturally, through the publication of Lucretius's *On the Nature of Things* which impacted the world like an exploding philosophy-bomb.

Jamison, Kay Redfield (1996). *Touched with Fire: Manic-Depressive Illness and the Artistic Temperament.* New York: Free Press. This brilliant set of biographies illustrates the upper right sector of the Pathos-Spiritus diagram, illuminating the case of artists struggling with high-pathos.

Lahood, Gregg (2010). "Relational Spirituality," parts 1 and 2, *International Journal of Transpersonal Studies*, 29(1), 31-78. This hard-hitting review of the history of Transpersonal Psychology traces the threads of many different philosophies, bringing together valuable insights to find the truth of the origins of transpersonal psychology, and to espouse the importance of relationship in psychology, not simply individuation.

Menasche, David (2014). *The Priority List: A Teacher's Final Quest to Discover Life's Greatest Lessons.* Touchstone. Overcoming adversity appears to be a story of navigating high pathos, but the deep stream involves lifting up through Spiritus.

McLuhan, Marshall (1994). *Understanding Media: The Extensions of Man.* Cambridge, MA: MIT Press. McLuhan presented his ideas in several books and articles.

Seligman, Martin (1995). *Learned Helplessness.* New York: Oxford University Press. One of Seligman's strengths is his slow systematic build-up of his system of thinking about behavior and how humans are trained to be helpless, and in later books (*Learned Optimism*, 2006, and *Flourish*, 2012) how we can reframe our entire approach to life.

Sheldrake, Rupert (2012). *Science Set Free: 10 Paths to New Discovery.* New York: Crown/Chopra. I recommend this work to everyone who would like to understand life in other than level #9 in my list of world-views at the beginning of this chapter. Sheldrake's is the best explanation of ten assumptions of materialistic science that should be questioned, not assumed. This book even gives the reader actual questions that can be put—courteously, of course—to materialistic thinkers.

Shepherd, Janine. In a series of books, including *Dare to Fly* (1998) and *The Gift of Acceptance* (2012), and in a YouTube video, this spunky young woman retells how she was incurably damaged by being run over by a truck (high Pathos). Through love of others and inner will, she becomes a pilot, and has many other adventures, finding the tragedy is a route to higher Spiritus.

Smith, Genevieve (2014) "50,000 Life Coaches Can't Be Wrong: Inside the Industry That's Making Therapy Obsolete," *Harper's Magazine*, May 2014, 29-34. This provides an excellent history of the origins of "life coaching" from Erhard Seminar Training (EST) and Landmark, and the promise from this approach that the training of the will can pull thoughts and feelings into line.

Tresemer, David, with Robert Schiappacasse (2007). *Star Wisdom & Rudolf Steiner: A Life Seen Through the Oracle of the Solar Cross.* Great Barrington: SteinerBooks. There are several biographies of Rudolf Steiner. This one approaches it from the point of view of astrosophy (star-wisdom).

Tresemer, David, and Lila Sophia Tresemer (2015). *The Sophia Elements Meditations.* From SophiaLineage.com.

Vitale, Joe (2013). *At Zero: The Final Secrets to "Zero Limits" The Quest for Miracles Through Hooponopono.* New York: Wiley. This follow-up to his 2008 book with Ihaleakala Hew Len describes further a process that cannot be explained by mainstream psychology, but can be understood by anthroposophic psychology in terms of soul and spirit.

Whitaker, Robert (2010). *Anatomy of an Epidemic: Magic Bullets, Psychiatric Drugs, and the Astonishing Rise of Mental Illness in America.* New York: Broadway Books. This well-documented overview of the forms of psychological discomfort and diminishment, their treatment, and the consequences of various methods has to be seen as a measure of the increasing pathos of our world—with some bright lights that can be understood as the rise of Spiritus.

CHAPTER 2

An Anthroposophic Psychology
by William Bento, Ph.D.

An anthroposophic psychology envisions the human being in his or her continual state of becoming, growth, and development. Rudolf Steiner, the Austrian philosopher who founded anthroposophy, used the term "psychosophy" to refer to an understanding of the innate wisdom of how soul life (*psyche* as Greek for soul) is related to both our earthly embodiment (a key aspect of *Sophia*, Greek for feminine wisdom), and our striving toward a spirituality of human-ness (which we may refer to as Anthropos, the possible human being), thus Anthroposophia. In this approach Steiner links soul life to earthly and cosmic phenomena.

In our times rampant mental illness has given rise to increasing levels of stress, depression, abuse, addiction, and trauma. Very few are exempt from these symptoms of a culture in crisis. Out of the inherent wisdom within an anthroposophic view of the soul, the contributors of this book address various ways in which we can bolster up our psychological resilience and engage in promoting mental health. Sharing these various approaches to anthroposophic counseling is not just meant for the professional counselor working with clients; the hope is that it will have value for all those who are called to advise friends in need of support. The approach taken in this endeavor is not to orient only to pathology, which we find one-sided. Rather we seek to meet the needs of the whole human being. This approach has been termed salutogenesis—creation (*genesis*) of health (*salut!*), a term that harkens back to the ancient Greek understanding that all healing was guided by an image of the wholeness of the human being, an image that comes from the beginning of creation. Rather than concentrate only on alleviating negative symptoms, salutogenesis emphasizes the positive healthy human being.

The content of this book arises from the collaboration of several of the faculty of Rudolf Steiner College's fledging Anthroposophic Psychology Counseling program—Dr. William Bento, Dr. Edmund Knighton, Dr. Roberta Nelson, and Dr. David Tresemer. It gives essential pieces of what was presented in an intensive held at Rudolf Steiner College from July 29 to August 2, 2013, transcribed and amended by the authors. In the years preceding this event, there were a series of conferences on the theme of Psychosophy, aimed at introducing key principles for the development of an Anthroposophic Psychology and Anthroposophic Psychotherapy. Along with the contributors of this publication, gratitude is extended to major contributors to these conferences: Robert Sardello, Cheryl Sardello, Dennis Klocek, James Dyson, and Orland Bishop.

Every attempt has been made to translate the proceedings of this week's intensive in as faithful and representative manner as possible. However, it is beyond the scope of this publication to deliver every word, nuance or experience generated through the artistic and movement exercises that accompanied each presentation. Despite the inevitable shortcomings of attempting to translate lively dynamic presentations into text, the book nevertheless offers every reader something of the unique nature found within an anthroposophic approach to psychology.

The four contributors shared a common objective in their respective presentations. Each stated their desire to create a bridge between anthroposophic approaches to counseling to what exists as best practices in the mainstream of counseling psychology today. Each contributor brought an experiential component to each topic, uniting theory with practical application.

One of the more predominant measures in anthroposophic therapeutics is the employment of a fourfold assessment approach. The organizational design of the week's intensive on anthroposophic counseling was derived from a selective unified perspective of four-foldness in the world of elements, in various paradigms of human experiences, in an appraisal of the core needs of a human being, in the four human bodily sheaths and their respective major organs related to soul life, and in the human being's four basic soul functions. Uniting these perspectives, the fundamental principle of salutogenesis was introduced. Each of these areas deserves extensive treatment. However, this book does not attempt an exhaustive explication of all the vital biological, psychological and spiritual components of human experience. Rather it demonstrates the correlations between ancient and modern perspectives in relation to an anthroposophical world view, as well as indicates an integration of these factors so essential to the make up of the human psyche.

Soul-needs undergo change of focus with every progressive soul stage throughout the human life span. Without an understanding of the themes and tasks that shape and influence the developing human being, emphasized in chapters 4 and 5, it is difficult to rightly assess the dramatic and dynamic unfolding of each life. This area of developmental psychology is greatly enhanced when an anthroposophic lens is applied to it. Distinct to the anthroposophic view is the organizing principle of examining the lifespan in seven-year cycles, the deep description of the unfolding of the physical, etheric, and astral bodies, the significance of the "I" in cultivating the inner dimensions of soul life, the capacity for growing consciously into states of spirituality, and the insights that are born out of following the principles of recapitulation and metamorphosis. Although not included in this exposition, it should be noted that one could add to this approach Steiner's groundbreaking perspectives on human karma and destiny.

Literature in the field of counseling psychology is replete with expositions on the many techniques a counselor may employ with different populations or with individuals with differing diagnoses. Even though research has shown that the most important factor in a counseling situation is the counselor's ability to establish a warm and trusting rapport, psychology as taught in many of the leading universities in the United States stresses techniques found in evidence-based practices without much of an understanding of the basis of the practice. It is as if to say, "You've got the evidence from studies that the technique works, now go through the steps with your client, and everyone will be fine." Yet the long-term success or failure of a counseling process depends more than anything upon the crucial factor of engendering warmth and trust, and not upon the counselor's capacity to deliver a particular psychotherapeutic technique. At the heart of an anthroposophic training of counseling psychology is the art of whole-soul conversation. One of our co-presenters, David Tresemer, has written (at www.apana-services.org), "The art of whole-soul conversation forms the foundation for the activity of *therapeia*, caring and support, what one gives as gratitude to the divine—at the altars in their temples, at the hearth in one's home, and on every meeting with another human being. True conversation—therapeutic conversation—differs from the usual loose talk, chit-chat, alarmism, careless use of words. The kind of conversation that deserves the gold king's aspirations—a conversation that can be helpful to another human soul—requires the development of several capacities in the therapist, who is the bearer of *therapeia*." (Dr. Tresemer gives more background to "the gold king" in chapter 6.) These capacities, necessary to deliver the techniques known to be successful with clients, are all derived from a discipline of genuine attentiveness to the other and the extrasensory phenomena present during the counseling session.

The various embodied exercises introduced in the proceedings of the seminar are here only briefly indicated. The value of whole-soul conversation cannot be translated into simple concepts recorded in words. It must be practiced with one's whole body and soul attention. We are dedicated to teaching counselors. However, what we give here will take them a long way toward understanding the theories and delivering the exercises that work the best.

Reformulating contemporary clinical issues from the vantage point of anthroposophic psychology requires a provisional acceptance of the linkage that Rudolf Steiner was able to make between bodily, soul and spiritual functions within the human being. The four specific clinical pathological conditions explored in this book extend and update the fine work of anthroposophic psychiatrist Rudolf Treichler in his book, *Soulways*. One element emphasized by all contributors is the importance of relying upon accessing the wisdom of the body to gain insights into unusual and/or abnormal states of consciousness. Psychosomatics, although underutilized in the mainstream of counseling psychology, is an essential aspect of any anthroposophic training. Not only does the clinician from an anthroposophic psychology background concentrate on sensations and the felt sense for gathering information, but he or she honors the feelings and thoughts that arise in him or her as well as those shared by the client. These elements widen and deepen assessments that are based solely on behavior.

Rather than using the term "diagnosis," we refer to this analytic activity as assessment. It still entails a weighing and judging, but avoids the connotation of labeling a human being. Diagnosis has unfortunately fallen from its original meaning of two-in-knowing to mean a determination made by an authority (clinician) that defines a person's mental illness. The result of this conception of diagnosis is usually a stigma attached to the human being. The diagnosis represents a summative investigation and carries with it a type of finality. By using the word assessment we are inferring that a formative survey is being done to understand the stresses and dysfunctions of a person in the present. No assessment can be adequately done without gaining the client's self-assessment. This latter point was emphasized throughout the seminar by both didactic explanation and participant exercises designed to demonstrate how assessments could be made and utilized for maximizing a course of counseling.

Based on the matrix of core needs and paradigms of human experience we explored the principles of assessment and the value of prognosis. We explored methods of intervention or treatment in the course of counseling individuals with personality traits that in a strict clinical sense could be called a disorder, as well as counseling individuals experiencing depression, addictions, and/or post-traumatic stress. Each of the above four clinical issues were addressed from the point of view of the *Diagnostic Statistical Manual-5* (2013) of the American Psychiatric Association as well as from the point of view of the phenomenological description from an anthroposophic perspective. In the latter approach a dimensional rather than a categorical model was employed. In the dimensional model, we realize how psychiatric disorders are really a matter of degree of severity of soul imbalances that have become problematic for the individual in some significant way. Through the many practical exercises introduced by William Bento and Roberta Nelson (chapters 9 and 10), it was made very clear that every human being has experienced aspects of these four clinical conditions in varying degrees of severity. The exercises have led and can lead the participant to discover the antidote to the dis-ease or to the soul dissonance.

Serious responsibilities and risks accompany everyone who attempts to engage in the activity of counseling. The tendency to be driven by diagnostic judgments often leads to misdiagnosis and premature conceptions of a client's true condition. The dynamics of projection versus introjection and transference versus counter-transference have their roots in the counseling experience. Being swayed by intense feelings, whether sympathetic or antipathetic, can place the counselor in a state of imbalance. Administering best-practice techniques at the expense of gaining consent from the client or assessing the range of approaches that could be employed often can create more harm than good. For these reasons alone, we repeatedly emphasize the importance of self-care for the counselor (chapter 11).

One route to assuring self-care is the employment of mindfulness and meditative practices (chapter 12). Knighton and Tresemer brought many activities to enhance sustained attention, as well as opening up avenues for engaging in meditations compatible with the practices of an anthroposophic counselor. A few of these practices and meditations have been included in the book to give the reader an opportunity to enter into the experience of its intrinsic value for the counselor.

Another reframe was given to pathology when Bento articulated the critical themes and phenomena of living in the Consciousness Soul Age (a term more rigorously defined in the first chapters). Referring to Rudolf Steiner's bold and prophetic statements aimed at the transition from the 20th to the 21st century, Bento points in chapter 13 to the fact that the esoteric condition of crossing the threshold into the spiritual world—normally a crossing that occurs at death or in very advanced meditation—is now a global event affecting all of humanity. This crossing, when experienced by those unprepared for it, has spawned increased pathology in every nation. The socio-cultural consequences of living in a world governed by technopoly, intent upon severing the human being from nature and into realms of energy for which they are not prepared, cannot be overstated. Learning to see the symptoms of pathology as signs of an initiatory process that all of humankind is going through can liberate the postmodern human being from the existential despair and dread that accompanies these changes. It provides a soul-spiritual context for re-discovering the meaning of life, as well as instilling hope in the future of humankind.

Expanding upon a lecture given by Rudolf Steiner, entitled "The Dissociation of the Human Personality through Initiation" (1909), Bento presents the dis-ordering of human society taking place in our time and the incessant exposure to evil, necessitating a greater wakefulness on the part of every human being. We make a plea in presenting an anthroposophic psychology to meet the ills of our time: to undertake a path of Christian initiation consciously and courageously, to be willing to see this approach to counseling as a pastoral path, wherein the sacraments of conversation carry the healing forces so needed in today's world.

For the anthroposophic counselor, the mandate is to find the healing spirit and invite its presence into each and every encounter. In the highest ideal this means to be a mediator between the divine Sophia (Wisdom) and that being who has endowed each of us with the spark of divinity, the "I AM," namely the Anthropos, the truly human. We conclude our book in the same way we concluded our seminar, with a deep gratitude for being able to celebrate the gifts given to us from Anthroposophia.

FUNDAMENTAL PRINCIPLES

INTRODUCTION TO FUNDAMENTAL PRINCIPLES
by David Tresemer, Ph.D.

In the seminars from which this book was transcribed and edited, and in all our work with anthroposophic counseling psychology, we emphasize the healthy, the true, the beautiful, and the good. Rather than detailing the strange and pathological things that people do, the quirky and the dangerous, we emphasize the normal and ideal course of development.

The foundations for a counseling psychology based on anthroposophy are not summarized in one place. The general introduction by David Tresemer (chapter 1) gives one way of speaking about it, as a quick list of key words—spirit, spirits, bodies, soul, the arts as portals, destiny, stars, and humor—each identifying a tip of an iceberg, each requiring further explanation. Though other aspects of fundamental principles can be found throughout the book, this section concentrates on those foundations. They give a good beginning, which we intend to follow in the future.

In chapter 3, William Bento proposes "salutogenesis," health-creating, as a foundation of understanding several overlapping four-fold schema that put the task of counseling into perspective. His analysis integrates the approaches of several other theories of human behavior and experience.

We have emphasized in chapters 4 and 5 the life phases of the human being. Some prefer the terms biological stages or life-stages, different ways of coming to understand the astonishing changes that occur over time in each of our lives. These two chapters bring forward the unique perspectives of these experienced authors. Each has an appendix that brings a wealth of additional information. In a teaching setting, we don't hand out papers such as you find in these appendices without thorough explanations, both theoretical and practical. However, the authors wanted to share their insights so we've added these pieces with the hopes that you will take the time to unpack these very concentrated charts. At the end of chapter 4, Roberta Nelson has shared her version of the seven adult learning processes fundamental to anthroposophy. At the end of chapter 5, Edmund Knighton has given a wide-ranging view of seven-fold processes and phenomena found in the world. Their virtue is that they can be overlapped one with the other, and with the sevenfold aspects of the human life span, for further insight into the task of each life period.

While in the seminar, both Nelson and Knighton recognized the power of prenatal and perinatal experiences. Elaboration of these areas will await a further publication.

In future, other aspects of anthroposophy can be featured as foundations. We begin with the mystery of the many lives within the one life, changing over the course of the years.

In chapter 6, the stage broadens to include the cosmos and the human being's relation to it. Anthroposophy is found in Anthropos and Sophia. Perhaps in politics the rule is "follow the money." Here, you have to "follow the concepts—follow the names—and follow the sounds" to find the origins and keys to a world in which soul and spirit matter.

In all, we emphasize the fundamental goodness of the human being, expressed most clearly in chapter 3. In this, we find support in "the humanist psychology of Fromm, Maslow and Rogers, where the humanum, the essential core of every individual, is considered to be always sound"—from the writing of Michaela Gloeckler, a leading spokesperson for anthroposophic medicine and psychology.

Suggested Resources for Further Study

Gloeckler, M. (2001). Preface. In H. Dekkers-Appel, A. Dekkers, & A. Meuss (Eds.), *Psychotherapy and Humanity's Struggle to Endure*. Dornach: Verlag am Goetheanum. I quote from page 9 of her preface.

CHAPTER 3

Salutogenesis: Foundation for Anthroposophic Counseling Psychology
by William Bento, Ph.D.

The anthroposophic approach to counseling is based on a very different paradigm of the human being than the one popularized in today's conventional understanding of psychology and counseling. I would like to frame our approach within the context of *Salutogenesis*, rather than within the modern picture of the human being as broken, fragmented, and disoriented.

The pathological orientation in mainstream psychology is not the best route if we are trying to reach some kind of healing or resolution. *Salut!*—health!, vitality!, life-force!—*Genesis*—the continual blossoming and development of this vitality. This leads us in a better direction. Salutogenesis means the capacity to see the human being as a whole being, as a being that has full potential and capacity for self-generation and self-healing. In the beginning—in the genesis of the human being—each was given all that he or she needed for wholeness and development. That should always be the guiding principle with which we work. The guiding question for us is: "How do we redirect ourselves to our wholesomeness and our innate movement forward as thriving human beings?" Salutogenesis guides us to look at accessing that which lies in the beginning, even if it's presently dormant. Through the lens of salutogenesis, we emphasize development of the capacity for self-determination.

The basic health of each human being lies in the background. In the foreground are the pressing needs of human beings. When we don't have the capacities to meet our own needs, or when we find ourselves in situations where our needs are not being met, then a kind of imbalance takes place between foreground and background. Something jars the foundation of human wholeness. As in our daily lives we emphasize the ability to meet our needs, let us start there. Of what basic universal human needs should we be mindful in this paradigm?

I propose a four-fold understanding of human needs, which will give us a framework for understanding salutogenesis, diagnosis, and treatment. Though Rudolf Steiner spoke about these matters, this view does not originate with him. It originates in the wisdom of our forebears, who knew that the world in its wholeness is composed of four perceptible and tangible elements.

I'll start with Plato. We know the four elements, Fire, Water, Earth, and Air. The ancients had given certain associations to these elements. When we look at the quality of fire, the Greeks had the sense that fire also existed in the inner nature of the human being. They called this inner nature of the human being, this interior place, soul. This warmth that we continually feel within us gives us our sense of Being-ness. In the condition of water, which is constantly within us, and always keeping us in movement, the ancient philosophers found qualities that they referred to as the spirit. The Air was associated with the mind. The Earth element was connected to the body. This formulation was a premise of Platonic thinking. The nature of the human being—body, mind, soul, spirit—was also experienced in the nature of the world.

A Platonic Vision of the Four Elemental Properties of the Cosmos: An Alchemical View

Fire = Nature of Soul	Air = Nature of Mind
Water = Nature of Spirit	Earth = Nature of Body

Domains of human experience were often talked about and brought into philosophical perspective. These domain terms were:

1. Psyche. Psyche is a longing and, one might say, the search for unifying the inner and the outer. This longing for unification is fundamentally a need. It's one of the basic needs of the human soul: the need for love. Rudolf Steiner formulated this picture in the November 1-4, 1910, Berlin lectures, entitled *Psychosophy: The Wisdom of the Soul*. From these leading insights from Steiner, we have drawn the foundation for an Anthroposophic Psychology.

Four Domains of Human Experience: Four Core Needs of Human Beings

Psyche: The Need for Love (Fire)	Ethos: The Need for Social Identity (Air)
Cosmos: The Need for Alignment & Grounding (Water)	Chronos: The Need for Bodily Sustainment (Earth)

2. *Cosmos.* With the sense of the spirit, it was very clear that the human being was embedded in the Cosmos. The human being was not separate from the water, air, fire, and earth. But the human being had to find relationship with this greater, encompassing wholeness, which we call the Cosmos. The human being has a fundamental need that we can call a need for alignment with the Greater Whole, what we could call spirit. For the Greeks, this was a sense of flowing-with, as with water, not just for aligning with what is above, but alignment also with what is below. It created our sense of verticality, a sense that we are connected with something much greater than just ourselves and/ or that which is visible within our horizon. For if our attention is only upon ourselves, we lose this sense of flowing-with and alignment, which is our spiritual birthright.

3. *Ethos.* The Greeks also understood that the radiant beings within our midst could share our ideas and thoughts. Thoughts and ideas, the powers of mind, which are really a kind of spiritual treasure for us, create the basic ethos, the basic values, the basic standards of relationships based on an innate need to have a social identity. We find out who we are when we engage with the other. We receive back a reflection, not only of who we are, but of who we could be, what we can become. The need to have a social identity, a role, a place, a confirmation, and acknowledge-

ment of one's meaningfulness to and with others—these are fundamental to our lives.

4. Chronos. In the bottom right location of our four-fold chart, we have the theme that the Greeks called Chronos. In Chronos, the sense of time exists, in whose realm everything undergoes constant change. This relates to our physical existence and the need for bodily sustainment, a vital need. On earth, we must sustain the earthy substance of our bodies. They will need to be fed—again, and again. With the solidity of earth forms comes the march of time, and the requirement to face our needs for survival over and over. And in the earth realm, there are other needs as well: With every human being, there are challenges in finding fulfillment in a loving situation, a situation that can give you a sense of your identity among others, a sense of your being-ness within a greater whole, and a sense that your very basic needs for security and survival are being met. Problems occur when needs are not met. People will find any way they can to meet their needs. Often what is seen as pathology is simply a striving to meet a need without the understanding or capacity to do so.

In that sense, all counseling has a kind of psycho-educational component to it. The salutogenetic approach requires we take a positive outlook toward human struggles rather than labeling them as negative and pathological. From a Jungian perspective, these four needs have to do with what Jung described as the four basic functions.

Jung's Four Psychic Functions in Relationship to the Core Needs

Soul Need for Love = Feeling	Mind Need for Social Identity = Thinking
Spirit Need for Alignment & Grounding = Intuition	Body Need for Existence = Sensation

Keep in mind that these various four-fold frameworks are meant to be super-imposed one upon another.

In the four basic functions, we have feeling, thinking, sensation, and intuition. Jung observed that we have a predisposition to rely on a particular function more than on the others. The task of integration is to bring the whole together in a balanced state, the art of applying salutogenesis. These functions orient the human being to meeting his or her needs. The frameworks given in these four-fold diagrams have been there for thousands of years. They have formed the basis of a philosophical understanding: the love and the wisdom of the human being, a worldview predating anthroposophy. We have to move that wisdom (Sophia) into Anthropos. Now we have to reclaim consciously what was given to us unconsciously. (This is taken up further in chapter 6.)

When I began counseling, I worked mostly with adolescents. Part of my training was with William Glasser, the founder of "Reality Therapy." I was very moved by the person and his work. Glasser had a view of basic needs, which he envisioned as six in number, and which we can now see as fitting our four-fold models.

William Glasser & Reality Therapy:
Basic Needs in Relationship to Core Needs

Love Needs = Relationships	Social Identity = Self-Worth & Empowerment
Need for Alignment & Grounding = Values	Body Needs = Security & Joy

One of Glasser's needs is security, basic bodily needs. With that also exists something you could say has to do with the inner sense of wellness. Not just being secure, safe, and having what you need, also an inner sense of wellness, that Glasser boldly called joy, being happy to be alive, and being grateful you have an existence: thus a deep sense of well-being.

Glasser spoke about the need for empowerment, your capacity to make decisions, to be able to see yourself to some degree as the director of your life. That sense of empowerment usually parallels your own inner experience of feeling you have value and self-worth. In this regard, what we see related to the air and mind element, he spoke about as self-esteem.

Glasser described a basic need of creating and sustaining meaningful relationships, which we can see related to our upper left quadrant. He named another need as living your own spiritual ideals, walking your talk, related in our view to the lower-left quadrant, that of water and spirit.

I have just given you a background of core needs. If you are a counselor or a friend, and someone comes to you for counseling, it's very important not to get caught up in the details of the story of woe and despair. The fundamental question to ask is, "What do you need?" This question does not differ from what we find in the Grail myth, where Parzival must mature to the point where he can ask, "What ails thee?" Rather than put the emphasis on suffering, it is much easier to see your client's struggles in a positive way as the striving to meet a need. In everything you do with the client, you can live the question: "How can I support you in what you need?"

Granted, many people come to counseling because they suffer from debilitating symptoms, so their attention goes to those symptoms, rather than to their needs. Many don't know what they need. We have to restore their ability and their right to articulate their needs. Some people have been in situations where that whole question of meeting their needs is foreign and strange, yet, it is a birthright that we need to honor.

When we take as our starting point for psychological assessment what is needed, we can emphasize the understanding of what needs are not being met. Then we can begin to develop a pathway to meeting those needs. Not that you directly give what's needed, but that you give them some guiding points. You as counselor can become someone who helps them articulate the map, which will help them navigate through the current storms in their lives.

I would like to speak about common paradigms of self-experience. The first paradigm is *Love versus Fear*. These paradigms of self-experience appear as polarities. In his seminal lectures of 1910 called *Psychosophy* (Part II of *A Psychology of Body, Soul, and Spirit*, see References), Rudolf Steiner stated that one of the fundamental experiences of the wounded soul experience is a quality of *Love versus Hate*. Under the notion of Fear we can put the word, Hate. We recognize this longing and striving for love as a fundamental need—closely related to the experience of fear to be intimate and a fear to lose oneself in the other. This fear often turns into hate. Hate is something you cannot logically know without having some experience of it. That is one paradigm of self-experience.

The tables below contrast the common paradigms of self-experience with Steiner's view.

Paradigms of Self-Experience

Love - Fear	Me - Not Me

Steiner's View of Psychosophy Seen in Polarities

Love & Hate	Memory & Forgetfulness

Another common psychological paradigm is *Me versus Not-Me*. Right away we are in a kind of relational dynamic. Who am I and who am I not? Who are you and who are you not? In Steiner's terms, this would engage us as *Memory versus Forgetfulness*.

To continue (see the table below), the core of so much of psychology is based on the paradigm of the experience of *Pain versus Pleasure*. Freud was obsessed with the dynamic of pain and pleasure. For Freud human beings lived entirely in this polarity. The "not me" was often identified as the pain that one did not want to acknowledge, and because it was suppressed into the unconscious, neurotic patterns were unleashed, patterns that shaped the personality. This important polarity belongs in the lower right corner, in our earth sector, for this polarity is something intrinsic to our existence on earth.

This four-fold approach could be overlapped with the other four-fold schema that I've given before.

Paradigms of Self- Experience

Love—Fear	Me—Not-Me
Good—Bad	Pleasure—Pain

Steiner's View of Psychosophy seen in polarities

Love & Hate	Memory & Forgetfulness
Wisdom & Ignorance	Pleasure & Pain

Our last sector of self-experience understands the world as *Good versus Bad*. In the Psychosophy lectures, Rudolf Steiner terms this the interplay of *Wisdom versus Ignorance*. Wisdom is fundamentally a principle of goodness, whereas what is bad or often termed as evil, is really the result of ignorance, the phenomenon of not knowing, of not having the wisdom to discern. This question of *Good versus Evil* is very loaded in our time. How Rudolf Steiner actually addresses it is quite unique to most people who have been trained to see these two as opposites, in a strict dualism. Steiner, like Aristotle, spoke of good versus evil as a threefold phenomenon with the good in the middle and with evil as twofold, one part an excess of a virtue and the other the lack of a virtue.

Rudolf Steiner brought something extraordinary to the anthroposophical medical path. That is where we in the anthroposophic counseling and the anthroposophic psychology work can find grounding for what we are doing. Rudolf Steiner spoke about the inner organs as spaces in which the soul lives. He spoke of four major organs that are connected to the four elements. Here are the main organs, organized in the four-fold schema that we have been following, and interlinking with all the other four-fold diagrams that have come before.

Steiner's View of Four Major Organs & Psychopathology

"I"—Heart—Personality Disorders	Astral Body—Kidney—Psychosis

Etheric—Liver—Depression/ Mania	Physical—Lung—Obsessive/ Compulsive

Steiner spoke of the heart in relationship to fire. The heart is the seat of warmth in the human organism; it is also the seat in which the "I" finds its home. For the king or queen within us, it's the throne from which we govern our entire life. With the heart we have a sense of the capacity of the "I" to direct life, not just in a physiological way. When we begin to understand this from point of view of the soul, we understand that the "I" has the ability to act as executive decision maker of what is purposeful and what is meaningful. The "I" governs the sense for destiny. This has a great deal to do with how we become who we are.

What can go wrong in the heart, the "I," in the fire sector? Personality disorders, as explicated over the course of the 20th century work by psychology, indicates how challenging it can be if the "I" is not able to be the warm glowing fire in the soul. (More in chapter 7). Twelve Personality Disorders have been recognized from 1951 to today. In each of these personality dispositions, the "I" tries to take control of the soul life in order to meet the needs of the human being. Personality disorders are distortions or exaggerations of our coping skills and our strategies for accomplishing whatever it is that has been meaningful to us. When these coping strategies are not well developed, and our capacities to meet our goals are limited and our needs have not been met, it's usually because we have fallen into a dysfunctional way of trying to get them met.

The whole idea of salutogenesis is that we look at the intrinsic wholeness; we remember that there is a part of us that will be able to relate to each of the dispositions of personality, even in their exaggerated or disordered states. This inquiry does not require filling out a checklist, such as many of us do as psychologists in the field. The diagnostic criteria are given, for example, "Here are nine symptoms; if you have four or five of them, you are a good candidate for being labeled such-and-such."

So many clinicians and counselors misdiagnose because they are only looking at one dimension, one category, rather than looking at something multi-dimensional. We really need to understand the severity of a person's suffering in any one category, and have the other categories in mind all the time, so we're never trapped in a box. When you are looking at psychological dispositions or styles, you can assess how you can lean toward one particular personality trait in the morning, and then, given certain circumstances of the day, you can express another personality trait in the evening. We will keep our eye on this flexibility, this movement and development as we look into personality formation. Indeed, the ability to change is a virtue of salutogenesis.

Personality denotes a capacity for a fluid interchange between the "I" and the astral body. The astral body is the body of movement. The "I" is the mover. Now I've added a new term, opening up another four-fold schema, to be superimposed with the previous, especially with the major organs and psychopathology just previous.

Rudolf Steiner's Image of the Four-fold Human Being

"I" (or Ego) Organization	Astral Body
Etheric Body	Physical Body

Behind personality, something much greater is at work. When we look at personality as really being the vehicle of the expression by the "I" or Self, we are looking at how each human being meets his or her sense of destiny. Most of the challenges and obstacles that we face in meeting our destiny come from within. All the outer situations we can point to are only circumstances that we set up in our pre-earthly life so that we can actually find resistance, so that we can be forced to develop. This self-accounting, the ability to weave through life responsibly while finding our way to our destiny, marks true self-development.

Let's return to the connection between the four organs and pathology that Rudolf Steiner brought into anthroposophic medicine.

The Fire element: As stated earlier the fire lives within us as a constancy of warmth. It is centered in the heart. The heart beats in a microcosmic rhythm of 72 pulses per minute, reflecting the greater rhythm of 72 years for the Earth's vernal point (location in relation to the stars of the Sun at spring equinox) to move one degree in the zodiac. This correspondence is not arbitrary. It is a cosmic indicator of how humanity evolves according to cosmic principles. To the extent that a human being lives one's life in accordance to these principles, one's destiny will find one. By living in accordance with the virtues of the zodiac, one can imbue one's personality with the right orientation to one's destiny. Falling out of these virtues leads to a life of vice and consequently to a life out of alignment; hence personality disorders arise.

The Water element: As did the early Greek physicians, Rudolf Steiner pointed to the liver as a kind of brain, a locus of intelligence, that knows how to discern all that comes into the human body. The liver is a kind of spiritual temple within the body. As the heart has so much to do with the "I," Rudolf Steiner said the liver has a lot to do with your etheric body, your sense of life. The wisdom that works in the human organism is a complex and intricate tapestry woven by the Gods. Understanding the liver's working was one way to understand how the mastery of the etheric body could be obtained. We take it for granted that our etheric body knows how to keep this whole complex organism working without difficulty. It is the times when we are in discomfort or in pain that we tend to think about the functions in our body. The same is true when we are undergoing soul travail.

In the realm of the liver, we have the intelligence for life, the ability to tap into vitality. Rudolf Steiner says the liver is a place where, if it is not experiencing that kind of healthy buoyancy, it can actually fall away, even falling into depression. Losing a sense of vitality and life is one of the indicators of depression. We will talk about the varieties of depression later (chapter 8).

The Air element: The kidney is the organ where the seat of the astral body exists. In as much as the seat of the "I" is the heart, the seat of the astral is the kidney. Through the kidney, we are able to bring a quality of relatedness between ourselves and all of the experiences we have in our lives. We could say that here is where reality-testing needs to exist autonomously. When it's not there, what we experience may be regarded as symptoms of psychosis, that is, not being able to see the whole, seeing only in fragments.

The Earth element: The lung exemplifies the circumstance of existence in the physical body itself. It relates to all our instincts, our obsessions, our compulsions. We will examine obsessions and compulsions, what one might call our instinctual nature. These unconscious drives hold the key to the mystery of addictions (chapter 9). We have seen this pathological situation in mental health growing in the last two or three decades. Significant numbers of people suffer from what we call PTSD (Post-Traumatic Stress Disorder, chapter 10). They are so shaken out of seeing and experiencing things that are inhuman, things that do not belong to the dignity of the human being, that they are deluged with images that turn into memories and specters that actually intrude into and dominate their psyches.

PTSD can also be accompanied by a kind of psychosis, not just memories and flashbacks that have taken hold of the person, but, due to being unexpectedly violated, the psyche opens to dimensions for which the person has no understanding. The trauma functions as a kind of push across the threshold into the spiritual world. Given an already unanchored sense of self, where the person's destiny has been interrupted in one way or the other, a psychosis can often accompany PTSD. When we look at our veterans, we can see very high statistics of people who have suffered this to an excruciating degree, living lives of quiet desperation.

From much of what Rudolf Steiner says about humanity's ability to meet the future, we know that we need to prepare ourselves to meet a culture that is dissolving into decay. A signature for this change would be an increase in psychopathology. Anyone can easily experience the influences of PTSD just by extending empathy to someone else suffering from it. The helper can experience that they accompany the suffering with the other whether they wish to or not. The pathology sticks, so to speak. These are the real and serious issues. I have called this not just a post-traumatic stress disorder (PTSD), but a *pervasive traumatic stress disorder* in the entire culture. No one really escapes this dreadful condition of our time.

This evidences a kind of unlawful crossing of the threshold into the spiritual world. We are all now having to get some sense of what psychosis is. It's an alarm, a neurological alarm in our amygdalas that just won't turn off unless we bring a lot of attention to ourselves, being in the here and now, and a lot of value to the fact that the maturity level of our consciousness can make an immense difference, to ourselves and to others.

This framework explains why we have chosen to work particularly with these four different kinds of pathological condition. We will present not only leading thoughts and cognitive ideas about each, but also opportunities to experience these phenomena.

From the approach of salutogenesis, we can bring a picture of holiness. Rudolf Steiner's view of the basic four-foldness of the human being showed his ability to see the interaction between the physical body, the etheric body, the astral body, and the "I." Each of these is related to the elements. These maps give us hints about how the pathologies develop, as well as pathways of return to fundamental health—salutogenesis.

The physical body is still a mystery, even though science has increased its understanding of it to a great degree. The physical body is the oldest body of the human being, the oldest member. It has the greatest wisdom. Knowing your body and how to take care of your body then becomes very important, particularly in the 21st century where we have already detached so much from our sense of embodiment that we no longer live in the beauty of God-given nature. Anyone living in an urban setting is seldom breathing the cleanest air, and is dependent upon food that may not be of the highest quality.

Our basic bodily needs for sustainability can be interrupted by our culture. It is most important for us to be in our physical body, this wisest member of our four-fold selves, to be here and now in the present in our bodies. Waves of cultural influences numb you down from being in your body, so you don't have the sense of things such as, "How is my right hand on my lap right now; what is the sensation of it?" Or, "What is this sense of my awareness of its capacity to feel, to move?" We take these things so much for granted that we even accept the persistent metaphors, such as, "The body is merely a machine." Or, "I can download memory from my brain." These metaphors are inaccurate and misleading—leading us away from our bodies. In our present world, the paradigm of the human body is no longer understood. It becomes labeled a machine. Or "the body is merely a sophisticated animal." And so forth. We have to renew our understanding of the human body and the care of the body, learning to pay attention to the fact that the body's wisdom lies in our ability to be awake to our senses and our sensations. That is what we will call a psychosomatic wisdom.

Edmund Knighton and David Tresemer will guide us into awakening the intelligence of the body (referring to actual exercises explained in part in chapters 11 and 12). Many clinicians and counselors do not pay enough attention to the body, the body of the client and their own bodies. Although there is a rising interest in the field of psychosomatics, it's still in its infancy in terms of what our ancient ancestors used to know about the body and the magic of just being able to heal oneself, or to calm oneself with learning how to breathe naturally.

So many of these things that once upon a time we could take for granted are now interrupted. We will return time and time again to the question and experience of embodiment. Rudolf Steiner gave much of himself to try to restore the loss of some of the vitality of the human body, through biodynamic agriculture, anthroposophic medicine, and eurythmy. So much of these renewed disciplines have the intent to safeguard that human beings do not prematurely excarnate, but stay healthy and present in the body.

With the etheric body, we have the sense of our interrelatedness. It's in our etheric body that we share a common life, and we will be doing a lot of things as a group in common. Just as with our awareness that extends beyond our body, we are actually living and moving in an etheric dimension. With very simple mindfulness exercises of bringing your attention outside yourself, you feel the expansion of dimensions. You start to feel your connectedness with all things. The result is a healthy etheric body that is not isolated in itself, but actually feels its interconnectedness with all things and everyone. (More at chapter 12.)

Thus we emphasize relationship. As soon as your client enters your office, you share a common field of life. To be able to work with that, to be able to begin with being in the here and now—we must open these potentials where you can always get to know your client anew and more than you knew him or her yesterday. You experience an increasing appetite and interest for keeping things alive. You become less interested in simply scripting what you need to do for the other person and running that script in the session. By becoming more alive yourself, you become open to having a common field of life with the other. This is salutogenesis.

Rudolf Steiner brought all kinds of things into the world for increasing this vital awareness. We know eurythmy is the art of living consciously with the etheric, living in it, moving with it. We as counselors need to have our own sense of inner eurythmy when we listen, when we pose a question, when we move to follow a person's story. All of this is the inner eurythmy of the soul life. We will have some opportunities to do that in counseling dyads where we can experience something of where we live in common in this etheric reality.

In the astral body, we are talking about the dynamics of consciousness: how consciousness and what we call general awareness is really our ability to be aligned with not just the thoughts, but also aligned with something that is formative and archetypal. If we are looking for healing, we need to be aware that healing is a wholeness activity, salutogenesis. This wholeness activity comes from where things began. They began in the Cosmos as archetypes. This is one of the great insights of Carl Jung, his ability to restore our connectedness, our grounding with the spiritual world and to begin to read the language of images.

Imagination allows the soul to have the wings of movement that go beyond the physical sensible condition. We can see not only what is present but, through a schooled astral body, we can create the opportunity to see the future in the present. One must not get caught up only in the *diagnosis*, for the real art of the future is a genuine sense of *prognosis*, knowing going forward into the future. What is coming to us? What can I do to be a support for your next step of development? I have to move with and beyond in order to reach that place, to bring the healing of what is the right next step to move on.

The highest sense of the "I" is what we can refer to as Self, with a capital S. This Self, which has an existence beyond what appears, and which has an existence prior to the physical body that is carrying it now, and which has an existence when the body is no longer here: That is the fuller meaning of the "I." This is the sense of a divine spark, of the "I AM." This is our greatest potential. Rudolf Steiner wanted us to be awakened to the potential of being co-creators of the future by coming to know our future Self.

If we keep these four bodies in mind and what their qualities are, it will help us in the translation of so many things, so many wonderful tools and techniques that are in the field of psychology and counseling. Then we can begin to integrate the details and bring them alive so that it is not merely a technique. We are not interested in a technique; we are interested in a path of transformation. This path of transformation is all about *being*. Life is not so much what you do, rather about what your path is. Life is more about how you are being with the other. That emphasis is ever so wonderful because it counteracts the disastrous tendency for human beings to be isolated from one another. We have the greatest opportunity to be together, overcome that isolation, and live in the joy of what has been given to us.

Appendix: Other Aspects in the Four-Fold Schema

One basic assessment tool in anthroposophic psychology for counseling lies in the ancient understanding of Four-fold-ness. Here are some other typologies that complement what I have already presented.

Psychological	Social Psychological
Spiritual	Sociocultural

Love Needs Communal Sharing Integration of Self (Family)	Social Identity Authority & Ranking Goal Attainment (Society/State)
Need for Alignment & Grounding Equity Matching Latency (Potential of Becoming) (Religion/Spirituality)	Body Needs Market Pricing Adaptation (Economy)

Our "I," or Ego, is who we think we are. It is based on Perception, on the way we sense a world outside of us. Here are aspects of what the "I" is and has to deal with:

Shadow	Mask (Projected Persona)
Superego	Body Image

Our Self is who we really are. It is based on Conception, on the way we intuit the world inside of us.

Natural Self	Sociable Self
Transcendent Self	Body Self

Paradigms of Self-Experience:

Love - Fear	Me - Not Me
Good - Bad	Pleasure - Pain

Steiner's View of Psychosophy seen in polarities:

Love & Hate	Memory & Forgetfulness
Wisdom & Ignorance	Pleasure & Pain

Rudolf Steiner's Image of the Four-fold Human Being:

Astral Body	Etheric Body
"I" or Ego Organization	Physical Body

Types of Addiction, Depression, Psychosis, and Personality & Identity Disorders can all be further delineated within these four-fold models.

Suggested References for Further Study
(in addition to the references at the end of the book)

Adler, G. (1979). *Dynamics of the Self*. London & Boston: Coventure.

Bento, W. (2004). *Lifting the Veil of Mental Illness: An approach to anthroposophical psychology*. Great Barrington, MA: SteinerBooks.

Cavalli, T. (2002). *Alchemical Psychology: Old recipes for living in a new world*. New York: Tarcher/Putnam.

Hillman J. & Von Franz, M.L. (1971). *Jung's Typology*. Dallas: Spring Publications.

Hull, R.F.C. & McGuire, W. (Editors) (1977). *C.G. Jung Speaking*. Princeton, NJ: Princeton University Press.

Johnson, R. (1971). *Existential Man: The challenge of psychotherapy*. New York: Pergamon Press.

Jung, C.G. (1971). *Psychological Types*. Princeton, NJ: Princeton University Press.

Lockhart, R.A. (1987). *Psyche Speaks: A Jungian approach to self and world*. Wilmette, Illinois: Chiron Publications.

Meier, C.A. (1986). *Body and Soul*. San Francisco: The Lapis Press.

Stein, M. (2006). *The Principle of Individuation: Toward the development of human consciousness*. Wilmette, Illinois: Chiron Publications.

Steiner, R. (1999). *A Psychology of Body, Soul, and Spirit*. Hudson, NY: Anthroposophic Press.

Triechler, R. (1989). *Soulways: The developing soul, life phases, threshold & biography*. Stroud, UK: Hawthorn Press.

Turner, R.G. (1996). *The Fire and the Rose: Human core needs and personal transformation*. New York: HarperCollins.

Wilber, K. (2000). *Integral Psychology: Consciousness, spirit, psychology, therapy*. Boston & London: Shambhala.

Wilber, K. (2006). *Integral Spirituality: A startling new role for religion in the modern and postmodern world.* Boston & London: Integral Books.

Wilber, K.(2007). *The Integral Vision: A very short introduction to the revolutionary integral approach to life, god, the universe, and everything.* Boston & London: Shambhala.

Chapter 4

Life Span Development:
A Brief Overview
by Roberta Nelson, Ph.D.

Anthroposophic principles, if apprehended and thoughtfully applied, can foster personal and professional development. From the viewpoint of human growth and development, one such principle is recapitulation. When we recapitulate, we repeat something. Recapitulation or mirroring is a fundamental principle within Rudolf Steiner's model of life span development.

Steiner identified three main phases in the human life span, progressing through seven-year periods, each manifesting distinct qualities within three main phases: physical or bodily development occurring from birth to approximately age 21; psychological or soul development from 21 to 42; and the potential for spiritual development from 42 to 63.

Spiritual development differs from bodily and soul maturation in that it is a capacity inherent to the human being, yet is not guaranteed. It occurs *if* a person intentionally engages in inner- or self-developmental activities. It is a possibility rather than a given. With spiritual growth we have choice. I often tell my clients that the Divine stands outside the doorway of our souls knocking without ceasing. The door knob, however, is on the inside. Because we are free beings, which the Divine respects, we have the option of opening the door, or not. If we decide to open the door, to take up spiritual maturation, the Divine will lead us forward towards what is good, true, and beautiful within ourselves.

Briefly, recapitulation means that we revisit in later life the themes, issues, and tasks from earlier in life. (See the diagram below.) When we apply the recapitulation principle to the three main phases of body, soul, and spirit, developmental tasks and themes from between the ages of 0 and 21 are taken up within a subsequent phase, from a different angle. Each new juncture or life phase generates the prospect of something new emerging in relation to what was encountered in the past. Recapitulation seen through an anthroposophical lens is not simply, "I get another chance at this." Instead, aspects and forces previously unavailable become accessible. In short, we revisit what we lived through earlier in our lives from the vantage point of a new place in development.

Through an anthroposophic lens, the study of life span development is inspiring and thought-provoking, as well as expansive. It adds another dimension to Erik Erikson's well known psychosocial developmental phases—it adds the spiritual picture. This addition dramatically expands our current psychological understanding by incorporating universal principles that support human becoming.

Here we can only give a brief introduction to life span development. Edmund Knighton will pick up this theme again in the following chapter. What follows is extracted from anthroposophical resources, particularly George and Gisela O'Neil's contributions as well as William Bento's materials given out at the Psychosophy Seminars.[6] We will end the session with a short experiential activity that takes us into our own life-span development.

As stated, the life span of a human being is divided into three separate main phases in anthroposophy: maturation of body, soul, and spirit. Each of these three are further subdivided into three succinct cycles. Each is assigned specific developmental tasks and themes that will be recapitulated throughout our lives from different standpoints. The subdivisions are divided further into seven-year intervals, beginning with birth to age 7, then 7 to 14, 14 to 21, and so on.

---

6 Some of these materials are in Bento's *Lifting the Veils of Mental Illness*, some in this book, and some planned for future publications.

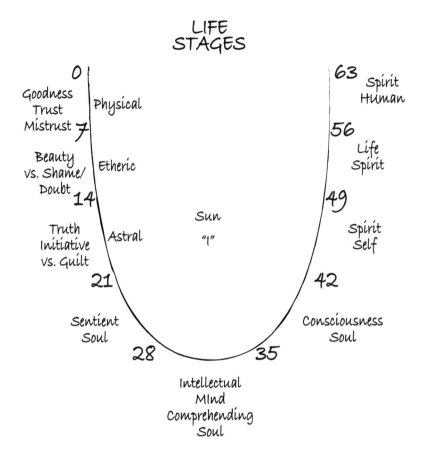

As these core constructs are sketched, begin to relate them to your own biography, asking: What was happening in my environment during this phase of life? Where is this point in my life now?

Physical Growth

Key components for the period from 0 to 7 years include the following:

    a. From birth to age seven, intense biological growth happens, evident in the creation of the physical body, a process that will continue for approximately 21 years.

    b. Three significant human abilities emerge during this

phase: uprightness, speech, and self-consciousness. "Here I am."

c. The child learns through imitation, emulating his or her environment. Hence ages 0-7 are characterized as the age of imitation. Do you remember when your 2 ½ year old began to read? I do. I thought he was a genius until I realized that he was even including my voice intonations when he read his favorite little book. Scotty was imitating me. He was imitating, not reading . . . not quite yet.

d. Awakening awe and reverence in the young child is crucial.

e. The installation of moral-spiritual values happens. Later in life these values will be *practiced* rather than *received* as they are during our first years of life.

f. The quality of will—what I usually term "doing" with my clients—in its early development is hinted at in the stage from birth to age 7, apparent in expansive energy and the willfulness of the young child. Exemplified in a common 2 ½ year old retort: "No, me do!"

g. Ideally, goodness is experienced with the child feeling loved and celebrated by primary caregivers. If this occurs, he or she is more likely to perceive the world as a place of goodness and safety. The presence, or absence, of goodness is related to the developmental crisis described as *trust versus mistrust* by Erik Erikson.

h. From birth to around seven years of age, development occurs within the dynamic tension between trust versus mistrust. Erikson introduced eight psychosocial stages. These stages fit into an anthroposophic view of development with modifications. Erikson assigned trust versus mistrust to infancy, limiting it to the first year of life, whereas anthroposophy expands this developmental crisis to the first seven years of life.

i. Recapitulation of the key aspects from birth to age 7, shown on the diagram, are taken up later in life, but from a dissimilar developmental level. From 35 to 42 psychological maturation is added. From 56 to 63 the potential for spiritual maturation becomes available.

Key components for the phase from 7 to 14 years include:

a. Physical maturation begins to slow down, which frees up vital forces transitioning into the age of identification. The loss of baby teeth heralds this new phase and ideally the child declares: "Everything is wonderful. I am glad to be here."

b. From ages 0 to 7 the focus was upon imitation. This stage emphasizes identification. We begin to discover our unique identity.

c. Physical maturation continues with the development of the life body, also called the etheric body. Fundamental habits, patterns, and gestures become visible. Temperaments can be observed.

d. Goodness was the ideal for ages 0 to 7. From 7 to 14 years of age, beauty or enjoyment in life becomes the standard.

e. Hopefully during this phase, social interaction, play, and creativity are encouraged. Instead our youngsters are often shuffled about from one organized activity to another and they are expected to sit in chairs at desks for long periods of time.

f. The psychosocial crisis taken up during this period is *autonomy versus shame*. Later in life the resolution of this developmental crisis will be experienced as *flexibility versus rigidity*. We can ask ourselves: Where am I with this developmental conflict? Do I tend towards flexibility or do I tend to be inflexible?

g. Ages 7 to 14 are recapitulated in reverse between the years of 35 to 28 adding psychological maturation; and from 56 to 49 offering potential spiritual maturation.

Now we enter the turbulent years of adolescence. Key components for the phase from 14 to 21 years include:

a. This time period is the age of independence where an adolescent's inner life is established as distinct or separate from his or her primary caregivers. It is the start of the life long search for oneself as a free being.

b. Understandably given the focus on independency, rebellion is often a hallmark of this developmental stage alongside the quest for knowledge and the development of judgment.

c. Development unfolds as the contest of *initiative versus guilt*.

d. It can be a time of intense emotional swings moving between extremes.

e. Analytical logical thinking is quickened enabling the acquisition of one's viewpoint or philosophical stance.

f. Physical growth culminates in the unfolding of the sentient or astral body.

g. Truth is the ideal for this period of the life span.

h. Recapitulation of key aspects of ages 14 to 21, shown horizontally on the diagram, are taken up again but from a different developmental level, from 28 to 21 adding psychological maturation; and from 49 to 42 offering spiritual maturation.

Soul Growth

Following physical or bodily maturation from birth to age 21 is the second main life span phase—psychological or soul growth. This period unfolds between ages 21 and 42. With the arrival of the second phase, forces previously expended in physical maturation are now freed up to unfold three periods of soul growth identified by Rudolf Steiner as the sentient soul phase from 21 to 27; the mind or comprehending soul from ages 28 to 35; finishing with the unfoldment of consciousness soul from 35 to 42 years of age. The theme during these three seven-year periods concentrates on what is coming towards us from outside, from the world, which meets what is within us. From this inner-outer tension we develop our life of soul, often aided by and moving from one crisis to the next.

Key components for the phase beginning around age 21 until 28 years of age center on the following factors:

a. Years of young adulthood are described as the age of adventure directed towards personal and outward discovering.

b. "I experience" is the motto for ages 21 to 28.

c. Learning about self through relationships becomes much more important.

d. This is the period of the sentient or feeling soul as well as the birth of the ego. In anthroposophic psychology the "ego" is differentiated from the Freudian or Jungian use of the term. Here ego refers to a soul sheath which permits the "I" to become embodied and thereby to experience the world. The ego functions as a director, organizing and maintaining continuity between sensations and experiences, between thinking, feeling, and doing. The ego develops by meeting and overcoming obstacles. We have a higher ego (the "I"), faithful to realizing what is good, true, and beautiful within our nature. And, we have a lower ego (the less-developed "i") committed to actualizing instincts, impulses, and desires.

e. The ego differentiates us from animals and presents the capacity for self-observation.

f. Development occurs within the dynamic tension between *industry versus inferiority*.

g. Competency in the world is a goal during these years. Abilities and skills are discovered and cultivated.

Between ages 28 to 35, the intellectual or mind soul unfolds. Key components for the phase beginning around age 28 until 35 years of age center around the following factors:

a. The age of working through experience starts around 28 with the motto: "I think."

b. Rudolf Steiner assigned mind or comprehending soul to this period, emphasizing thinking, judging, objectivity, and rationality.

c. Development occurs within the dynamic tension between *identity versus role diffusion*. Discovering one's own inner authority arises often alongside becoming proficient in whatever trade of discipline we take up.

d. Ego organization is expanded, influenced by our existential circumstances.

The last soul or psychological phase is named consciousness

soul. Key components for the phase arising around age 35, extending to 42 years of age, concentrate on the following factors:

a. "I" consciousness is awakening, evident in discovering self and others. Goodness, beauty, and truth are recognized by the "I."

b. In the anthroposophic literature, this period is referred to as the age of loneliness with the motto "I will do." This is a time of action and responsibility.

c. Now the call towards spiritual development strongly beckons us forward. We might ask ourselves if our heads, hearts, and limbs are aligned with what is true, beautiful, and good? What are my circumstances entreating? What can I do differently to make it better instead of expecting others to change?

d. The psychosocial conflict occurring within this seven year span is summarized as *intimacy versus isolation*.

Spiritual Growth

Now we move into the three seven-year phases of spiritual maturation with the possibility of transforming our body and soul nature. The primary psychosocial crisis from age 42 to 63 happens within the dynamic of *generativity versus self-absorption*. Key components for the phase arising around age 42 and extending to 49 years of age center on the following factors:

a. The birth of what Rudolf Steiner termed the *Spirit Self* is dependent upon inner or self-developmental activities. Realization of this dimension of spiritual maturation is not granted. It is attained.

b. Recapitulation at a higher level of psychological maturation from 28 to 21 and physical growth from 21 to 14.

c. The goal is the acquisition of sense-free thinking, named *Imagination* by Steiner.

d. Truth is the ideal, with generativity or service to others as the principal aim.

Key components for the phase arising around age 49 and extending to 56 years of age, a time referred to as *Life Spirit* by Rudolf Steiner, concentrates on the following factors:

a. These seven years recapitulate or mirror 35 to 28 as well as ages 14 to 7.

b. Community, mentoring others, and responsibilities continue as themes throughout this cycle.

c. The goal is qualitative thinking or *Inspiration*.

d. Beauty is the ideal, as it was during the phase from 14 to 7, but with a change. In our youth, beauty was about enjoying life. Spiritual maturation shifts the focus towards the art of living while inspiring others.

e. This is a time to decide to resume conscious spiritual impulses. Birth of the *Life Spirit* entails intentionality as well as inner or spiritual developmental activities such as, but not limited to, Steiner's so-called six subsidiary exercises or his revisions of the eight-fold Buddha Path. William Bento has amended the eight-fold Buddha Path, creating a version appropriate for our times. Michael Lipson, in *Stairway of Surprise,* takes up Steiner's six subsidiary exercises. (See chapter II for more on these exercises.)

In closing, the last phase of spiritual maturation, named *Spirit Human* by Steiner, addresses key components for ages 56 to 63. This cycle takes up the following:

a. Recapitulation of age 42 to 35 and 7 to birth takes place during this cycle of seven years.

b. Goodness is once again tackled but with a difference. In childhood the focus was upon being loved and celebrated by our primary caregivers, which in turn, launched a view of the world as a place of goodness and safety. Since the overarching theme for these three seven-year periods is spiritual maturation *creating* and *giving*, goodness is accentuated rather than receiving, the reverse flow from what occurred during the first seven years of life.

c. Another theme is reverence. Again there is a mirroring going on. From 0 to 7 moral values were laid down. Now, at ages 57 to 63 we *realize* or *practice* our moral values.

d. *Intuition* (thinking with the heart) and community are goals to strive towards.

e. Once again, the unfoldment of *Spirit Human* depends

on our willingness to take up activities that foster inner development or self-realization, as Abraham Maslow entreated us to do.

Beyond 63

Of course the life span does not necessarily culminate at age 63. The recapitulation continues with 63 to 70 mirroring 63 to 56. From ages 70 to 77 the period from 56 to 49 is echoed. From 77 to 84, the years from 49 to 42 are recapitulated, and so on.

When I started this review of life span development through an anthroposophic lens, I stated that the forthcoming developmental principles can be personally as well as professionally beneficial. How is that so? What I have presented is an abbreviated map, please note this, identifying several core constructs for what anthroposophical practitioners refer to as biography work. It's a protocol that includes mainstream counseling biographical concepts, while adding spiritual tenets derived from Rudolf Steiner's spiritual science. These additions possess the potential, if studied, of enlarging our view of who we are and how we develop—primary themes in mental health schooling and practices.

The viewpoint of life span development, as given by Steiner, is a threefold one, taking in our physical, psychological, and spiritual nature, which is seldom assimilated in mainstream mental health literature. With the incorporation of the spiritual dimension, the reviewer will discover that the inclusion of Spirit amends the knowledge we already possess of our physical and psychological nature. The thoughtful reviewer will deduce, as many have, that well-intended clinicians are regrettably diagnosing and counseling from a reductionistic view of human nature. The biography work outlined today has the possibility of moving us towards a holistic practice grounded in spiritual developmental principles. Such principles possess a key that can unlock healing forces, transforming self-destructive behaviors evident in addiction, anxiety, or mood disorders.

Although counseling literature stresses the importance of

inner or self-development, I am aware that this often does not occur in our schooling processes. From my perspective, this is a significant oversight with far-reaching consequences. I work in a residential treatment facility functioning as a mental health addiction clinician. I journey alongside adult clients who have been diagnosed with co-occurring disorders. In other words, every adult that I see has more than one diagnosis. All are struggling with addiction plus mental health disorders such as, but not limited to, depression, bi-polar, generalized anxiety, and post-traumatic stress disorder. Many clients exhibit personality disorders such as borderline or obsessive-compulsive personality disorder. Almost every client has experienced neglect or abuse in childhood. For them the world is not a place of safety or goodness. They understandably mistrust not only others but sadly they mistrust themselves.

Inner development practices, including biographical study, are invaluable. Because I have had the opportunity to look at my life through an anthroposophic lens, I perceive my issues as well as impressions of my clients' possible diagnoses as opportunities rather than pathologies. Bernard Lievegoed characterized development as the process of meeting and overcoming obstacles. William Bento has described pathology as a *path of initiation*, a pathway towards becoming all that we were intended to be. Our lives hold a treasure chest filled with gems *if* we choose to plumb the depths and the heights of who we truly are.

Since I struggle with self-awareness and change, with viewing the recesses of my soul, its ups and downs, I am not unlike my clients. We share a common destiny entitled: "Meeting and Overcoming Our Obstacles." I experience that they sense this commonality. They know that we are comrades. (This does not mean that I disrespect ethical boundaries.) Consequently I do not take on a hierarchical relationship with the men and women that I counsel. I do not adopt the voice of authority; instead, I proceed as Roberto Assagioli advised students of Psychosynthesis: The clinician's goal is to awaken the latent wisdom dwelling within the client, rather than a platform for the therapist to espouse his or her own knowledge.

In the residential treatment facility where I work, I witness arrested development over and over again. What is meant by arrested development? It is development that has stopped prematurely. It is stuck. How does arrested development manifest? Imagine sitting across from a 6'2" male, who is 27 years old, yet unable to hold a job, although he seems intelligent. He is homeless. He has no idea what he would like to do with his life. He has little understanding of who he is. Getting along with his peers is difficult. In fact, he is rather clumsy in social settings. He is constantly experiencing perceived and real rejection although he is an attractive likeable young adult. Instead of self-sufficiency, he is dependent. It can be quite confusing for those who meet him and most importantly for himself. On one hand, he presents as a young adult; on the other hand, he is not functioning as one. His development was arrested usually around the time when he began to abuse drugs or alcohol.

When such clients are shown the life span developmental map designed by George and Gisela O'Neil, briefly outlined today, the client lights up. I will usually be swiftly asked: "Can we do this? How do I get this chart?" It surprises me how rapidly a client, with little or no coaching, begins to construct meaning from a previously unknown map of the human life-span. The jargon does not seem to snag them, another surprise. Instead they are eagerly hoping to understand and heal their own developmental processes. As friends and clinicians we have the opportunity to aid their search for meaning.

Listening

Before we move into the experiential activity, I would like to pause for a moment in order to introduce the phenomenon of listening, which we will be doing shortly in the activity. Time will allow only a brief introduction to a major activity—listening. Most of us listen to speak instead of listening to hear.

To illustrate this statement, I speak to my clients in the following way: Imagine this scene. Most likely you all can do so because it has happened to you. You've had a tough day at work. Somebody said something to you that was shocking. It was said without kindness. Maybe your heart is breaking. Or maybe you are angry. You call up your best friend, asking him or her to meet you for dinner, adding: "I really need to talk about what happened today." Your friend agrees to meet you at a favorite restaurant. You manage to order your food but have no desire to eat because inwardly you are hurting or angry. Maybe both. You can't wait any longer to talk about what happened. You tell your friend the details. When you're all through, possibly on the verge of crying or yelling, your friend leans forward announcing: "I know what you mean. Just last week a person I work with pulled me aside and told me . . . ."

After I present the scenario, I ask the clients what just happened. What occurred for you? Their responses always echo a version of the following: "This has happened to me! I become a nonbeing. Unimportant. Unheard. Insignificant." Clients quickly resonate to this scenario, and agree that it's extremely important for us to listen to hear, rather than listen to talk. They recognize that the quality of our listening, that is, our ability to momentarily sacrifice our own agendas, creates an empathic resonance between the speaker and the listener. As we proceed with the forthcoming exercise, I invite you to practice listening to hear.

Experiential Activity

Instructions:

1. Please pair up with someone that you do not know in the group. Move your chairs into a space where you can have a bit of privacy. Create your own special space in the room, just the two of you.

2. As you practice listening to hear, silence your voice of judgment. Please do not analyze or attempt to solve anything. Instead warmly receive what your partner shares, listening with an open heart and mind. Ask questions, if appropriate, to gain clarity and to show interest.

3. Another point that is critical is confidentiality. Whatever is shared, respectfully hold it. Do not discuss or divulge what your partner has disclosed. Later on, you will be in-

vited to talk about your experience but not about the content of your partner's story.

4. We will be sharing a glimpse of our biographies with one another in order to begin to digest the material which has been given. We will do this by asking ourselves: Where is this aspect in my life?

5. As you hear the forthcoming information, select one psychosocial crisis that you would like to explore and discuss with your partner. Select the aspect that you will be comfortable sharing.

6. Three psychosocial crises or developmental conflicts have been identified. *Trust versus mistrust* occurring between birth and age seven. *Autonomy versus shame* occurring between the ages of 7 and 14. *Initiative versus guilt* as the psychosocial challenge between ages 14 and 21.

7. For today, select one cycle and its corresponding psychosocial challenge. Write it down on paper—the issue and some of the details about what happened regarding the selected psychosocial challenge. Maybe one event summarizes this conflict for you, and maybe several. Write down the main points as they appeared in your life.

8. Now ask yourself four questions: Where is this challenge presently in my life? Has it been resolved? If so, how? If not, what are you willing to do?

9. Take a few moments to record your insights and questions.

10. Begin to share with your partner, each person talking for about ten minutes each. I will announce when the ten minutes are up.

11. After you've both had a chance to speak, share with each other what you have learned from this process and this exchange.

Discussion

[a sampling of responses and comments]

[Participant #1:] What is the opposite of doubt? It might be certainty.

[William Bento:] Trust is usually relational; doubt is very subjective.

[Edmund Knighton:] With the passage of the earth into individuality, that is, with the passage of human consciousness into what we can call the Consciousness Soul Age, we move from ignorance or the guileless into doubt. Eventually it will become blessedness. The sequence is ignorance, doubt, blessedness. That doubt is an inner characteristic. It appears to have nothing to do with the world. It has to do with Parzival himself. As you recall, Parzival is the central figure of the tale told by Wolfram von Eschenbach. He begins in ignorance and must pass through doubt, years of doubt, before finding blessedness. He doubts the existence of the Spirit. He doubts the existence of blessedness. Mistrust is about the first year of life where I get my basic needs met, or not. Doubt comes later.

[Participant #2:] Around age 8 or 9 or so, I was surrounded by doubt. I would fall asleep and wake up and doubt would be around me. It would be like a seizure or something. It would impair the right side of my arm and then disperse. I would wake up in the morning with doubt. I would have to say, "I'm OK!" But I wasn't. It was worse during those few years. Today, I do physical yoga as a four times a week practice to repair and balance that. I haven't had any seizures since that time. I notice that in my approach toward sleep, I no longer fear it. Now I welcome sleep.

[Edmund Knighton:] Notice how difficult it is to come to a question. It takes an effort to contemplate this. "Where am I now with this?" So, what is the question, now, the question that pulls you forward?

[Participant #2:] The question that pulls me forward is: "Why don't I fully take the power for not having that doubt? What is it that stops me?"

[Edmund Knighton:] If you have a question, pose the question. Find the question that guides you. Write it down. A gentle guide is this: "Why" takes you into your head. "What" tends to take you into Roberta's pulling you forward with what is more phenomenological.

[Participant #2:] I just now changed my question to "Who." My

living question is "Who am I living for?"

[Roberta Nelson:] Yes, "What can I do to develop deep trust in somebody?" This is how questions can lead to useful movement—at this moment, yet in relation to any place along the developmental stages of the full life-span. Then I can use the adult learning processes to work with the question.

Appendix. Seven Adult Learning Processes

I rely on the seven adult learning processes as introduced by Rudolf Steiner. They have clear connections to the life phases of human development. I use them in every aspect of my counseling practice. Each of these processes requires the activation of self-observation or witness consciousness, a function of the "I AM" or transpersonal self. I have summarized and condensed these processes based on the brilliant interpretations by Coenraad von Houten.

1. **Observing:** What we objectively observe through our 12 senses. Facts. What do I hear/see, etc.?
   a. Anything that strengthens the active use of the senses
   b. Observation exercises
   c. Developing pure observation skills
   d. Developing openness, wonder, and reverence
2. **Relation/Warming:** How are we experiencing or connecting to the information/observation? What did we warm to? What were we cooled by?
   a. Learning to generate enthusiasm
   b. What are the moments that I was inwardly touched?
   c. What is important/unimportant?
   d. Where am I resistant?
3. **Digesting/Assimilation:** An active step. Taking the information and breaking it down. Analyzing. Dissecting. What does the information, or my reaction to the observation, say about me?
   a. Assimilate through thinking: Try to think the opposite.
   b. Assimilate though feeling: Express in an artistic manner.
      i. Listening to your feelings
      ii. Learn to listen for a "sense of truth"

    c. Assimilate through the will: Here fundamental beliefs are confronted. Is this right? Is it morally justifiable from my point of view?

        i. What significance does the information have within the framework of my biography?

       ii. Why did I not meet it before?

      iii. How does this content relate to what I am really looking for or who I really am?

    d. This process is a struggle between old/new and warmth/coldness.

    e. Courage is required to continue processes.

    f. What are your underlying intentions/motivations?

4. **Individualizing/Absorbing**: Open, active, attentive space. Listening inwardly. Review and release preceding information into silence. Listen into the spiritual world. Reconnection with the Divine. Seek new questions, insights, impulses. Caution: New awareness can evaporate; therefore record quickly.

    a. This process is a quiet contemplation so that something new can break through.

    b. Acceptance enters allowing for ownership.

    c. New understanding, new way of sensing, new way of valuing

    d. Sets up a will impulse. An understanding becomes an intention, a decision, or a new question.

    e. Accomplished through:

        i. Creating a learning review. What are the essential things that I have learned today? How did I learn them?

       ii. Group processes are supportive. Invite participants to help each other find their individual goal or true question.

      iii. Questions are helpful rather than answers. True questions have a future.

      iv. Transitioning into the fifth process, accomplished by awakening the drive to understand, the drive to develop, and the drive to improve.

5. **Practicing**: The new impulse, question, or insight needs to

be incubated. Nurtured. Brought into the will. What does this information have to do with my life now? How do I work with it?

a. If something is to be "maintained," it must be repeated or practiced.

b. To practice is to develop, to learn, and to grow.

c. Practice is founded upon previous steps. (Steiner: "Every idea that does not become an *ideal* destroys a force in the soul; every idea, however, that does become an ideal within us creates life-forces.")

d. Create a sacred space for your exercise/practice.

e. It is supportive to fashion a practice by incorporating the essence of the Six Subsidiary exercises (given by Steiner):

    i. Exercise takes in concentration (willing into thinking). Not automatic pilot or repetition but engaged, full concentration and attention.

    ii. Develop regular variations that are stimulating such as imaginative practices rather than an arbitrary playing around (thinking into willing).

    iii. Rhythmical practicing instead of routine.

    iv. Develop love of practicing for the sake of the practice instead of boredom or sense of duty.

    v. Create an exercise that is balanced, including periods of silence or inner quiet, not one-sided or exaggerated.

    vi. Harmony as a whole. Many exercises may be tried. Remember, if a rhythm is established, spiritual beings will unite at night with the exercise, thereby reinforcing and improving.

6. **Developing/Growing a New Faculty**: Implement a practice so that the new faculty can be developed.

a. Development is occurring in the night leading towards a new ability or faculty.

b. Pay attention to your resistance, remembering that learning/developing has to do with the experiencing and overcoming of resistances.

c. Incorporating practical situations are supportive: Project work, practical learning, learning through experience.

   d. Pay attention to how "resistance of reality" enters into your life or practice since these so-called obstacles often support the "birthing" of a new ability.

   e. Artistic activities are helpful.

7. **Creating Something New:** As a result of processes 1-6, something new will be created, fashioned in your life.

Suggested Resources for Further Study
(in addition to the references at the end of the book)

O'Neil, George and Gisela. (1990) *The Human Life*. New York: Mercury Press.

Lievegoed, Bernard. (1984) *Man on the Threshold: The Challenge of Inner Development*. United Kingdom: Hawthorn Press.

Lipson, Michael. (2002) *Stairway of Surprise: Six Steps to a Creative Life*. Great Barrington, MA: Anthroposophic Press.

Van Houten, Coenraad. (2000, second edition) *Awakening the Will: Principles and Processes in Adult Learning*. London: Temple Lodge.

CHAPTER 5

Seven Life Phases
and Seven Levels of Will

by Edmund Knighton, Ph.D.

Rudolf Steiner describes seven life phases and seven corresponding will phases. Each phase includes the focus of body, soul, and spirit. We will touch on the important points here, as this is a very large study.

We will access these life-phases first through meditation. It is a form of meditation that is definitely helpful to a counselor, and could also be used with clients, depending on their receptivity to this kind of meditative work. You may be surprised at how many people can do this kind of work. At the end of the chapter is a chart offering qualities and practices related to each of the life phases in relation to many other indices important to human beings and to our world.

Meditation has many benefits. I use it with groups and with individuals to find what's essentially going on with them. I speak about some dangers of meditation and counter-indicators to its use in chapter 12. Assuming that you've prescreened your client or clients, then you can use this approach.

To begin: Set an intention with yourself to return to the seminal pieces evoked during this meditation, later, when you are alone. Have a blank piece of paper and a pen in front of you. Write down or sketch any information that comes to you as we progress through the meditation: images, songs, colors, memories, sensations, pictures, moods.... We will be flowing back and forth between writing, not in sentences, but perhaps images in a word or two or three, and then moving back in the space. Notice movements, associations, perceptions, thoughts, particularly those that surprise. It could be an expression that finds its way to your face—make a face! And note that. Whatever it is, become curious and open to the experience, without judging it or trying to figure it out. If something presents itself to you, take a moment with it. Make contact with it. Write a word or two, sketch an image. If you do not experience anything, that is fine. If you do not understand the image, or the line of a song comes to you, write that down. It does not have to make any sense or have a logical meaning, e.g., first you came into form in the womb from the spiritual world, now you come into the physical world through birth. Take another few moments to finish that thought enough so that you will remember it when you return to it later, like writing down a part of a dream.

Please begin by placing yourself in whatever position is comfortable for you in a meditative practice, whether your eyes are closed or open, focused on something or focused inwardly, that is your choice. Take a moment to center. Bring yourself into a space of openness. I am going to lead you into a life-phase meditation. We will travel through seven periods; each is seven years long. We are going to start before birth.

Lunar Instinctive Wisdom (Age 0-7)

Begin by imagining yourself before you inhabited your present physical body. Wish the body away. Imagine yourself expanded out into the cosmos, before birth. (We could take a much longer time here in spaceless timeless reality.) If you like, move a gesture, write a word, or sketch an image or symbol on your paper.

Now, notice the transition from that space into inhabiting the body for the first time. A very, very tiny, fluid body. Notice sensation. Do you sense comfort in structure? Limitation? Something else? How do you find yourself arriving into form, the first experience of development? Allow the effort to impress itself upon you.

Unite yourself with manifesting into embodiment, appearing into form from the freedom of the cosmos. Again, sketch, in a word or two, a brief image or movement. Not a full picture or description just yet. It may be a taste. You will be able to return to it later and flesh it out on your own time.

Now, return to your space of reflection, back into your nest, now that you have a body to nest into. Enter into the first period of life, the moment of birth. The spirit has entered into form, gestated, and now the moment of birth, from womb to world. Notice that moment, entry into one world and of leaving another world, at the same time. Sketch any impressions if you have them.

Return to your meditation. Imagine lying in the horizontal plane as an infant. Experience this plane of space ... the world as horizontal.

Transition from horizontal to vertical, the upright plane. Remember arriving at standing for the first time, that first moment of precarious balance. From this point forward, write or draw an image whenever it suits you as you emerge from the meditative space. Again, give yourself a mere hint, then shift back to the moment when you found yourself upright in the world. What was that like?

Discipline yourself to be brief, to flow backward and forward in time. Transfer from standing to walking. Initiate your first step forward. Notice this in your body, the movement forward in the world. Which leg did you use, which knee lifted? Can you recall? Or gain an impression? Where was your gaze? What mood was in your heart as the first step happened?

Now remember your first word. What was the mood of your first word, even if you do not remember the word? Even if you do not remember the mood, invite it to be present around you now. The first word is here, around you, around the body ... the mood of the first word.

In the next few years of childhood, learning comes through the body and as a direct imitation of those around you. That imitation takes the form of play. Play with movement. Explore.

The instinct of body rules you. The forces of the Moon hold sway and all of this information is in your hands. Remain with the encounter: Me and the Moon, my life with the Moon. Dwell in your experience of the mood of will called instinct. What is your relationship with instinct?

From a wonderful book by Nancy Tillman, "On the night you

were born, the Moon smiled with such wonder, and the stars peeked in to see you. The night wind whispered, 'Life will never be the same,' because there had never been anyone like you, ever in the world. So enchanted with you were the wind and the rain, that they whispered the sound of your name. The sound of your name is a magical one." Say it out loud before we go on.

Say your name out loud. Remember the first time you said your name. The first experience of an "I" occurs often around the third year... "I" and then the world.

This is the first seven year period of life, harkened back to so often in all of psychology for good reason. As much as possible, inhabit the mood of these years as we proceed. Face the Moon mood. Gaze at the full Moon's face.

Mercurial Healing Impulse

Contact the transition from Moon to Mercury, from 7 to 14, the will mood of impulse. Dwell in the impulse mood, the mood of urge, in my voice as it changes from the reflective slowness of the Moon, to a more mercurial childhood quality. Become a little more sanguine. Let your body be light, easy.

If we were focused on "the good" during our first seven years, now we focus on "the beautiful." Our etheric life of well-being opens up as an early physical development completes itself at least for this stage. Transit from the will phase of instinct into impulse. What is the difference in your body?

Instinct? Impulse? Note the transition in you between instinct and impulse. How are these different in you? How are you active instinctively? How impulsively? Link yourself to your childhood years from age 7 to 14, and invite an image or memory to arrive as a kind of quintessence of you, as the hallmark of this time for you. Again, if it is a picture form, sketch a little picture of it. If it is an activity, commence the movement with your limbs or trunk.

Live in the mood of play. Enter the mood of exercise. So activity proceeds from imaginary play, to exercise. Play incarnates, enters into the body deeply. Now I look for the beautiful; my life body seeks to exercise itself.

Venusian Desire for Love

Progress now from Mercury to Venus, to the adolescent years, the realm of will called desire. How do those words strike you—"adolescence," "desire"? Rich in imagery, perhaps memory? Age 14 to 21, the third cycle, in the realm of Venus. We moved from the good, to the beautiful, and now we look for truth. Try on different personas like cloaks: One week the March Hare, the next week the Gothic Coat, the next the mannerisms of your favorite teacher, the next an incredible crush on a movie star. Try these things on lightly and move on. Seek truth. Activity changes from play, to exercise, and now to work.

What is your experience of work? Your body absorbs these concepts. You do not need to reflect them into the brain; they are already there. Live into the mood of work. Work in your thinking in school. Work in your first job. Work in your relationships. You are caretakers of your first love, your friends; steep yourself in the mood of work. Yet maintain the mood of play that pervades the mood of work. What is your heart's desire?

Embody an image, a word or two. Whatever it is, write that down for this third period, the Venusian period. Look for truth wherever you find it.

Solar Motive of the Sentient Soul

Now you are at age 21, the age where the "I AM," what is often referred to as the ego or the sense of self, consciously enters the body, where spiritual traditions allow individuals to enter their gates, in order to consciously work toward what psychologists call ego development, or toward dissolution. You move out of the astral suit of adolescence into the soul life, the life of the Sun, for the next 21 years from age 21 to 42. What is your relationship to motive? Can you feel it in your body? Where? Take a moment to describe this phenomenon in a sketch, a movement, or in words.

Observe the transition from Venus to Sun in yourself. Wish farewell to Venus. Welcome the Sun Being into your life. You are an adult. Your body is permeated with the adult mood.

The desire you had in adolescence changes into the will mood of "motive." What are my motives sensing in the world? Invite the dawning of the sentient soul, the sensing soul that wants to assimilate the world without the need for intellect. Sink into this mood as it manifests from 21-28, a Sun mood of motive, a sentient mood, exploration of the world. Invite an image or thought or memory to arise in you.

The movement of work travels into the creation of art. The ability to work as a laborer clarifies itself a bit to more of a craftsperson, or perhaps even artistry. Not only painting or clay, but additional senses of arts—the art of relationship, with yourself, with the other, with the world. Dwell on your art of movement, how you show up in the world, how you think artfully about the world. Perhaps you have an image that arises in terms of your artfulness in these years, or a word or two that describes this to which you can return later.

Solar Motive of the Intellectual Soul

Forward to age 28, continuing in the realm of the Sun. The sentient soul releases its hold. The intellectual soul dawns. Perceive the intellectual soul inhabiting you now. Immerse yourself in this age heralded (at 29 ½) by the return of Saturn to the place where it was at your birth. Reflect on the course of your life. Analyze it—Saturn's mode of inquiry within this realm of the Sun.

What arises in you with the sense of the intellect being born? Remember your life from 28 to 35. Transit from the sense of creating art, to, for the first time, requiring a meditative mood in order to soften and temper the intellect so that it does not become too analytical, too sharp, too cutting. Meditation helps to widen our perspective. It is a healing balm as the intellect gains hold of the person.

How does motive feel different in the intellectual soul as distinct from the sentient soul? Inhabit this intellectual motive mood for a time.

An image arises of the intellectual soul. Work with sympathy and antipathy, what you like and what you dislike, what attracts you and what repels you. The intellect strives to overcome that duality of thinking, but struggles. Discover a sense of your life from 21 to 28, through this healing life of the sentient soul. Consolidate it. If you haven't found a livelihood or a partner, perhaps the need arises in this time. Now, at age 28, intellect begins to order your life... or not. Find order.

Solar Motive of the Consciousness Soul

Your task now is to progress from this logical thought, to a kind of living thinking, a consciousness soul that is dawning at age 35. How do I bring warmth to my intellect? You are doing this in a linear way, but remember these things are like a spiral, we circle back around to them. Even if you are 56 right now, you may be struggling with bringing warmth to your intellect yet again. You circled around again, and beneath you, on the layer of the spiral, is that intellect warming need. You get another chance, analogous to going back to crawling.

Enter the consciousness soul phase; expand the intellect, widening out. Add the need to meditate, our new form of play, exercise, work, and creative art. Now we add to meditation the need, as consciousness widens us out, to concentrate. The opposite of meditation turned inward is attention, focus, and concentration turned outward.

You may discover a need to practice a concentration exercise at this time, when consciousness widens you, as you become aware of this complementary motion of concentration or one-pointed focus. Seek that in yourself at this moment: transit from the softness and emptiness of meditation to being filled with one-pointed determination.

How does motive feel now in this third aspect of soul, of consciousness soul? Feel consciousness-motive will-mood.

Martian Wish of the Spirit Self

At age 42, we draw away from the Sun, expanding our capacities. Thank the Sun with deep reverence. Gratitude warms the heart and settles the nervous system as we recede from the Sun.

Jung, Steiner, mystics, and occultists suggest that about midlife, age 35 to 42, we reach the bottom of the arc of development. Our angel leaves us in freedom, gives us distance, space to create our own destiny. The angel gives you space, leaves you alone, which are the same. Some may experience this as being forsaken, while others may experience it as a gracious spaciousness. Many find it both positive and negative at different times.

Notice the angel withdrawing. Notice Mars approaching as the Sun, and the being of the Sun, recedes from you, draws away from you and Mars approaches. You are 42. Affiliate yourself with Mars as a being.

You begin to move out of soul phases and into spirit phases. Find the shift from soul to spirit in you, a miraculous shift of consciousness. You emphasize the body in the early years until 21, then the soul until 42, and now you experience a conscious need to grapple with your own spirit life. Rudolf Steiner calls this phase Spirit Self.

In the level of the will, we change from motive to wish. From 21 years of motive during the Sun stage, now shift to wishing. How do you experience will-in-wishing? What is your relationship to your Spirit Self? It does not matter if you are presently younger than 42, or if you are out of this phase, the knowing is still alive and active in you at this moment. These things do not dry up and leave us.

Steiner suggests that at this stage it is now possible for us to awaken our imagination. What is my relationship to Mars? It is a very important relationship to come into the world with Mars at this time, from 42 to 49. The soul is working hard and Mars is helping to bring the full force of the personality into the world.

Is there an image arising for you at this time, that you would like to capture for later reflection? The image does not have to make sense. If you do not have one, invite your pen to start sketching something, anything.

It discovers you. You do not have to know. You do not have to figure it out. Let yourself be sorted out by the speech and active power of Mars. What does the wishing-will feel like?

Jupiterian Intentionality

At age 49, note the shift from Mars' intensity to intention, to the ponderous, dominant expansiveness arising from relationship to Jupiter. Goodbye to Mars! Here comes Jupiter! Jupiter approaches in you. What is my relationship to Jupiter at age 49? It might include dominance in the highest sense of the term, to be ordered in a logical and clear way, not by some ruthlessness or force.

Jupiter becomes active in you. Travel from imagination to inspiration, inspired between the ages of 49 to 56. Willing transfers from wishing to intention. Mars bestowed this gift. Absorb the previous quality and it leads into the next quality, interlacing in reciprocal enervation.

The intention of will comes through inspiration. Did you play as a child? Play in the earliest time has characteristics of inspiration, not arising from images, but from sudden inspirations. Play leading to creativity; work imbued with play. Thought matures from knowledge into understanding and thirdly into wisdom, the grown-up, the elder dawning in you: the mystic, the gnostic, the occultist, or the transcendentalist.

Invite an image, a thought or mood, or be surprised by the pen on the paper, whatever comes to you. Dwell in this mood, the mood in Jupiter of intention and of inspiration. If you are not chronologically this age you may have to imagine it, but there are many indicators of age. You have an emotional age, physical age, developmental age, mental age, spiritual age, old and young souls. They are all open to your understanding and participation.

Saturnian Resolve

At age 56, Jupiter begins to recede. Who comes to you? Saturn, offering an opportunity to complete something quite profound, that you started much earlier. There are two chances to meet the Grail in life, at age 18, and later at age 56. These opportunities relate to the return of the Moon node. The Moon's orbital path creates a plane of Moon-Earth. That plane crosses the plane of Sun-Earth (the so-called ecliptic plane) at two points called the Moon's nodes. Those two intersecting planes move in relation to each other, and return to the same orientation to the wide heavens every 18.6 years, just over 18 and a half years. When the Moon nodes come back to the same orientation as they were at your birth, you feel the strumming of the strings of destiny, the same relation of the Moon, Sun, and heavens that happened at your first breath, what I have called an opportunity to meet the Grail in life. The first return occurs at age 18.6. This can be felt ahead of time and lived through at an earlier age, even at age 16. Every individual will differ in exact timing.

On the initial visit, the Grail castle comes to you as a dream, at the edge of consciousness or below in the unconscious. Often we miss this first opportunity, sleeping through the opportunity, depending on a combination of soul development and current life conditions.

We search for the Grail for the rest of our lives.

One can seek the Grail consciously at age 56, the third return of the Moon node to its place at your birth. At 56 years and nine months, the Moon node returns for the third time. This celestial event marks the beginning of the eighth seven-year period, the entry to the Saturn years. It prepares you for the return of the planet Saturn to the place where it was at your birth for the second time at 59 years. I sometimes use the phrase "16 and 60" as an easy (though only rough) reminder to refer to the early and the later encounter with the return of the Moon nodes and the return of Saturn, the opportunity to realize the Grail in life.

In these encounters you have the well-earned possibility to transit through the suffering and trials of ignorance and doubt, toward a sense of blessedness. The tale of Parzival instructs us about the unfolding of this process.

Invite Saturn to yourself, who rules Parzival, the fearless knight in you. Yoke yourself to the mood of the birth of individuality.

Here are the opening lines of the tale of Parzival as told in the thirteenth century:

> If unfaith in the heart find dwelling, then the soul it shall reap but woe;
>
> And shaming alike and honor are his who such doubt shall show,
>
> For it standeth in evil contrast with a true man's dauntless might,

As one seeth the magpie's plumage, which at one while
is black and white.

And yet he may win to blessing; since I wot well that in
his heart,

Hell's darkness, and light of heaven, alike have their lot
and part.

But he who is false and unsteadfast, he is black as the
darkest night,

And the soul that hath never wavered stainless his hue
and white!

This my parable so fleeting too swift for the dull shall be,

Ere yet they may seize its meaning from before their face
'twill flee,

As a hare that a sound hath startled: yea, metal behind
the glass,

And a blind man's dream yield visions that as swift from
the eye do pass,

For naught shall they have that endureth!

A brave man yet slowly wise is he whom I hail my hero,

The delight he of woman's eyes. Yet of woman's heart ...
the sorrow.

Imagine 24,810 lines sung with full instrumental accompaniment, from town to town by wandering minstrels and trouba-
dours in this way. You heard the first lines. Note this mood in you
at this time, the birth of the individuality on the planet, from the
dark ages to birth.

Saturn greets you. The council of beings on Saturn is with
you, awaiting you as the brave man or woman—brave one slowly wise! Now is the time of life for wisdom. Become aware of your
relationship to the council of all beings. Use imagination to cognize inspiration as it repositions to intuition. Transformations
in the pituitary and the pineal gland lead to our future development. See if you can sense these glands in the center of your
brains, active.

Welcome intuition. Welcome Saturn. Experience the activity
of will as it transfers to intention. Resolve. "I resolve." Your op-

portunity for the Grail castle opens to you. The choice you make: Am I a knight of the sword or am I a knight of the world?

Your final image arrives at this time, ages 56 to 63, in the realm of Saturn. Resolve, intuition. Freedom dawns. Thinking frees. Feeling is free. Body free. The world, the planets, recede. Whatever image or concept arises in you, write down for later reflection.

Later Stages of Freedom

When you are ready, return to your meditative state for a second childhood in the years 63 to 70 and beyond. The planets draw away and leave you in freedom. The planets recede. They withdraw instead of swaying you with the harmony in their spheres. You can create disharmony and enjoy that to the extent that you would like to, and to the extent that you are working with your own karma. The view of the seven naked-eye planets (Moon and Sun, and Mercury through Saturn, those that can be seen by the naked eye, without telescopes) recedes from your sphere and leave you as a star—alone. Feel the possibility of playfulness and all its purified joys of stages of work—creativity of artistry, the harvest of imagination, the harvests of inspiration and intuition. The fruits are yours. Feel a second childhood. Contact the sense of decline, destitution, meaninglessness. Connect these polarities—decline and meaninglessness on the one hand, and fruits of inspiration on the other. Bring both poles present in you, sometimes during long moments when you work with others as clients, friends, and colleagues. The entire spectrum is now yours.

We have the heights possible of the second childhood; we have the depths possible of utter darkness, in the sense of oblivion and lifelessness. Feel yourself stretched between these two poles and inhabiting the space of balance between them. For those whom you work with, your clients, especially the ones you struggle with, you realize something profound:

> Create for yourself a new indomitable perception of faithfulness.
> What is usually called faithfulness passes so quickly.

Let this be your faithfulness.

You will experience moments, fleeting moments with the other person.

The human being will appear to you then filled and irradiated with the archetype of her spirit.

And then there may be, indeed will be, other moments, long moments of time, when human beings are darkened.

But you will learn to say to yourself at such times, "The spirit makes me strong. I remember the archetype, I saw it once. No illusions, no deceptions shall rob me of it."

Always struggle for the image you saw.

This struggle is faithfulness.

Striving thus for faithfulness, we shall be close, one to another, as if endowed with the protective powers of angels.

Recite this Rudolf Steiner verse to yourself before the toughest clients have their hand on the door knob as they come to see you. Then you are ready for them.

Review

You stand in the sea of the spirit in the last three seven-year periods. The spirit continues. An image comes to you for now until the end of life, from 63 until death. Imagine yourself as old as you can imagine yourself to be. Invite an image or a thought, set of intentions, what you would like to be, be placed on your paper as a final key note for the story of your life that you have written here on a page.

[The following can be used as a template for working with a group who has gone through the exercise of this chapter together.]

When you are ready, take a minute to look backwards through the images and the words. Do not try to understand them; invite them to play inside of you. Feel the pictures, the sketches you have created. Feel in your body the sense in the words. Let it affect you. Do not think about them. Let them think into you. If one particular mood or life period strikes you, note that.

We are going to take a little time for each person to share one aspect of his or her life. What is present for you in this moment as you have gone through the whole of your life in the last forty-five minutes?

When you are ready, popcorn style, whoever is ready to give us the essence. Obviously we will not have time for you to begin to have a biographical sharing of this life period - but give us the essence of a particular mood you have been living in and the rest of us will hold that and take that in for you. If you have a memory that surprised you, I invite you to go along with it.

[Participant #1:] "Well for me, I work a lot with life transitions in that 42 to 49 period. Midnight of the soul, the image is very powerful for me. For the first time I loved what happened. I went from 'midnight of the soul' to 'mid knight of the soul,' and so I took it in as my own and I'm 68, so for me, it is this free place to be knight of the soul."

[Edmund Knighton:]

Let me speak to that with a quote from the great teacher Karl König:

> There is a knighthood of the twentieth century, whose members do not ride through the darkness of physical forests as of old, but through forests of darkened minds. They are armed with a spiritual armour and an inner Sun makes them radiant. Out of them shines healing, healing that flows from knowledge of the image of the human being as a spiritual being. They must create inner order, inner justice, peace and conviction in the darkness of our time.

[Participant #2:] 28 to 35 was probably the hardest time in my life. I felt like I was falling apart completely. My whole world shifted. It made me mad; it was not what I was used to. But around 35 I was able to come to something at the culmination of the intellectual soul time period. I'm 40 now.

[Edmund Knighton:]

That is called intelligence. Feel free to hold the seven-year periods lightly. These are indications or tendencies only. The actual timing varies with the individual. I may enter my intellectual soul phase later than you do, say at age 30; you may have entered the sentient soul phase later than your friend. Steiner preferred to use the term "description" rather than "definition." The world does not fit neatly into boxes. It is messy. Terms such as tendency, indication, propensity, help us know that the world is in flux. This sevenfold structure is constructed; it does not exist objectively. The phases are indications for things that we tend to enter into and out of, a starting point for a conversation. We have to have a linear viewpoint and this is one effort at a typology of development.

[Participant #3 spoke concerning death and pregnancy, leaving the world and entering the world, and Dr. Knighton replied as follows.]

The death you describe is a nice way to go out. Being able to bless others at the end. At the pre-natal time, between conception and birth, Steiner suggested that you take care of your own development and not try to do anything with the baby. No tinkering. Focus on yourself. That in itself is all that is necessary in the pre-natal period.

[Participant #4 said she was 36 years old, and spoke about her sentient soul and intellectual soul experiences.]

It's not unusual for that to happen on both sides of the intellectual soul period. The sentient soul and consciousness soul—you can feel softness of both of these, blanketing the intellectual soul period from either side. The muse is a little more available to you. You are carrying a little bit in that sentient soul muse time, in your enthusiasm you get carried away, and then in the consciousness soul you have a little bit more ground to meet with the muse, thanks to your developing intellectual soul. You were developing what you needed to.

[Participant #5:] In my Mercury stage (7 to 14), that was interesting for me. I got an image of a tree, and I have trouble incarnating. The Moon was being sad, but I could see the tree as an image that is helping me to incarnate. The tree of life was always a strong symbol for me. When that came in, I could see why, why that had been so important to me.

[Edmund Knighton:]

One more thing: We moved quite quickly given that we had a limited time to move through a whole lifespan here. I would never move a client this quickly. You get a taste of this progression. The deepening of it you can do on your own if you would like to. You could take one seven-year period or one year, or one experience or moment of your life, into a meditative mood. Certain special moments in our lives can feel like a whole lifetime.

Suggested Resources for Further Study
(in addition to the references at the end of the book)

Crain, William (2011). *Theories of Development: Concepts and Applications*. Boston: Pearson.

Eschenbach, Wolfram von (1980). *Parzifal*. New York: Penguin.

Howard, Michael. "Educating the Will." Available online: <https://sites.google.com/site/healingeducation/home/contents/pedagogical-background/educating-the-will---michael-howard>.

Klocek, Dennis. "Mystery Wisdom Introduction." <http://dennisklocek.com/lectures/mystery-wisdom-introduction>. Set of seven audio recorded lectures.

Lievegoed, Bernard (2008). *The Spiritual Rhythms of Adult Life*. Forest Row, UK: Rudolf Steiner Press.

Steiner, Rudolf (1996). *The Foundations of Human Experience* (previously published as *The Study of Man*). Hudson, NY: Anthroposophic Press.

Wade, J. (1996) *Changes of Mind: A Holonomic Theory of the Evolution of Consciousness*. Albany, NY: State University of New York Press.

Appendix: The World from a Sevenfold Perspective

I would like to share other ways in which our world is organized in a seven-fold manner. You can see many correspondences between the various categories and the stages of a life.

Systems of Seven-Fold							
Planet	Moon	Mars	Mercury	Jupiter	Venus	Saturn	Sun
Days of week	Monday	Tuesday	Wednes-day	Thursday	Friday	Saturday	Sunday
Age Cycle	0-7	42-49	7-14	49-56	14-21	56-63	21-42
Chakra	Base	Throat	Spleen	Brow	Solar plexus	Crown	Heart
Will (with numbers representing the level of will)	Instinct[1]	Wish[5]	Impulse[2]	Intention[6]	Desire[3]	Resolve[7]	Motive[4]
Karma	Purify sin via Angel	Spiritual karma of talent	Healing	Spiritual karma of talent	Love	Spiritual karma of talent	Moral karma
Hierarchy level	Angel	Thrones	Archangel	Cherubim	Archai	Seraphim	Exousiai, Dynamis, Kyriotetes
Planetary symbols	☽	♂	☿	♃	♀	♄	☉
Metals	Silver	Iron	Quicksilver	Tin	Copper	Lead	Gold
Colors	Violet lilac	Red green	Yellow blue	Orange blue	Green pink	Purple yellow	White black red
Counter-life processes	Replication	Hardening	Premature rotting	Combustion	Encapsulation	Consuming	
Teaching & leadership	Evaluate review, summarize, reflect	Initiate, speak, organize, contract, social	Examples, humor, stories, life	Ideas, concepts, structure, clarify, content	Nurture, listen, support, question, interaction	Planning, goal orientation, holding direction, procedure	Harmonize, truth
Time	Timeless	Future	Present	Present	Timeless	Past	Timeless
To heal self	Silence	Nature walk-life	Sunlight	Bathe	Breathe	Fasting	Earth garden plant
Gender	Fem	Masc	Fem	Masc	Fem	Masc	Neutral
Temperament	Phlegmatic	Choleric	Sanguine	Melancholy	Phlegmatic	Melancholy	Sanguine

Sins	Lust	Wrath	Greed	Pride	Gluttony	Envy	Sloth
Liberal arts	Grammar	Music	Dialectic logic	Geometry	Rhetoric	Astronomy	Arithmetic
Tree wood	Cherry fruit	Oak	Elm	Maple	Birch	Conifers. White beech. Hornbeam	Ash
Grain	Rice	Oats	Millets	Rye	Barley	Corn	Wheat
Organ	Brain. Reproductive	Gall bladder	Lungs	Liver	Kidney	Spleen	Heart
Virtues	Hope	Prudence	Justice	Faith	Temperance	Charity	Courage
Soul types	Occultism	Voluntarism	Transcendentalism	Logicism	Mysticism	Gnosticism	Empiricism
Parzival characters	Orgeluse	Gawain	Repanse de Schoye	Fierefiz	Condwiramurs	Parzival	The Grail
Holy spirit gifts	Capacity for creation, fear of lord (timor domini) wonder, awe	Assertive counsel (consilium), right judgment, fluency of language	Sense of self, piety (pietas), reverence	Understanding (intellectus)	Purest Loving sacrifice of knowledge (scientia)	Deep inner contemplation of wisdom (sapientia)	Balance of all fortitude
Archangel	Gabriel	Samael	Raphael	Zachariel	Anael	Oriphael	Michael
Influence (quality)	Life forces, growth, propagation	Strength and energy	Sociability and interaction, healing	Overview	Beauty and love	Responsibility	Healing wisdom
Activities	Bread baking	Building and gardening	Eurythmy and drama	Crafts	Painting and beeswax	Cleaning	Stories and music
7-fold path	Right speech	Right action	Right livelihood	Right endeavor	Right recollection	Right conception	Right resolves
Governing god	Artemis; Diana	Mars; Hephaestus	Hermes; Mercury	Zeus; Jupiter	Aphrodite; Venus	Chronos; Saturn	Apollo; Helios
Musical key	B	C	D	E	F	G	A

Life pro-cesses (see ch. 4)	Gener-ating: creating the new as a spon-taneous outcome	Nour-ishing: taking in to be respon-sible (in the face of fear)	Growing: cultivat-ing the transfor-mational process	Warm-ing: per-meating experien-tial space (in the face of cynicism)	Main-taining: support-ing the develop-mental environ-ment	Breathing: sensing phenom-enological polarities (in the face of doubt)	Secreting: sorting essential from the inessen-tial
Epochs	Polarean	Hyper-borean	Lemurian	Atlan-tean	Post-at-lantean (our own)	Sixth great epoch	Seventh great epoch
Post-atlantean cultural ages	Indian age—Crab, Cancer 7227—5067 BCE	Persian age—Twins, Gemini 5067—2907 BCE	Egypto-Chaldean-Baby-lonian age—Bull, Taurus 2907—747 BCE	Greco-Latin age—Ram, Aries 747 BCE—1413 CE	Anglo-Saxon and Ger-manic age—Fish, Pisces 1413—3573 CE	Russian, Slavic age—Wa-terman, Aquarius 3573—5733 CE	American age—Sea-goat, Cap-ricorn 5733—7893 CE
Adult learning processes	Observe	Warm	Digest	Absorb	Practice	Develop	Creating some-thing new
Ages of Humanity	Adam to Noah	Noah to Abraham	Abraham to David	David to the captivity	The captiv-ity to the birth of Christ	Nativity to the second coming	Apoca-lypse, general resurrec-tion, final judgment

CHAPTER 6

Soul and Spirit—
and Counseling Psychology
in the Light of Anthroposophia

by David Tresemer, Ph.D.

Soul and spirit. Mainstream science says you don't have these. If, however, you find them, what do you do with them? And how does this discovery assist a counselor? These statements and questions, though oversimplified, will be familiar to anyone who has dealt with phenomena beyond the physical/chemical structures assumed by science to be the causes of our behavior. To address the situation more accurately, we have to build up to these questions from more familiar foundations.

Three Functions

The philosophy given by Rudolf Steiner called Anthroposophy designates three domains of soul function: thinking, feeling, and willing. Such a triumvirate is not new. Peter Mark Roget— of Roget's Thesaurus, first published in 1852—divided all words between *cognition*, *affect*, and *volition*, the same three domains as, in more familiar terms, *head*, *heart*, and *hand*. Each of the three interacts with the world differently. Thinking—pictures of the world, concepts of what's going on, ideas, beliefs—would like to convince us that the other two are subcategories. Many modern civilized persons have been taught that everything can be thought, or ought to be thought, or ought to be captured by words. They deny the other two functions. The third—willing, volition, behavior, deeds—has nothing of thinking in it, and simply acts, the deeds themselves being proof of its prominence. We can fool ourselves that feelings can be thought—"I love you!" or "That's disgusting!" as pictures and concepts—but pure feeling is not thought. Perhaps you know an adolescent who feels and demonstrates that feeling is the only function. Anyone who assumes that only one of these functions accounts for everything will have surprises ahead that could be uncomfortable.

Several psychological theories posit the same three functions, for example, David McClelland's division of human needs into need for achievement (based on evaluations of the merits of one's work, that is, on thinking), need for affiliation (feeling), and need for power (one purpose of willing).

From an anthroposophical perspective of the human being, these three functions are considered the triumvirate of the soul. They come from beyond the body. You don't receive true thinking, feeling, and willing as part of your physical equipment. Some people function as automatons, getting by on the bare minimum. More than that requires a greater capacity, from a realm beyond the body that we can call soul. A surprise given by anthroposophy is that these three capacities come from beyond, and at death separate and go off in different directions. During our lives each of us depends on a cooperation of thinking, feeling, and willing.

Different forms of contemporary psychotherapy favor one of the three functions. For example, the modern form called Cognitive Behavioral Therapy or CBT concentrates on the cognitive structures that determine behavior. Behavior—deeds in the realm of will and feelings expressed—is seen as thoughts-made-visible. Thoughts are seen as things that can be rearranged, and then the side-effects—the symptoms—will disappear. Other modes that depend on re-organizing your thinking are Albert Ellis's Rational Therapy (also called Rational-Emotive Behavior Therapy, REBT, the precursor of Cognitive Behavioral Therapy or CBT), Victor Frankl's logotherapy, and Gelatt's Decision Theory (based on mathematical game theory).

Here's an example of the dominance of thinking: A doctor friend told me a story about a patient: "I told the woman that her test results showed a genetic predisposition to breast cancer. I explained very carefully that she could reduce her chances of breast cancer by 70% if she quit smoking. 70%! The studies showed it. I explained it to her. I said, 'If you stop smoking, you will decrease your risk by 70%.' She didn't change. She didn't stop!" He wagged his head from side to side and threw up his arms. "Amazing!" The unspoken sub-text from the doctor was, "The studies are there. They're expensive and thorough. We now know so much more about genetic predispositions than we used to. This knowledge is precious and she's ignoring it. She just needs to think it through. She doesn't have breast cancer now, but she surely will get it." And finally, the unspoken judgment, "She's irrational ... impossible!," summarized in his gesture of frustration. This is a picture of someone who is certain that thinking is the one and only sphere of the inner life of a human being.

It helps greatly to understand such deeds as smoking as coming from their own sphere—the will—unimpressed by any gymnastics in the sphere of thinking. Behaviors deep in the will such as smoking or any other addiction cannot be understood or mastered through thinking, but must be approached on their own terms, through deeds, through the will. This is where the notion of "soul" found in rhythm-and-blues finds a home, through movement, through dance—as soul!

Modern fascination with screens—computer screens, movie screens, television screens, mobile phone screens, even windscreens on cars—has sat us down and turned off the will, and muted the feeling function. We are fascinated by the stimulation of our perceptions and of our thinking. But even that is diminished. Television has dumbed us down so that only a small bandwidth of our thinking capacity is used. In that small bandwidth, a lot is happening, but it is a small fraction of our whole capacity. Try this: Watch someone at one of these screens. Don't watch the images; put in earplugs so you aren't lured into the enchantment. Simply watch someone and feel the level of their life force. Now watch someone—same earplugs or hands over your ears—who is having a conversation with another person, a whole-soul conversation. Compare these two activities.

The thinker who thinks that the will is only a figment of thought should try this: Decide to stop breathing. After you've found yourself unable to stop your gasping for breath, be happy that the whims of thought aren't in control. Or, another one: Think yourself standing up. You can think it hard, and yet you have to engage the will to actually stand up. Or, another one: Walk over rugged terrain, and marvel at how your feet pick the right path that, were you to think about each step, you wouldn't make it through.

Approaches based on pure will emphasize activity without thinking. Examples are dance camps where students mutely follow a mute choreographer. Athletic training and military training have long stretches of work in the realm of the will.

The mediator between thinking and willing is the sphere of feeling, and thus, oversimplistic but true, the necessity for psychology.

Some modes of therapy specialize in feeling, such as the warm and compassionate listening of nurses and empathic counselors. Carl Rogers and Harville Hendricks emphasize the simple and warm practice of listening to the client. Support groups seem often to mimic the traditional role of one's ideal grandmother, with her warm hand on yours and a warm smile.

Albert Ellis (the father of CBT) insisted that thinking was the master of all the realms, and re-organizing your irrational beliefs the key to transformation. However, I have a friend who was Ellis's first assistant for some years; he describes Ellis as actively listening, funny, confronting, charismatic, engaging—in short, as having a very active feeling and willing in his demeanor. Now you can see YouTube videos of some of psychology's great teachers, ranging from presentations of the heart-oriented philosophies to the cognitive-only philosophies. If they have created a movement in the name of their formulation, they have succeeded in developing charisma, a combination of all three functions.

Rearranging thoughts-as-things can be called thoughting. True thinking opens up realms of creativity that integrate feeling and willing as well. Carl Jung's archetypal psychology, especially when working with an analyst who emphasizes an imaginative encounter with dreams and fairy tales and ancient mythic structures, can be understood as living within the realm of true creative thinking, a thinking related in a healthy way to powers of heart and movement.

A whole-soul conversation includes all three functions: thinking, feeling, and willing.

But there are challenges to this view. Perhaps thinking, feeling, and willing are merely pre-conditioned responses of a mechanism. I have to decide as a therapist, is this bio-mass sitting across from me a pre-programmed robot that needs a tune-up, or is it a soul that enlivens water and earth for a purpose beyond its present troubles?

The Behaviorist Mechanistic View

A strictly behaviorist view would be that what sits in the client's chair is programmed matter. Reprogram it, and the pesky symptoms disappear. Cognitive Behavioral Therapy or CBT is very successful in many settings ... to an extent. CBT is presently the mainstream method of therapy and teaching. In the general field of psychology, you can find small percentages of very interesting approaches such as Jungian archetypal psychology. But in what the government-funded agencies provide, in what the Veterans Administration provides, you won't find much Jungian psychology or other alternatives. The job of the agency is diagnosis of behavioral symptoms and the alleviation of those symptoms. As recent research by Mayo-Wilson and others has shown, dwindling budgets means that people who have gained a diagnosis will be met only by the most cost-effective (in the short term) methods, with set CBT protocols, or more often with psychotropic drugs—to the long-term detriment of the client and of society.

I worked with B.F. Skinner a little bit when I was in graduate school. He has been dubbed the father of behaviorism. He walked his talk, a strict behaviorist. I once said, "Gosh, Professor Skinner, I'm really looking forward to your lecture this evening!" He responded, cooly, always training the student to see the situation properly, referring to the word-behavior that just came out of me, "Well, that's simply a behavior." The feelings I thought that I was having of excitement and anticipation were simply forms of behavior, without meaning beyond that, in fact, without any meaning at all. His persistent analyses were disconcerting. Feelings were behaviors—merely behaviors—as were thoughts. For him, there wasn't a thinking or a feeling realm. All was reduced to the area we're calling here the will—deeds, behavior. He was also a warm, loving father who went out of his way to protect his infant daughter by putting her in a Plexiglas box. He did this to shield her from all unplanned stimulation, including from childhood diseases. These days we know the best thing to do with a small child is take her or him to a farm and let the kid eat dirt. That's the very best way to develop the child's immune system. Skinner was doing the best he could with what he knew. (By the way, she turned out fine.)

From the point of view of behavioristic materialistic science, the human being is mechanism. Your senses are like little windows or lenses into the environment that serve as entry points for stimuli that trigger automatic responses. These responses can be trained, making you a useful commodity whose labor can be sold as a "job." Or they can be replaced by machines that do these things more efficiently.

You come into this world preprogrammed or "hard-wired" for certain behavioral patterns, indicated by the gears in the illustration (below). You learn certain patterns of behavior early in life, also thought of as "hard-wired," that is, traceable along pathways of physical nerves. These wirings set up the buttons and the gears. When a button is pushed by a stimulus arriving through one of your sense windows, the gears go click, click, click, and the mechanism causes observable behavior. You behave in the way that you've been conditioned to behave, all through hard-wiring. "Hard" here meaning actual dendritic connections from one nerve cell to another, just as you would find if you opened the back of a telephone or any other hard-wired device.

Through the little windows of your senses, certain frequencies enter your field. Some act as stimuli to pre-conditioned patterns: The stimuli push buttons. When you talk to a true behaviorist, it gets that simple about how the human being is put together.

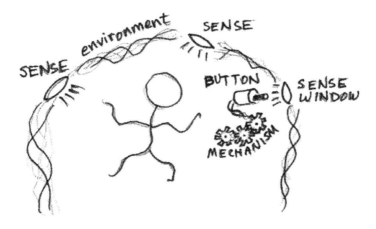

In the materialistic worldview, there are occasional hints of something else out there, a sort of vague sense of woo-woo. Someone in authority has an experience that confirms that there might be woo-woo in the world, something that we can't identify: We don't know what it is but it's something! The neurosurgeon Eben Alexander technically dies, has experiences, and comes back to write a best-selling book and to go on lecture tours. Materialistic scientists conclude that such experiences were anomalies or simply what brain chemicals do when you die, giving you illusory experiences, should you survive to recall them. They give out names—"Those experiences are merely a dump of N,N-dimethyltryptamine (DMT) into the system" or "They come from an endogenous glutamate blockade with excitotoxicity mimicking the hallucinatory anaesthetic ketamine"— that would scare off the average person. Alexander knows the language and answers these theories and others. Because Alexander appears to have broken ranks with the materialists, people perk up and listen to him more than the dozens of others who have written about similar experiences.

A surgeon, Sam Parnia, has recently written *The Lazarus Effect* (also published with the title *Erasing Death*). He has had a very high success rate of resurrecting (which is his term) people who have died. If he can get to you within three hours of your heart stopping, he has ways to bring you back. He picked that name, Lazarus Effect, as in the raising of Lazarus by Jesus. However, he rejects all the reports that he gets from his clients about the experiences they've had in that zone of time—those minutes or up to three hours. He rejects any further connections to Lazarus. He admits that his clients report experiences. They can accurately describe things that have happened in the room during those three hours, or at a distance that can then be verified. But he says it's irrelevant, he doesn't care about that stuff, and he is adamant about having no religious or spiritual leanings. He just wants to be a clever doctor. The name "Lazarus" is meant only superficially, though he must know that it turns the heads of the majority who are not materialists. Thus materialistic thinking maintains its position of not-knowing about anything beyond the behavioristic model of the human being. Given the three-hour limit, some people have chosen to live near him.

Oliver Sacks, the brilliant science writer who has written about neurology from many points of view, has recently written *Hallucinations* in which he concludes that all religious experience comes from chemical imbalances, either intentional, as in drug use and abuse, or hormonal. He believes that experience is all chemistry and brain cells, in other words, materialistic.

These two join Richard Dawkins, author of *The God Delusion* and other attacks on anything but scientifically measured reality. They are adamant about rejecting anything having to do with spiritual experience.[7] These authors represent the world view of materialism, one of twelve world views noted by Rudolf Steiner. We don't need to review those world-views right now, simply to note that there is more than one way to understand the world around us.

As I said before, CBT understands behaviors outside of

7 Dr. Parnia surmises that the brain undergoes a process that is merely chemical, that there is nothing past the veil of death. *Psychology Today* has concluded (October 2014) on the side of the materialists, admitting that there are some as yet unexplained phenomena, with the attitude that soon these will be "explained" chemically.

the model of cognitive-causes-behavior as anomalies. Those anomalies can accumulate and become a problem. A friend and colleague specializes in therapy for CBT therapists. Here's the pattern: A young CBT therapist hears hours of stories of war experiences from Iraq and Afghanistan. The therapist designs CBT protocols to address the soldiers' traumas by changing cognitions and, therefore, in that model, changing behavior. At the end of the day, the therapist goes off to an active night life. Yet over time the therapist begins to have trouble sleeping, and the dreams are disturbing. There is no room for this in the CBT model. Sometimes the therapist "burns out" and can't do CBT with clients anymore. Sometimes the therapist finds someone such as my friend, who introduces him or her to a realm assumed in CBT not to exist—the realm of soul.

A Larger Picture

Anthroposophy gives us a detailed and coherent vision of what these other people have called the "woo-woo zone," those phenomena that don't fit the behaviorist or materialist models of reality. The materialists call them anomalies or exceptions, illusions not to be noticed. In that view, the human physical body has borrowed substance from the earth, and is an extension of the mineral world, rising up from algae to fish to rodents to apes to human beings, yet keeping many of the old patterns in place.

I must address the mythic structure of neo-Darwinism at least briefly. Suffice it to say for now that the predominant models of who we are and where we came from (and therefore where we're going) are inadequate to explain our own experiences, and the many extraordinary experiences that materialist science names "anomalies." When the "anomalies" are one or two, they might perhaps be dismissed. When they number in the thousands of well-documented phenomena that don't fit the dominant paradigm, then a review of the paradigm is in order. The book *Forbidden Archaeology* is worth studying in this regard, as well as more recent discoveries of large architectural structures dated to times when human beings were represented by the dominant paradigm as far too primitive to accomplish such things. Eben

Alexander's very accessible book, *Proof of Heaven*, details the experiences of a neurosurgeon in realms deemed impossible by materialists; Appendix B in that book lists the materialist objections to the possibility of his experience, and refutes them one by one. The neo-Darwinist creation story begins to fray and fall apart.

The earth is more than a big ball of inert matter. It has a "living-ness" to it, a quality not explained by traditional neo-Darwinism. I have come to consider the earth as the living being of Sophia from whom we've borrowed substance for our bodies. Our bodies have more than mineral elements and water. They have vitality, livingness, activity, a glow. If you have an opportunity to be near a corpse, you learn quickly the difference between physical substance versus substance imbued with livingness. An honest appraisal of our situation is that there is "something else" besides physical matter. Names given by different observers for that "something else" differ. We will use the ones from anthroposophy.

Anthroposophy has names for this invisible "something else" that interpenetrates and animates the physical: the vital body, life body, or etheric body. Science has been unable to mimic or replace this quality of livingness that animates matter for plants, animals, and human beings. Science has just begun to describe this quality of livingness.

Another kind of vitality emanating from the human being has been termed the astral body. The astral body focuses the soul functions of thinking, feeling, and willing through the other bodies, into deeds on earth. Where do these soul functions live? They interweave in subtle spaces within the earth sphere. In the illustration, I show them interweaving though distinct. If I showed all the interweaving completely, it would be more difficult to perceive any one aspect. You can tune in to different layers because they all have specialized frequencies. Feelings, thoughts, and deeds can be refined or coarse, all interweaving around and through us. We can tune into and express many kinds and varieties of these soul functions.

The human being by its nature stands on the earth, takes in

and sheds mineral substance, breathes in the air, is made mostly of water, generates warmth, and thus lives within the bodies of the being of the earth, Sophia—those bodies that we call the "elements." (*The Sophia Elements Meditations* works specifically with these different bodies of Sophia.) And the physical human body has sensitive etheric and astral bodies to animate it and relate it to the environment.

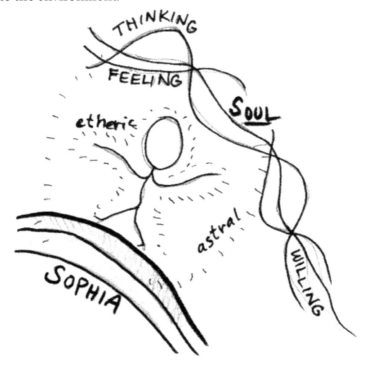

We can picture the continually moving and interweaving of the ability to cognize, the ability to emote—have affect—and the ability to do—to act, each with more refined and more coarse versions. All of these interpenetrate. Within this realm, we can see the effects of the movements of the planets in relation to the soul functions, both at birth and afterwards. The planets in their movements stimulate soul forces to move and express. Continuous movement, mostly rhythmic yet also creative, typifies the working of the soul forces. As the organism discovers patterns that effectuate desired goals, and lay them into permanency as personality, the risk is that the soul forces become hardened.

Beyond the Soul

The "I"—our true individuality, our highest self, the foundation of our being that has endured many lifetimes and many educational opportunities—lies beyond the physical. This ability to say "I am!" and "I exist!" lies also beyond the realm of soul. The "I" is more rarified than soul, yet works through the functions of soul into the bodies on the earth. This is the true individuality of the human being, something that shows its radiant promise in a youth, and really lands in the vehicle of this life and this personality after a couple of decades of preparation. Rather than say, "my soul," it is more accurate to say, "my 'I' working through realms of soul." But that terminology is cumbersome. We can continue to use the word "soul" to refer to the "I" working through the powers of soul realms. Your "I" is both elusive, floating as in the picture beyond the sphere of Saturn, and yet it's right here and available at any moment. The "I" endures beyond this particular physical body and this particular life.

Ad and Henriette Dekkers have worked for many years to create exercises that help you distinguish between the four bodies—physical, etheric, astral, and "I"—and have summarized their work in their new book, *A Psychology of Human Dignity* (cited at the end of the book). In anthroposophic psychology, the four bodies are meant to work in balance in service of the development of the human being. Contrary to the aims of many religious and spiritual movements, one can have too much "I" in expression in one's life. An excessive "I," lording over the other bodies, can lead to stress on the other bodies, showing as the schizotypal "space-cadet," hypersensitive, dazed and confused, and not functional. Sometimes the self-cutter can be understood as too much "I" trying to find the essence of life through the blood, the carrier of "I" forces, and through exploration of the borderlands of death; the self-cutter feels an immensely strong pull to discover the essence and foundation of life itself. Such an insight is true and profound, but also not true, certainly very impractical. The intimations of advanced states, and experiences of them, require integration. Balance of the four bodies leads to a more secure development over the long term of this and subsequent lives.

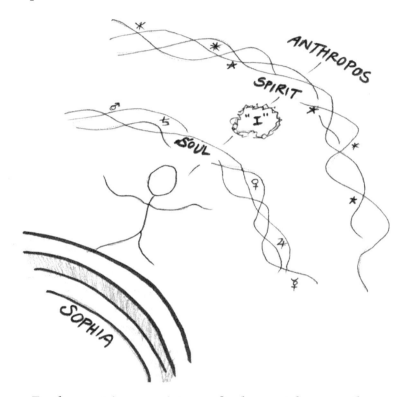

Further out in our picture—further out because they are more refined, and actually more universal—is Spirit, a reality far more refined and powerful than Soul, a reality also with several kinds of functions. We can use the mysterious names for them from ancient wisdom traditions: manas, buddhi, and atma. Or we can name the spirit functions as Rudolf Steiner did: Spirit-Self, Life-Spirit, and Spirit-Man. Or we could name them by their main characteristics: true Imagination, true Inspiration, and true Intuition.

The Nature of Consciousness

The previous diagram can clarify a much greater range of psycho-spiritual realities. Yet it fails by suggesting that spiritual development requires a linear journey, as in a Newtonian paradigm where you have to travel from here to there, across a distance that takes time. In reality these states interpenetrate both in space and time. Everyone has experienced momentary "anomalies" of brilliant insight, glorious revelation, great strength, prescience, and healing love. However, we should not conclude so easily that "you're already there"—enlightened, holy—and then with a satisfied smile, cease trying, as I have experienced with more than a few New Agers and non-dualists (not all, by any means). We continue to learn, to explore, to develop, in service of development of the "I" and of the "I" of the other.

We can learn from quantum physics, a paradigm that has been developed for many decades, though it has not influenced the mainstream Newtonian thinking. True, we can experience any state of the diagram at any moment. And, also true, we have tendencies to familiar modes of consciousness. The task is to make them all accessible.

In the quantum world, particles can be "things" in one place, or energy waves pulsing over a distance. When waves interact, patterns emerge. Things disappear in one place and appear in another; they don't move visibly from one place to another. You speak of knowing where something is, say an electron, with higher or lower tendency. (I prefer the term tendency to probability, because the term probability has implications for what sort of beings are in charge of the phenomenon. That's a teaser, and this topic will just have to wait for a presentation on statistics and the notion of randomness.) The more you know where something, say an electron, is, the less you can know about the strength and quality of its energy. The mysteries of quantum phenomena occur at small scales, at the level of atoms, the foundations of matter. Yet these phenomena occur also at the levels built on those foundations, the scales with which we are familiar. Consider an advanced cancer patient who asks for one more test before going into surgery. The tests reveal that the tumor has disappeared—gone, nowhere to be found. Had this happened only once, it would be disregarded as an "anomaly." Yet sponta-

neous remissions have happened many times, still a small percentage of the whole but far more than a few.

Now examine the qualities of your own consciousness. It
might take a weekend of Vipassana training to help you notice
what's happening moment to moment in your awareness. Or
you can do it now. Notice how impressions and pictures arise
and fall, and how diverse they are. Rather than see this as an ir-
ritant—as discursive mind or "monkey mind"—anthroposophic
psychology understands this as a natural scanning through the
various realms of soul, "I," and spirit (more on this in chapter 12),
a process that can be expanded to include more zones of being.
The scanning is normal. When the scanning becomes tightly
constrained, it appears as perseveration, or insistent repeated
patterns. Expansions of the scanning can help you incorporate
vast realms into your own sense of "I."

The "I" is not a point of existence in a specific time and place.
The individual is not a score on a depression questionnaire or on
a GAF (Global Assessment of Functioning) scale. Your client is
not just a lump of protoplasm sitting in the chair opposite. The
"I" is a wave form of tremendous power that can appear here
and there. One of the best sound bites I received from a spiritual teacher is: "I am here; I am there." Simultaneously present,
both here and there. The "here" is closer, more familiar, perhaps
something calling for my attention such as a crying child. The
"there" is another zone or realm or state, which appears as there
but is "here" too. The quality of our own consciousness, and its
ability to travel far and wide in an instant, guides us toward an
experience of ourselves and of our client that is far more creative. This is why relationships are, from the point of view of anthroposophy, so important: The various wave forms of each of us
overlap to make astonishing patterns that can be worked with
actively. That is, if we notice and engage.

Wave-forms and other aspects of the approach of quantum
physics can explain spontaneous remissions, as in disappear-
ance of a tumor or a disease. This view can also explain why
we have difficulty in the consensual paradigm of psychology in
knowing how to repeat a spontaneous remission. A wave-form

understanding of the range from body to spirit can also explain spontaneous madness, once named a "nervous break-down" and whose incidence is predicted by some to increase in our time as environmental stresses increase.

The counselor's responsibility is to continue to master the full breadth of experience of all states and realms, moving freely between them all—and then to assist others in that process. We can call this the development of Spiritus (from chapter i). The greater the sense of Spiritus, the greater the capacity of the counselor to hold on during spontaneous movements in one's clients, either for good or ill, and then to help them understand what happened.

The spirit functions (Spirit-Self, Life-Spirit, Spirit-Anthropos) interpenetrate with the zone of the great fixed stars, distant from one point of view, and very present in the resonances that they emanate to our Sophia. The great stars Aldebaran and Antares, Spica the Goddess Star, Regulus the heart of the Lion, and many others, have a deep effect on our existence. Interwoven with those levels of refined power lies a great being that was sent by even greater beings from the center of our galaxy: Anthropos, the possible human being, the becoming human being, the template set into the cosmos by the great creators at the core of our galaxy.

The imagination by ancient peoples of a template for humanity—Anthropos, sometimes called Adam or Adam Kadmon—means that something greater is working through the "I AM" of each individual, something arising from the wellspring of humanity itself—Anthropos, the possible human being. Now you can understand why I translate Steiner's ultimate capacity not as "Spirit-Man," rather as "Spirit-Anthropos." The question then becomes, "How can 'I,' as an individual imbued with blessings from realms of spirit, working through my soul capacities—how can 'I' further the task of Anthropos on this earth?"

Sources

This picture comes from four important influences. Firstly, my own critique of neo-Darwinian evolution. This predominant creation story of our times does not cohere. The many exceptions or "anomalies," the gaps in the fossil record, the inability to embrace or explain consciousness, and many other challenges erode its predominance. Though helpful to explain processes of change, it does not explain origins. I have written about this extensively as a preface to my play, co-written with my wife, *Darwin in the Dreaming,* and in a position paper "Monkeys on the Mind." When you let go of the dominant story, you are for a time story-less. Then you can see better where the story has been taking you. If you see yourself, as one does in the daze of Darwinism, as the product of random genetic mutations selected by the violent happenstances of living conditions, surviving only in order to procreate, thus passing on "selfish" genes, then your only purpose, especially after child-bearing, can be to stimulate your senses toward pleasure. You can ask, "Who profits from me thinking of myself in that way?" You can ask that question of every creation story. For Darwinism, you can ask, "Who profits from me thinking of myself as random and insignificant, the product of violent competition yet without purpose?"

The second influence on this research came from the fourth-century texts left in a large jar found in 1945 near Nag Hammadi, Egypt. These are not the same as the Dead Sea Scrolls, found also in a jar near the Essene settlement at Qumran. In the Dead Sea Scrolls one finds a kind of aggressive, zealous writing and a violent rejection of any other than the chosen few. The Nag Hammadi texts are completely different, written by various sects of Gnostics, a Greek word meaning "Knowers," or "Those Who Remember." There were extreme Gnostics also, though nothing as extreme as the authors of the Dead Sea Scrolls. The authors of the Nag Hammadi texts wrote about Sophia as a divine being, how she became the body of the earth. They wrote about Anthropos as being sent from the galactic center to assist Sophia. They wrote about Christos, the divine masculine counterpart to the living being of our earth, Sophia. They wrote about retarding anti-life spirits, who have plagued humanity since the beginning. John Lash has been an important interpreter of these Gnostic texts.

The third resource for this picture comes from the inspirations of the philosopher Rudolf Steiner, sometimes through his vast panoramas of philosophy—that common word meaning love with the quality of intimate friendship, *philia*, of Sophia—and sometimes through integration of little hints found here and there in his six thousand lectures. Most of the terms in this picture come from Steiner, and also from the fine interpretations of Steiner from Robert Sardello and William Bento. What's new in this presentation is a deeper understanding of the name that Steiner used for his philosophy of life: anthroposophy. In the picture that I present, we see Anthropos in relation to Sophia, with the human in the middle.

Though Steiner did not have access to the Nag Hammadi texts, he comprehended similar truths about the origins of the world. His name for the most developed spirit function is often translated Spirit-Man. The word Man should be seen in its fullest, as Anthropos. The final stage of human development should thus be termed Spirit-Anthropos, that part of the individual that has come through Spirit to encounter its source in Anthropos. (Steiner's term Spirit-Man works more easily in the German language, where "Man" [*Mensch*] is seen as much more general, and as indeed a promise of what human beings can become, in other words, as Anthropos.) When the human being becomes conscious in spirit at this level of refinement, that human being knows his or her roots in Anthropos, and understands the task of connection with Sophia.

The fourth and most important resource for this picture comes from my own inner reflections and meditations, encouraged by the recently emerged Lineage of Sophia. I had to verify this grand picture through personal experience. The Gnostic texts state that Anthropos has a task in relation to Sophia, working through the lives of individual human beings. For me this has been a revolutionary concept, and one that I have sought to verify and deepen through my own experience. All creation stories are myths, unproven and unprovable from our little vantage point. One must choose the mythos that resonates (literally sounds in a harmonic manner) with one's own inner life.

Soul and Spirit

What does this picture tell us about the difference between soul and spirit? I attended a wonderful conference that began two days before December 21st in the year 2012, the dreaded day of the predicted end of the world, according to some readings of a Mayan calendar (one of the several calendars that the Mayans used). On December 20th the conference organizers announced, "Isn't it awesome that this is the last day of the old era and the whole world is going to change tomorrow on December 21st? All the conflict and pollution will be gone—tomorrow!" On the next day they announced, "Isn't it wonderful?! This is the first day of the New Age. Everything is different now. We will receive all that we deserve: freedom, light, love, peace, simplicity." In that astonishing display of naiveté, I realized something profound about the difference between soul and spirit.

Those traits—freedom, light, simplicity, peace, love—are traits of spirit. They exist as truths, outside of time and outside of space. They exist everywhere and eternally. The speakers were correct in claiming these as our birthright. The realm of spirit is our birthright. That has been the clarion call of the New Age for decades. Here's the problem: Many people realize that they don't have these features prominent in their lives. They then make the mistake of feeling guilty—"I don't have my birthright because I am a bad person"—or blaming—"So-and-so is the reason that I don't have freedom, light, and all those other things that I deserve." I have observed this guilt and blame burdening many people. "I must have done something wrong because I've not realized freedom, light, ... (etc.)." Some modern philosophies and sects make it even clearer: If you don't have these things, indeed if you're not wealthy, then God does not love you.

This is a mistake! Light, freedom, love, and the rest can be attained by traveling a path of development (what I call the rise through Spiritus in chapter 1). Through the difficulties and challenges, we mature into wiser and more loving beings. We polish the rough diamond to reveal the true perfection that was always there. The path toward revelation of spirit involves the work of the soul. To fulfill its task, the soul is very attracted to darkness, bondage, complexity, grief, difficulty, strife, the frustrating crunch of inadequate time, death—whatever the opposites are of all the traits that belong timelessly to spirit. The soul—through the capacities of thinking, feeling, and willing—puts us into a setting where we can learn through challenge in the domain of Time. We learn to transform the putrid kitchen scraps of our lives into life-affirming compost. We can know that our birthright in spirit is to know bliss and freedom and so forth, and we can speak of "return" to that idyllic place, but that's not the way to grow and mature. From your soul's struggles in the messiness of life, you can learn to become a better human being. If you really had a life that was right now full of light and peace and bliss, you wouldn't make use of your opportunity in this lifetime to work on yourself. We can touch upon the purity of spirit in every moment, and certainly in between lifetimes. Then we decide to come back again and work some more in the realm of soul, using the memory of the soul, traditionally named karma.

The relation between one's everyday life and one's "I" unfolds over an entire lifetime. The "I" does not seat into the human being very strongly until the age of 21, and even then it comes and goes. In childhood, the parents or parent-figures can sometimes hold the child's "I" in trust, so to speak, supporting the knowing of the child's divinity until the child is ready to take it on himself or herself. A "guru," which means "light-from-dark," traditionally had the same responsibility: to hold the "I" of the student or "chela" in trust, while the student developed further. The "I" held in trust by the elder is meant to be released after maturation has been attained, though often the chela has to wrestle free from the guru or the young adult from the parent. These dramas in the realm of soul have as their prize the presence and power of the "I."

The "I," the enduring part of oneself that plunges us into earthly existence, has the task to mature the less developed vehicles of the human being. One develops one's individuality. The frequent mentions in workshop advertisements of "find out who you really are" promote a true goal, yet one not easily attained in a weekend workshop. I enjoy the cleverness of the sound bite,

"Be who you are; everybody else is taken," yet the flippancy of this invitation and command conceals the difficulty of the journey to find this truth.

For the more mature, the "I" assists in the relation of Anthropos and Sophia. Human beings slowly improving their grasp of spirit become a better and better bridge between Anthropos and Sophia.

Anthropos-Sophia is the true root of the term Anthroposophy, the philosophy that guides you through the hard knocks of this lifetime. Anthropos exists as a spark in each and every one of us. We all have a purpose coming generally yet persistently from Anthropos, then more specifically through our "I," the part that endures through lifetimes, and finally most specifically through the "I" clothed in the powers of soul in this lifetime in this place on earth—soul as the clothing of the "I" at work in this messy school called life. As individuals we work through the "I," working in concert with others, to link Anthropos and Sophia.

There is another force in this picture, Sophia's consort, a divine masculine to her divine feminine. Some term this partner, this twin flame essential to her wholeness, *thelete*, some as Christos, some as Christ-light. In this view, the linking of Anthropos to Sophia becomes the catalyst to the marriage of Christos and Sophia. It becomes complicated to invoke the name Christos in our age, as so few can expand to first-hand experience, beyond the dogmas of their religions either for or against the name Christ. I have not included Christos in the illustration because that would require maneuvering the many misconceptions of the true Christ, and such an explanation would require going all the way to the center of the galaxy, to what the Gnostics called the Pleroma—the fullness, the all-and-everything. We will explore that another time. For now we can take refuge in a little saying from Thomas Aquinas (the "doctor" of the Catholic Church, and an important figure in anthroposophical philosophy): "One may never have heard of the name 'Christ,' but be closer to God than a priest or nun."[8]

---

8 That helpful little saying comes from David Ladinsky (2002), *Love Poems from God*. New York: Penguin Compass, p. 125. He has several sayings

The mechanistic picture provides a much smaller view of what it means to be a human being. In the mechanistic picture, there isn't any purpose to your life. You are the product of random selection pressures working on random mutations in a tiny backwater of a random galaxy. If there's no purpose, then what else is more important than pleasure, base sensual delights? In truth the mechanistic picture functions as a concept or a dream, an illusion in the mind of the human being that distracts us from realizing the larger picture.

In the larger picture, how is this for the human being birthing and growing up, drawing in the etheric substance from the Sophia atmosphere and the mineral substance from the Sophia earth? How does this human being feel the interaction with the planets of the solar system cycling round and round? How does my physical-etheric existence draw up from the earth, water, air, and warmth of Sophia? How can I help draw in my "I" into my bodies, in such a way that Anthropos can come streaming through atma, through Spirit-Anthropos, then through buddhi and manas, to meet with Sophia? In that context you can see the darkness and struggle in the soul realm as the appropriate meeting ground for these fiery influences. Then you feel connected with the purpose of humanity as a whole as it streams into the density of your life here. Your personal destiny finds its place in that larger purpose.

Our life on this planet is meant to balance between soul and spirit, in ever-new circulation between the ethereal and the mundane. In this way we grow. A verse from Steiner summarizes some of this picture:

> My head bears the being of the resting stars.
> My breast harbors the life of the wandering stars.
> My body lives and moves amidst the elements.
> This am I.

The head can feel the being-ness and beings of spirit. They move through thinking and the sphere of the head. *My head*

---

of Aquinas, who lived from 1225 to 1274, and wrote the immense *Summa Theologica* still used as the foundation for the Catholic Church.

bears the being of the resting stars. Then, at the soul level, we can feel the moving of the planets: *My breast harbors the life of the wandering stars.* Feeling in the torso, centered in heart and lungs. Finally, to the level of earth and its substances, its elementary forms, and elemental beings: *My body lives and moves amidst the elements.* And the conclusion? *This am I. This am I.* The "I" finishes and completes the whole.

Human Senses

Let's take another look at the senses. In the mechanistic view we have little windows onto a portion of reality, only a portion of reality because most of reality we don't perceive. In the larger anthroposophical view, the senses aren't just little windows; they are whole zones of awareness that actually move between the physical level through the etheric, astral, soul, and right into spirit levels. Every sense has capacities beyond the commonly agreed limits of sight, of hearing, of touch—limits that can be called the con-sensual, meaning shared sensory, and often termed the "normal range." We have the ability to sense more than the tip of the iceberg of reality; we can sense its entirety. Every sense has a window, yet more than a window—the sense provides a pathway that can connect us deeply to a certain aspect of the reality of spirit in matter. When people say "what you see is what you get," they are typically trying to limit the situation to what the dullest person could describe. I respond to "what you see is what you get" with "well then, learn to see better; open up your sight." Open up all of your senses. Especially in this age when the senses are being shut down by overstimulation, open them further! A long and wide sensory window can link us into the phenomena of the bodies of Sophia in all her elements, mineral, water, air, and warmth (fire).

The recognition of Anthropos does not mean that there are human beings on a distant planet sending down little messengers that look like us. Anthropos has a mission—a mission from the galactic center to assist in a marriage, a reaffirmation of the partnership of Christos and Sophia. There are others engaged in this drama. The archangel-become-archai Micha-el is often mentioned. We each have to find our way to the reality of the larger picture through our own experiences.

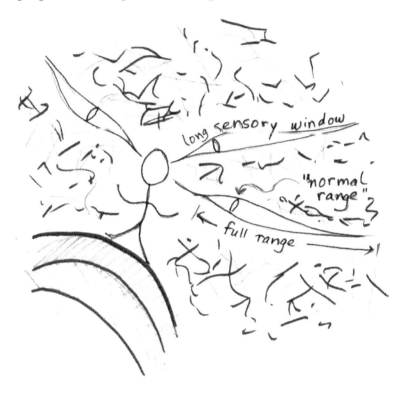

I haven't put retarding or adversarial spirits on this map as they can cause confusion. That's often their role, to create confusion. Once you understand the enormity of the relation between the individual "I" to the cosmos, then you can begin to tackle the forces that attempt to work against that understanding, and against any positive development in your life and in the world. I also haven't put in the human shadow or double, complications that we can take on at another time.

Applications to Counseling Psychology

Many secrets of human psychology, including guidance for counseling psychology, can be found in this map. I have presented this level of complexity in order to give the notion to you that, when you're dealing with another human being, both you and the other have these dynamics. Neither you nor your client are islands, independent and unconnected entities standing on the surface of the earth, mechanistically pulled this way and that from programmed responses. In mainstream therapy, the goal of the therapist is to assist the client to get rid of negative symptoms and adapt to social norms. However, when you touch the possibilities in the larger picture you realize, "Every moment and every thought is important. I'm in a streaming current of moving energies. There is a through-line beyond my present circumstances. My through-line is partly in this day and week and lifetime. And it goes beyond all those. I can and must ponder my next lifetime; everything I do or think or feel affects that lifetime. I can do my very best to attune to what is streaming through me, and do my best not to obstruct, nor sabotage, nor harden that sacred life streaming force." I find this vantage very helpful in the consulting room. It turns symptoms from obstacles to living the pleasurable life into treasures that have awakened the individual to his or her own true being. You can then understand, for example, punishing guilt as coming from the struggles of soul with the world, whereas conscience comes from more refined spiritual realms, where certain beings take the trouble to mirror to you the consequences of your actions on other sparks of Anthropos. Too often the pain of guilt mistakenly causes people to throw off all responsibility, including conscience, thus losing connection with their own more developed selves. As a therapist, you can guide clients to the difference.

With this larger picture in my mind and personal experience, sitting with a client becomes an immense privilege. I'm sitting across from a human being who also has a sacred "I" and is a conduit to Anthropos in relation to Sophia. The client may be completely identified with the hungers of the body, with the smallest mechanical picture of what it means to be human: survival panic may grip them in its ebbs and flows; they may curse their lives, or the lives of others; success may look like, "I've got mine, everyone else can bugger off." Thus the client may not realize his or her sacred foundations. Yet I can know that those foundations are solidly present, and available for discovery. The method of discovery is whole-soul conversation.

Gold, Light, and Conversation

From a fairy tale we have a confirmation and refinement of this picture. The great writer Johann Wolfgang von Goethe spent much of his time attending to requirements of his government position (privy council to the duke, looking at highways, silver mines, construction of government buildings) and necessary decisions for his large household. On the side he wrote scripts for plays, including a play-script of the legend of Dr. Faust that he revised right up to his death. He also wrote *The Green Snake and the Beautiful Lily*, in the style of fairy tale, allegory, and fantasy. At one point in the story, the mystical snake, having spoken with the bronze king and the silver king, meets the gold king. The gold king asks, "What is more precious than gold?" A king by his nature likely considers himself at a peak of social development, and this one has passed beyond the stages of bronze and silver. Gold! One must hold it in its 24-karat pure state to understand its great value, the highest regal function of the mineral kingdom. In the great tradition of dragons and plutocrats, one can feel satisfied with such a treasure. To be made of gold must bring with it a sense of fulfillment, the radiating warmth of the heart, and the preciousness of high value.

Yet the gold king asks, "What is more precious than gold?" It might have been a mocking question, but unfolding events show that this king asks in sincerity, implying that a characteristic of gold, once achieved rather than merely yearned for, is a kind of humility.

The snake, whom we later find at the end of the tale is the messenger of the most powerful spirit realms, does not hesitate to answer, "Light!" This implies that beyond the pinnacle of corporeality—in the mineral kingdom, gold, and in the social realm, kingship—one can seek and perhaps become pure light. A verse from Rudolf Steiner begins, "In purest outpoured light shimmers the divinity of the world." Before manifestation in this world of any thing comes the shimmering of divinity through light. One can recall the auras and halos depicted by great painters and one's own experiences of radiance from some of the things in the world. One becomes aware of the mystery of light, its action sometimes as wave and sometimes as particle, and its intelligence—how it seems to know when the investigator is looking. Light sets the standard for the ultimate in velocity, the key relation between matter and energy ($E=mc^2$), as well as the goal of spiritual practice. Light is the carrier of blessing. We are blessed by light. From the snake we learn that light is the more precious precursor of gold and kingship.

In this tale, we have the shortest answer for what is soul and what is spirit—gold for soul and light for spirit. Gold tells the tale of the "I" working with the soul's help in realms of densest matter. One begins with mineral substance, and must refine that substance. All metals are hidden in rock and must be teased out with water and fire. The alchemist struggles to refine further and further, to find the metals in the slag, and to elevate those metals to gold. Carl Jung thought that the medieval alchemists' writings were not about chemical processes but about psychological processes, refining the slag of the inner world further and further, ending with gold. Others insisted that the alchemists' symbolic language concerned chemistry. For the tasks of the human being on earth, it works both ways. Gold is both psychic and physical, symbol and shining metal—the summary of the work of the "I" through the realms of soul.

Light summarizes the work of spirit. It reaches into our world of senses, yet beckons toward the inner light of inspiration and intuition, what the Gnostics called "organic light." The accomplishment of the soul as gold requires a light that dips into our world, and blesses us, revealing the shine of the gold. In the Waldorf School curriculum for the eighth grade, the teacher warms a piece of gold in flame to the point that it glows. The quality of that glow can never be forgotten.

I feel satisfied with the snake's answer, pointing from soul to spirit. But the gold king surprises me by inquiring further. The gold king asks, "And what is more precious than light?" The snake immediately replies: "Conversation!" The king does not ask again, as he has found the final answer.

In this brief and potent exchange, there is a trajectory from the common people to the refined power of kingship, from the mineral earth to its highest refinement in gold as the height of the soul, from king and gold to light as emblem of spirit, and now... to the exchange in speech, gesture, and feeling between two human beings. This trajectory gathers all that came before as a foundation for what comes next. The final includes the former. The most comprehensive is exchange of spirit-filled words, creative words, in the sense of "In the beginning was the Word." From this comes the marriage of Anthropos and Sophia and Christos.

The Most Precious Sophia

Rudolf Steiner rarely spoke of Sophia directly. In one lecture, he made it clear that she is the most precious of all. Here from Steiner's lecture of February 13, 1923, lecture 4 of *Awakening to Community*:

> The term "Anthroposophy" should really be understood as synonymous with "Sophia," meaning the content of consciousness, the soul attitude and experience that make a man ['man' meaning the individual human being of either gender] a full-fledged human being.

Thus, Sophia assists the individual to mature into Anthropos, the "full-fledged human being."

Recalling that the translation of the Greek word Sophia is wisdom, and that the translation of Anthropos is "the becoming human being," or "the possible human being," and together often are translated as "wisdom of the human being," we can follow Steiner as he continues:

> The right interpretation of "Anthroposophy" is not "the wisdom of man" [again, 'man' meaning human being in general], but rather "the consciousness of one's humanity." In other words, the reversing of the will, the experiencing of knowledge, and one's participation in the time's destiny, should all aim at giving the soul a certain direction of consciousness, a "Sophia."

Thus Anthropos and Sophia work conjointly through the soul to assist the development of human beings who, in turn, assist Anthropos and Sophia to fulfill their (and our) destiny. Steiner names three tasks here. First is the "reversing of the will," which means meeting the stream of will-force streaming from the future, and disciplining it; through inhibition of impulsive reactions, one frees powerful will forces for creativity. Second is "experiencing of knowledge," which means opening to the kinds of revelations that are available not only to thinking, but through the three functions of thinking, feeling, and willing, and their more refined counterparts, Spirit-Self, Life-Spirit, and Spirit-Anthropos. Third is participation in the destiny opportunity of one's time, that is, what is happening in the world and where one can find one's place to engage in the world. These combine to give a place for Sophia in oneself and oneself in Sophia. As with many statements by Steiner, this one requires pondering and trying things out to find one's way to its gold, light, and exchange through conversation.

Whole-Soul Conversation

In anthroposophic psychology, we work via "whole-soul conversation." By this we mean the "I" of the therapist, working through capacities of soul, inspired by spirit, and finding its higher self within the mission of Anthropos, all levels of "Self." The "I" of the therapist regards the "I" of the client in the same way. The therapist is interested not only in the symptoms and their alleviation, but with the client's "I." A whole-soul conversation essentializes all those words into what happens when you choose to sit across from another human being in need, whether it's a friend or a client. You engage thinking, feeling, and willing with each other. You remind each other about spirit. You remind each other about something very rich that you share—more precious than gold or light. You share the mission of Anthropos, the possible human being. Through conversation, you come to know yourself—the "I" comes to know itself through another "I"—gold comes to know itself, also with light, also with kingship/queenship.

Studies have shown that the most powerful mode of therapy to help another is conversation. Several recent studies have admitted that being held by another—even if in the strictly limited encounter of the protocols of Cognitive Behavioral Therapy—is superior to psychoactive drugs; the confession is that drugs are cheaper and therefore used more often. A whole-soul conversation parallels the discovery by Werner Heisenberg that you can't know both an electron's position and its level of energy. Once you measure either position or energy, you've interrupted the system to the extent that you can't know the other property. This came to be called the Uncertainty Principle. We can reframe this here. Once you attempt to assess yourself or another, the act of articulation and of listening alters the other attributes of the client. Self-knowledge as a process or an active verb alters even the parts that are not being observed nor described. For both therapist and client (or uncle and nephew), whole-soul conversation has an impact on the underlying states that move far beyond the issues apparently being discussed. In the crucible of whole-soul conversation, "uncertainty" becomes the developing freedom from fixity.

Does the kind of story-telling that we've been using with *The Green Snake* derail the intelligent skeptic, or does it help one come closer to soul, and eventually to spirit? The use of metaphor (George Lakoff), of narrative psychology (Michael White, Theodore Sarbin, and others), of reframing (Milton Erickson and the NLP systems), Open-Dialogue Therapy (from Western Lapland in Finland), the work with concentric circles by my wife and me—and their predecessors in mythic psychology (Carl Jung), Gestalt psychology (Fritz Perls), even Rational Emotive Behavioral Therapy (Albert Ellis—"What are you telling yourself?"), as well as many unnamed others—become more powerful in the framework of Anthroposophic Psychology—as initially framed by Rudolf Steiner, and interpreted by the authors of this book and those mentioned in the readings at the end. A specific approach through anthroposophy to biography is now taught in several places. And now the development of Anthroposophic Psychology: Whole-soul conversation includes the story of oneself—of one's "I"—as it finds its way into this world, through the smaller stories of one's daily life. It relates one's personal story to the story of creation of the whole world. One understands one's own story in relation to the minutiae of this moment and to the grand gestures of the cosmos, the story of Sophia and Anthropos.

"Talk therapy," for which Freud, Adler, and Jung became famous, thus doesn't function only by helping the individual find a path to the individual's own "I." Talk therapy can initiate whole-soul conversation that connects "I" with "I," and through that a connection to the cosmic power of Anthropos.

It is so much easier to hold a client or friend, suffering in your presence—to hold this sufferer in the warmth of whole-soul conversation—when you accept soul and spirit and work actively with their powers.

Exercise to Discover These Greater Influences

An exercise can help reveal aspects of this grand view of the human being. This is not whole-soul conversation but can become a prelude to it. The method is called the Repeated Question form, which I learned from the Diamond Heart approach, and now present with gratitude to those teachers. It goes like this:

David: What's a favorite dessert?
Respondent: Ice cream.
David: Thank you. Tell me, what's a favorite dessert?
Respondent: Chocolate.
David: Thank you. Tell me, what's a favorite dessert?
Respondent: Apple pie, with a glaze of maple syrup on top, and cooked so that the crust is crunchy.
David: Thank you.

And so it goes. I have obviously picked a mundane question for illustration. Your answers should be relatively brief. The coach's tone should be neutral. No matter what the respondent says, it's not for the coach to fix her or comment on the wisdom of her choices of dessert. Stay neutral and more interesting responses will arise. Always say "thank you" and then repeat the question. We'll do that one way and then we'll do it another way, three minutes each. Please find yourself in pairs facing each other.

The repeated question is: "What makes you feel most like your true Self?"

[This exercise is a very useful way of finding out about your images of your Self and how expanded and contracted that Self can be. They may reveal your relation to soul, spirit, Anthropos, and Sophia. And you are advised to learn this technique by beginning with something less daunting, such as your favorite dessert!]

Resources for Further Study
(in addition to the references at the end of the book)

Alexander, Eben (2012). *Proof of Heaven: A Neurosurgeon's Journey into the Afterlife*. Simon & Schuster. This supplements the comprehensive research by Raymond Moody and others on NDEs (Near-Death Experiences), in a very accessible manner. Appendix B of his book lists the standard materialist explanations for NDEs, with Alexander's systematic rebuttal.

Cremo, Michael A., and Richard Thompson (1998). *Forbidden Archaeology: The Hidden History of the Human Race*. Los Angeles: Bhaktivedanta Book Publishing. This nine hundred page book details the many well-documented "anomalies" that are not possible in the conventional model of evolution of human beings and societies. Cremo and Thompson have gone on to publish other pieces on this theme.

Dawkins, Richard (2008). *The God Delusion*. Mariner. It's important to understand the arguments of the materialists. When in chapter 4, Dawkins rejects reliance on one's own experience, it becomes very complicated as to what or whom to believe. Dawkins has written many other books, including *The Selfish Gene*, a concept referenced in this chapter.

Ellis, Albert, and Robert Harper (1997). *A Guide to Rational Living*. Chatsworth, CA: Melvin Powers Wilshire Book Co. This is a fully revised version of the original 1961 book that expressed the manifesto of the intellectual or mind soul, and gave the foundation for Cognitive Behavioral Therapy (CBT). The ten Irrational Beliefs and their antidote are a potent guide to thinking your way through problems, though, from the point of view of anthroposophic psychology, not the full picture of the human being.

Fromm, Erich (1979, recent edition 2013). *To Have or To Be?* Bloomsbury Academic. Fromm, the dock worker who wrote insightfully about social-psychological issues, describes the selling of one's life to a "job" in exchange for stuff. The possessions you own become the key to how you identify yourself. He contrasts this with being, in other words, with a life that acknowledges soul and spirit.

Lahood, Gregg (2010). "Relational Spirituality," parts 1 and 2, *International Journal of Transpersonal Studies*, 29(1), 31-78. This hard-hitting review of the history of Transpersonal Psychology traces the threads of many different philosophies, bringing together valuable insights to relate these streams, and find the truth of the matter.

Lakoff, George, and Mark Johnson (2003). *Metaphors We Live By*. Chicago: University of Chicago Press, second edition. The new epilogue for the second edition is especially helpful to understand story-telling in politics and the general culture, a form of myth-making.

Lash, John (2009). *Not in His Image: Gnostic Vision, Sacred Ecology, and the Future of Belief*. White River Junction, VT: Chelsea Green. Lash's main website, metahistory.org, has many resources on his approach to the wisdom of the Gnostics.

Lawlor, Robert (1991). *Voices of the First Day: Awakening in the Aboriginal Dreamtime*. Rochester, VT: Inner Traditions.

Lawlor, Robert (2014). *The Geometry of the End of Time*. An e-book available from Amazon, though expected as a print version at some point. Though challenging to read, the gems are worth the struggle to understand the relationships between the wisdom of the true Gnostics and the living Sophia.

Mayo-Wilson, Evan, Sofia Dias, Ifigeneia Mavranezouli, Kayleigh Kew, David M. Clark, A.E. Ades, and Stephen Pilling (2014). "Psychological and Pharmacological Interventions for Social Anxiety Disorder in Adults: A Systematic Review and Network Meta-Analysis," *Johns Hopkins Public Health Magazine,* spring 2014. Referred to at http://www.jhsph.edu/news/news-releases/2014/talk-therapy-not-medication-best-for-social-anxiety-disorder-large-study-finds.html

McClelland, David C. (2010) *The Achieving Society*. Martino Fine Books. The original of this work goes back to the 1970's. Daniel Goleman was a student of McClelland for some years.

Parnia, Sam. (2013) *The Lazarus Effect*. Rider.

Parnia, Sam. (2014) *Erasing Death*. New York: HarperOne. The thrust here concerns Parnia's abilities to bring the dead to life up to three hours after they have ceased functioning. He also has asked people to recall what happened during their time technically dead. Parnia's methods of study are reminiscent of J. B. Rhine's attempts to demonstrate ESP (extra-sensory perception) in which one person asks another to guess the pattern on a playing card—such as the six of spades. In our terms, the soul is simply not very interested in playing cards, but will demonstrate telepathy and out-of-body knowing when something dynamic engages its interest, such as emergencies for a loved one.

Robinson, James (1990). *The Nag Hammadi Library.* New York: HarperOne. Other versions of these documents are available, sometimes referred to as the Gnostic gospels (as in Elaine Pagels's work).

Sacks, Oliver (2013). *Hallucinations.* New York: Vintage.

SophiaLineage.com includes many of the references to Sophia, in relation to Anthropoε.

Steiner, Rudolf (1974). *Awakening to Community.* Spring Valley, NY: Anthroposophic Press.

Tresemer, David, and Lila Sophia Tresemer (2014). *The Sophia Elements Meditations.* From SophiaLineage.com. This publication, with related audio presentations, offers a step-by-step approach to the bodies of Sophia expressed in the elements of earth, water, air, fire, and the fifth element, love.

Tresemer, Lila, and David Tresemer, two DVDs—*Couple's Illumination* and *Brain Illumination*, both giving excellent pictures of energy dynamics beyond those perceived by the normal senses.

Tresemer, Lila, and David Tresemer (2015). *The Conscious Wedding Handbook.* Boulder, CO: Sounds True. This book about relationships is pertinent in this chapter because of its presentation of the concentric circles exercise, as a way of understanding the mythic structures behind your everyday experiences.

Tresemer, Lila, and David Tresemer (2010). *Darwin in the Dreaming.* Play script and Study Guide, available from David-Lila.com. This is further supplemented by David Tresemer's paper "Monkeys on the Mind," also available from David-Lila.com.

Weintraub, Pamela (2014). "Seeing the Light," *Psychology Today*, October 2014, 70-77, 88. This sides with the materialist views of near-death experiences (NDEs) as chemical experiences in the physical brain. Anomalies—such as detailed reports of events in other places during the NDE—are seen as anomalies not yet explained.

REFORMULATING CONTEMPORARY
CLINICAL ISSUES

INTRODUCTION TO CLINICAL ISSUES
by David Tresemer, Ph.D.

The earliest writings from ancient times show that human beings have created typologies and categories to try to understand each other. The earliest preserved theatre script, from Sumeria, found on clay tablets that have survived for five thousand years, depicts a disputation between hoe and plough, assigning qualities of human psychology and character to each. The Hoe-type and the Plough-type argue back and forth, each seeking to justify its character, to glorify its superiority, and to diagnose the other as unfit.

Each new attempt at classifying human beings into types and kinds creates a comprehensive theoretical framework, and then sees people and their behavior within that framework. One classification presents the Oedipal-type.[9] Another presents the Puer-type.[10] In one system that I enjoy for its utter simplicity, the counselor asks if the client is a Never-Enougher or a Super-Trooper.[11] The systems, each one in itself a model of coherence and beauty, usually don't integrate with each other (though Ken Wilber has attempted to integrate everything in his *Integral Psychology*). Discontent with previous systems leads to the creation of new systems. Wilhelm Reich perceived people as tending toward schizoid, oral, rigid, psychopathic, or masochistic, which was made practical by the Barbara Brennan School of Healing,

9 From Freud's psychodynamic theory based on the notion that the male child is sexually attracted to the mother and harbors often unexpressed antagonism for the father.

10 From the Puer-Aeternus archetype, one among many archetypes described by Carl Jung.

11 From Jack Rosenberg's very dynamic approach to human relations through sexuality, which in his view extends to every other aspect of life.

wherein these five tendencies were given pictures in internal and external energy fields. Isabel Myers and Catherine Briggs (a daughter and mother team) put Carl Jung's personality types into their Myers-Briggs Type Indicator, distinguishing between extraversion/introversion, sensing/intuition, thinking/feeling, and judging/perceiving. The Enneagram divides people into nine types, complete with healthy and unhealthy modes of expression. Alice Bailey's "Esoteric Psychology" identifies seven rays that influence behavior, finding different rays working in the individual at etheric, astral, and soul levels. Anthroposophy has a romance with the four traditional temperaments: Melancholic, Phlegmatic, Sanguine, and Choleric. And there are many more typologies. Each seeks to identify different human modes of being and expression.

In recent times, all of these typologies have yielded in whole or part to the mighty DSM.

World War II offered a great opportunity to evaluate large numbers of people, as everyone was mobilized in one way or another. People were shocked when 1.75 million Americans were rejected for service because of mental disability. In 1952, the American Psychiatric Association built on work done by the military in World War II to publish the *Diagnostic and Statistical Manual of Mental Disorders*. Extending to 130 pages, it defined 106 mental disorders. Its fifth edition, abbreviated DSM-5, was published in 2013 and numbers 950 pages. Even the quick reference version numbers four hundred pages. Over five hundred different disorders are named and numbered. A parallel publication put out by the World Health Organization called the International Statistical Classification of Diseases and Related Health Problems (ICD) is in its tenth edition; an eleventh is due soon. Perhaps most impressive in these classification encyclopedias are the lists of contributors, and the "task forces" of many professionals, on each of the topics. Diagnoses are defined, given numbers (for example, Histrionic Personality Disorder, ICD-9 code 301.50, ICD-10 F60.4, the codes cited in the DSM thus linking DSM and ICD). Eligibility for a diagnosis is less often measured by increasing frequency of one behavior, and more often from the presence of, for example, at least five of eight "criteria," each of which is qualitatively different from the others. Because "mental disorder" is seen on a continuum of seriousness, what I refer to in chapter ɪ as the Pathos Scale, these categories have entered the common language.

The etymology of *diagnosis* means to know (gnosis) as different (the sense of splitting from the prefix dia-), to discern, to recognize as separate. That's something we do every moment. The challenge comes when the diagnoses stick. Categorization dulls the brain. If you've named it, your warm interest is no longer engaged. This issue is addressed in every chapter in this section.

What are the driving forces behind this passion for a taxonomy of mental disturbance? Partly it comes from the desire to put some kind of order into the panoply of human experience. When someone says, "Oh, you're so 'OCD'!," from the DSM category for Obsessive-Compulsive Personality Disorder, or, "Oh, you're so 'three'!," often without referencing the system being used, it tells you that the labeller is seeking order in what is felt as a churning sea of chaos.

Another driving force is to know about the state of society. Trends change. Homosexuality was seen as pathology, and now isn't. Passive-aggressive behavior was seen as a problem, now is seen as normal. People want to know how the social fabric is holding up, how it is changing over time.

A major driving force for a central organizing principle of human behavior comes not from an academic or research organization but from an unexpected source: insurance companies.

Insurance companies are asked to support therapies for customers or employees of customers who are suffering. The company would like to validate if there really is a problem, a reasonable request, and now often requires a certification of dual (also called co-occurring) diagnosis—in other words, two problem areas—before it pays anything for treatment. One serious problem isn't enough. Entire institutes and treatment centers have sprung up because of these clauses in insurance arrangements: If an institute can attract a clientele that gets diagnosed with two numbered ailments in the DSM-5 (or the ICD), they have a thriving business. A reasonable request on the part of the insurance companies has had consequences for how human beings are perceived and treated. It's not that difficult, with so many overlapping named and numbered pathologies. Each of us could qualify to be placed in two or more boxes.

These manuals, the DSM and the ICD, have extraordinary power in our world. Both are used internationally. Their language has become common. Seeing psychological experiences as physically based aberrations that can be named, just as physical medicine does, has led to the codification of psychology, and to the mammoth increase of psychotropic medications—a kind of certainty that the insurance companies prefer. Product X is given for diagnosis A, product Y for diagnosis B, etc. This has led to some very big changes in a short amount of time. In the 1960's, for example, very few children were prescribed psychotropic drugs for anything; now the number is four million in the United States, and rapidly rising. Approximately one in every eight adults takes a psychiatric medicine for anxiety, bipolar depression (previously termed manic-depressive), or unipolar depression—despite the studies investigating the long-term effects of these drugs showing this to be a sad road down which to travel. Robert Whitaker's well-researched study, *Anatomy of an Epidemic*, documents the wreckage and calls for alternatives. The relegation of all psychic phenomena to physical biology has led to some very poor choices. When one takes on the perspective of anthroposophic psychology to include the dynamics not only of the physical body, but also the etheric and astral bodies, and the soul in the higher astral realm, then one can understand the symptoms within a broader context and respond in more appropriate ways, and with more than the current most popular drug.

There are many disorders identified by common sense as well as by the DSM-5. We cannot discuss them all. We have chosen common problems in order to cast them in the light of anthroposophy, both for appraisal about the dynamics underlying the syndromes, as well as for guidance in treatment.

Chapter 7 deals with twelve major personality disorders, from histrionic (which a hundred years ago was called hysteria), to schizoid (which is on a spectrum with the more serious schizo-phrenia), to narcissistic. Some are common terms used in common speech—narcissistic, obsessive-compulsive—and some are more difficult to understand—schizotypal, for example. Even though the Axis system from DSM-IV has been done away with in DSM-5, people continue to speak of Axis I (depression, autism, schizophrenia, etc.) and Axis II (personality disorders). Bento relied on the Axis II system in DSM-IV for his dissertation work, which he describes in chapter 7, in a brilliant study that brings the whole issue of personality disorder under the wing of somatic psychology and anthroposophy.

In every case, Bento's piece makes the so-called disorders of personality more intelligible and accessible.

Robert Whitaker criticizes the DSM for trying to make psychology into a medical profession—with named diagnostic categories that are defined materialistically for which medicines could then be targeted. For example, let us ponder "Social Anxiety Disorder," not one of the main twelve personality disorders but illustrative nonetheless. Social Anxiety Disorder in DSM-5 had been "Social Phobia" in DSM-IV. Before that, for centuries this syndrome had been seen as shyness or clumsiness around people, which most people simply grew out of. Suddenly in 1998 it became "the third most common psychiatric disorder in the United States, after depression and alcoholism." Once named and numbered, drugs were discovered to address that (new) syndrome. What had once succumbed to maturation, to a process of ensoulment, has become a cooperation between insurance companies, drug companies, physicians, and government. What about the side effects, and permanent changes to the sufferers' neurological systems? Whitaker's critique calls the entire system into question. Though Bento uses the naming system of the DSM, he loosens it, and opens it up again to larger contexts of soul and spirit, in a sense reclaiming these "disorders" for human beings. Anthroposophic psychology must recognize the predominant system of the culture while embracing a larger understanding of the human being.

In chapter 8, Edmund Knighton and William Bento address

depression, a widespread phenomenon in our time. They are less interested in differentiating between the twenty-two categories of depressive disorder from the DSM-5, and more on casting it in entirely new (anthroposophic) terms. The syndrome then opens up in a new way for understanding and treatment. This is sorely needed, because the research on anti-depressant drugs has shown that the medicalization of what has always been known as episodes of melancholy can lead to increased dysfunction.

Chapter 9 gives Roberta Nelson and William Bento an opportunity to grapple with addiction and its relation to the soul forces of the human being: thinking, feeling, and willing. Roberta Nelson shares some of her techniques for dealing with addiction which will be welcome to anyone who has had to confront this in self or other.

In chapter 10 Roberta Nelson and William Bento address trauma and post-traumatic stress, leading to Post-Traumatic Stress Disorder (PTSD). Though PTSD is given a single category in the DSM-5 (ICD code F43.10), Nelson and Bento find these dynamics much more widespread in our culture—widespread, often hidden, and often occurring later in adult life. "Delayed expression" to the mainstream means, "These dynamics live in the neurology, somehow, we don't know how, and we won't worry until the behavior shows up." "Delayed expression" or "delayed onset" instead ought to be a way of saying, "These dynamics live in the soul, and can be accessed not only through belief systems (thinking), but also through willing and feeling." The brilliance of Nelson's and Bento's approach is that it applies to everyone to some degree, for we have all experienced trauma (also noted in chapter 14 in relation to the trauma of birth). Anthroposophy has a unique approach to memory, which is the basis of trauma, and the beginnings of that understanding are laid out here.

The presentations in these chapters create openings for understanding the syndromes better, and bringing them into a context wherein the counselor knows the broader picture of what the client confronts. The approach of rank-ordering of anxiety-provoking stimuli and the systematic desensitization to those stimuli as found in Cognitive Behavioral Therapy (CBT, not to be confused with Closed Brain Trauma) have their place in therapeutic responses to the client's needs. And yet the understanding of the deeper dynamics of the psyche helps keep the counselor fresh and aware, not simply running the CBT protocol. The approach here completely undermines the proposal that we should mechanize delivery of CBT routines to be delivered by robot. In the hands of a practitioner alive in her or his thinking, feeling, and willing, the insights of CBT (and DBT and all the other cognitive techniques) come alive. One can sense this in the depth of these authors' understanding of psychological phenomena.

A counselor struggling with depression, addiction, PTSD, or any of the personality disorders in his or her clients may be frustrated by the absence of quick one-pill solutions. There are hints in these chapters, well worth following, that lead one to a ripening, an unfolding, a path. Anthroposophic psychology does not have formulaic protocols for these kinds of suffering. In all of these, one must understand the imbalance of the four bodies (physical, etheric, astral, and "I") and work to restore balance. In these chapters, hints are given about how to accomplish this task. Repeatedly, one is brought to the touchstones of anthroposophic counseling psychology: emphasis on the healthy, on salutogenesis (chapter 3), on soul and spirit (chapter 6 and throughout). From the firm ground of the good, true, and beautiful, a sufferer's soul-struggles can be appreciated and a pathway through can be found. One grows in spiritus and comes to terms with pathos (from chapter 1). One matures.

Resources for Further Study

Each of the chapters has references, as well as the general references at the end of the book. Here are a few of the other approaches referenced in this introduction:

Almaas, A. H. (2000 to 2011). *Diamond Heart*, Books 1, 2, 3, 4, 5. Shambhala. Almaas has written many other books on his "Diamond Heart" approach, though this series from his lectures to students is particularly helpful on specific themes.

Bailey, Alice (1971). *Esoteric Psychology, volumes 1 and 2.* New York: Lucis. Bailey's psychology is extensive, a comprehensive system revealed in these two volumes and in many other places in the five thousand pages of her work.

Brennan, Barbara. (1988) *Hands of Light: A Guide to Healing Through the Human Energy Field.* New York: Bantam. From her clairvoyance, Brennan was able to develop methods of healing, and a school for healers numbering in the thousands.

Frances, Allen (2014). *Saving Normal: An Insider's Revolt Against Out-of-Control Psychiatric Diagnosis, DSM-5, Big Pharma, and the Medicalization of Ordinary Life.* New York: William Morrow. The head of the task force that issued the fourth version of the Diagnostic and Statistical Manual of the American Psychiatric Association (DSM-IV) strikes out at the changes in DSM-5, finding it too much influenced by the combination of insurance companies, drug companies, and government to over-diagnose and then over-medicate the population.

Rosenberg, Jack (1986). *The Intimate Couple.* Turner. Rosenberg authored several books with a similar theme, and presented at Esalen Institute during those years.

Van der Kolk, Bessel (2014). *The Body Keeps the Score: Brain, Mind, and Body in the Healing of Trauma.* New York: Viking. Van der Kolk, a medical doctor, a "traumatologist," and a fine therapist. His insights prepare one for the approaches of anthroposophic psychology to trauma, as begun in chapter 10.

Whitaker, Robert (2010). *Anatomy of an Epidemic: Magic Bullets, Psychiatric Drugs, and the Astonishing Rise of Mental Illness in America.* New York: Broadway Books. This important book, summarized in this introduction, and referred to elsewhere, has pictured the failures of modern mechanized medicalized treatment, and opens the door for a psychology that recognizes soul and spirit.

CHAPTER 7

Personality Disorders Reconsidered
by William Bento, Ph.D.

Before I consider the disorders of personality, let me make a few remarks about how personality has been regarded by the discipline of psychology. There are dozens of theories about personality, each with its own definition of what personality is and is not. In the broadest view, there are five main theoretical models: Biological, Behavioral, Psychodynamic, Humanistic, and Trait-Based. To these I will add a sixth, Anthroposophic Psychology.

The Biological view suggests that genetics shapes the personality and endows it with the enduring traits of personality. Hans Eysenck (1916-1997) is a representative theorist of the biological model. In that view, the introvert type results from high cortical arousal (in the reticular formation—the brain stem, midbrain, medulla), leading such a person to avoid additional stimulation; the extrovert type results from a low cortical arousal causing such a person to seek out stimulating experiences. The personality is thus largely innate to the biological structures; it is governed by genes and chemistry.

The Behavioral perspective posits that personality is the result of interaction between the person and the environment. The behaviorist takes into account only observable and measurable behaviors, dismissing all personality theories that attribute traits to thoughts and feelings. Key theorists in this model are B. F. Skinner (1904-1990) and John B. Watson (1878-1958). This approach has enjoyed a recent renaissance in the name of Cognitive Behavioral Therapy. Personality is seen as patterns of behavior learned and reshaped by conditioning from the environment.

Within the Psychodynamic theory, heavily influenced by Sigmund Freud (1856-1939), personality is considered to arise out the unconscious mind and the impact of childhood experiences prior to or at the edges of recollection. The two most prominent approaches are Sigmund Freud's "psychosexual stage theory" and Erik Erikson's (1902-1994) "stages of psychosocial development." Both Freud and Erikson emphasized the increasing capacity of what Freud called the ego (the sense of "I") to navigate through stages of development. In Freud's view, the ego moderates between the demands of the id (instinctual needs and urges), the superego (ideals and morals), and reality (the consensual context of ongoing situations). Erikson postulated that the ego was involved in the maturation of the personality. For him the personality progressed through a series of stages with certain universal conflicts and themes arising at each stage. The notion common to psychodynamic theorists is that for each rocky road a person climbs, there is an opportunity to become stronger from the experience. Carl Jung (1875-1961), initially a student of Freud's, expanded these dynamics to greater heights and depths, finding in the dramas of a personal life the pictures of mythic good and evil.

The Humanistic theory of personality pivots around the importance of "free will" and life experiences unique to each individual. For the humanist, these two factors contribute to the development of personality. Core to the idea of personality is the concept of self-actualization, a concept that assumes that each person has an innate need for personal growth toward a sense of mastery—an ideal missing from Biological and Behavioral models. The humanist attributes this desire to grow to the motivation behind behaviors. Carl Rogers (1902-1987) and Abraham Maslow (1908-1970) pioneered this model, with many practical applications in counseling, to guide the personality towards greater degrees of self-actualization.

Trait-Based theorists state that personality is made up of a number of broad traits. Traits are the relatively stable characteristics that drive an individual to behave in certain ways. The five-factor theory of personality formulated by Paul Costa and

Thomas Widiger is one of the most recent advancements in the realm of personality development. It departs from the categorical approach and advocates a dimensional approach, which more aptly accounts for the variations of personality types.

From the point of view of Anthroposophic Psychology, personality is the animated expression of the astral body, the body of movement and the innate qualities of soul life. Just as the Greeks referred to persona as the mask through which a person spoke—"sona" means sound and "per" means through, "persona" being the name of the character mask used in Greek theatre—so Anthroposophic Psychology regards the personality as an expressive instrument formed by both intrinsic and existential factors in a person's development. Although current day views on personality have abandoned the term character, Anthroposophic Psychology recognizes its fundamental importance, including its origin in realms far more vast than the genes and chemicals in the individual. Similar to the view of James Hillman (a major voice in Jungian psychodynamic psychology, 1920- 2011) on character in his book, *The Soul's Code*, Anthroposophic Psychology includes the concept of karma in the description of what constitutes character. Karma indicates the greater drama of destiny working through the individual's relationships and circumstantial challenges.

Anthroposophic Psychology does not reject outright the five conventional theoretical models of personality; however, it accounts for them by understanding the polarities at work in the soul, the four temperaments (phlegmatic, melancholic, sanguine, and choleric), and the interplay between the three primary soul forces: thinking, feeling and willing. One can indeed contemplate a continuum of expansion in the following terms as determinative of human experience:

DNA (and chemicals, serotonin, etc.)—behavior—complexes—patterns—personality—character—karma—soul.

Anthroposophic Psychology understands that all levels are true at all times; emphasis on one level may be more useful under certain circumstances, and thus arise the many theories that I have introduced.

We could consider many other factors in determining the unique configuration of each personality, but that would lead us into too much complexity concerning the personality disorders for this writing. We will emphasize a salutogenic approach to personality development (from chapter 3), and come to see the category of personality disorders not from a fixed pathological condition, but from a disruption or imbalance in its development.

From a taxonomic audit of how personality disorders have been clinically defined, we arrive at five fundamental notions. A personality disorder shows the following:

- A major mental disorder as found on Axis I (which includes depression, bipolar disorder, schizophrenia), but manifesting a less severe set of symptomatic traits. This particular definition was proposed by Kraeplin and Kretschmer and adopted by the American Psychiatric Association. A couple of examples within the *Diagnostic and Statistical Manual (DSM)* of this concept are represented by schizotypal personality disorder appearing as a part of a schizophrenia spectrum and obsessive-compulsive disorder appearing as a part of an obsessional-compulsive spectrum.

- The failure to develop important components of personality, as is confirmed by Cleckley's (1976) concept of psychopathy as the failure to learn from experience and to show remorse. Psychoanalytic theories postulate persons with defective superego development and failure to acquire specific structures and processes, inclusive of problem solving skills and coping mechanisms, are prone to personality disorders.

- Kerberg's (1984) concept of borderline personality organization sums up a third definition of personality disorder. It consists of identity diffusion, primitive defenses, and poor reality testing.

- Robins's (1966) concept of sociopathic personality as the result of the failure of socialization emphasizes the social deviance aspect above and beyond any cognitive dissonance arising from incompatible behaviors.

- Personality disorders considered as abnormal personality types (in the statistical sense) are represented by models of personality disorder derived from "normal" personality structures. These models conceptualize disorder as extremes of normal variation.

Liberating our notions from the pervasive categorical fixations of personality disorders allows us to see the human being behind the mask. In an anthroposophic view we adopt a multidimensional approach. In other words, we all have attributes of every personality, and therefore of every personality disorder. I will demonstrate this later when I introduce the somatic attributes of the disorders—somatic exaggerations which everyone will find familiar. Coming to "disorder" is really only a matter of predisposition and degree of severity given particular life contexts. For instance, I may awake feeling on top of the world and project a narcissistic personality, but by noon I may develop an apprehension about a certain social situation that I am ambivalent about and project a histrionic personality type. And then by mid-afternoon my apprehension may be so intense I adopt an avoidant stance. Being distanced from this social situation, I may return to it and start to think in a paranoid way about where I stand with regard to others in the social situation. Moving from narcissistic to histrionic to avoidant to paranoid dispositions is not necessarily pathological. It is a fairly normal process when we survey the many differing social situations we encounter in a day. This demonstrates the fluidity of personality, the natural capacity of the personality to be adaptable and not fixed in its behaviors. This underscores the innate drive in personality to grow, learn, and change according to what is necessary to meet realities and to achieve established goals.

Although our intent in this seminar is not to teach clinical diagnosis of personality disorders, it is nevertheless important for you to know some of the basic criteria that are used in the field today. With all the five prevailing definitions of personality disorders, four basic criteria comprise a common set of standards of evaluation:

- Ways of perceiving and interpreting the Self, other people and events;
- The range, intensity, lability, and appropriateness of emotional responses;
- Interpersonal functioning;
- Impulse control.

These criteria, thought necessary to diagnose a personality disorder, are problematic for they are too vaguely worded to translate into reliable measures. They also lack a rationale based on an understanding of the functions of a "normal" personality. Instead, the customary clinical practice merely catalogues features that characterize a wide range of psychopathology, naming common symptoms that one might observe or be told about by the personality presenting as a client. The categorical approach amounts to little more than a checklist method, wherein, if you have more than 50% of the symptoms associated with the personality disorder under consideration, you are awarded the diagnosis disorder. (The verb "awarded" is intentional, for there is often a status in getting that diagnosis, as well as a monetary value.) This method does nothing to stimulate a clinician's capacity for critical discernment, not to mention how such a check-list bypasses the clinician's intuition. Unfortunately this categorical approach only reinforces a pseudo-scientific premise that the objective empirical method involves numbers, weights, and measures—even at the expense of knowing the whole person. In recent research done to write the *DSM-5*, a blind study was executed to see how many clinicians could diagnose personality disorders accurately. The rate of accuracy was an appalling 35%.

This leads us to the need to reconsider the whole proposition of making clinical diagnosis and basing our counseling interventions on the data derived from this categorical approach. The field of psychopathology is based on the abnormal person; it offers very little understanding of what the normal and ideal person's profile looks like. From a salutogenic paradigm and an understanding of an Anthroposophic Psychological view of the human being, we can enrich what has been put forward as criteria for determining personality disorders without becoming caught in rigid stereotypical labeling, which so often becomes an artificial dead end for a person's development. For instance, let us re-examine the four main criteria noted above from an understanding of the fourfold human being.

The first criterion: "Ways of perceiving and interpreting the Self, other people and events" can be regarded as an assessment of the executive function of the ego in the most expanded sense of the word, that is, the "I" of the person.

The second criterion: "The range, intensity, lability, and appropriateness of emotional responses" can be regarded as an expression of a person's astral body.

The third criterion: "Interpersonal functioning" can be viewed as the innate tendencies of the etheric body to be in relationship with others with whom one shares space and time.

The fourth criterion: "Impulse control" can be viewed as the human being's capacity to manage the instinctive drives of the physical body.

Implied in this revisioning of the criteria are the ideals of growth in the four areas of "I," astral body, etheric body, and physical body. Thus psychopathology becomes an investigation of arrested development toward those ideals, rather than a list and catalogue of symptoms of inadequacy.

When our observations are referenced to a guiding image of the human being, there is no need for creating abstract categories. The whole proposition of ticking off boxes in a checklist in order to satisfy the demands of a clinical diagnosis can be abandoned in favor of thinking about the person in his or her circumstances as on a rocky road of development. If we are schooled in making phenomenological observations of the human being in various natural and social contexts, the observations themselves will lead us to behold the meaningfulness of certain components of the personality that are ordered or disordered. One of the primary characteristics for determining personality has been an emphasis on orientation. Yet in the history of diagnosis, and in the guidelines for determining *DSM–IV* Axis II personality disorders, one of the most basic orientations has been overlooked—spatial orientation.

In my doctoral dissertation for the Institute of Transpersonal Psychology, I proposed a correlation between the twelve personality disorders (ten from the *Diagnostic & Statistical Manual-5* and two personality disorders that were in *DSM-IV* but were removed in *DSM-5*) with orientations in spatial movement. The latter is based on the three dimensions in space (frontal, horizontal, and sagittal) and the four types of movement to be found in each of the dimensions, hence 3 x 4 = 12. Here is an excerpt from the abstract to my doctoral dissertation, *A Transpersonal Approach to Somatic Psychodiagnostics of Personality: A Contribution Towards Its Development, Dis-ordering Tendencies, and Embodied Transcendence:*

> This dissertation explores how the body's movement in spatial orientation may play an influential role in the dis-ordering tendencies of personality. The somatic psychodiagnostic approach to personality presented in this dissertation advances the case for a more rigorous examination of the body/psyche dynamic in the formation, assessment and treatment of personality issues. The hypothesis of this study is that stimulation of the motor/sensory system in movements through various spatial planes substantially impacts perceptions of self, others, and the world. These perceptions form the basis of the evolving personality. Rather than viewing personality as a set of fixed traits, personality is viewed as a state of consciousness on a continuum of adaptations to self, others, and the world. Research findings of this study with seventy research participants indicate that fixations in movement correlate with fixations in personality. In this schema a causal comparative relation between twelve fixated spatial orientations and twelve clinically recognized personality disorders is demonstrated in matrix, tabular, and textual formats. The findings point to exciting possibilities for the further exploration of a somatic oriented clinical psychology.

It should be noted that the *International Classifications of Diseases - 9ᵗʰ Revision - Clinical Modifications* (ICD-9-CM) retains all twelve personality disorders. The American Psychiatric Association decided to strike the Passive-Aggressive Disorder from the *DSM-IV* list on the basis that it was perceived as a normative personality disposition in the American population. They also removed the Multiple Personality Disorder and elevated it to an Axis I pathology, a major pathological diagnosis, known as Dissociative Identity Disorder due to the severe dysfunction it provokes in one's life.

In an Anthroposophic Psychology the widely known dictum, "Man is a microcosm of the great macrocosm," is more than a poetic phrase. It is an essential correspondence for understanding the intimate relationship the human being has to all aspects of the cosmos. With the cosmos we can say its archetypal existence in space is mirrored to us in the expanse of the zodiac, a twelve-sectioned circle wrapping itself around the earth. The ancients saw this correspondence to the human being as a twelve-sectioned column with the human being standing upright in the center. The astronomical/astrological sign of the Ram (or Aries) was associated with the head; the sign of the Bull was associated with the neck; the sign of the Twins was associated with the arms; and so on. In this correspondence of cosmos and the earthly human being, prior to birth the human being exists in the sphere of the cosmos and descends into the sphere of the womb of its mother in an embryonic form. After birth and into the first year of life, the infant struggles to find its uprightness and assumes the form of a flexible and upright column. Once achieved the human being gradually explores and inhabits three-dimensional space.

Space is not just something that can be measured in inches or centimeters. It is not only quantifiable. Space also has quality. It matters to our consciousness if we are walking forward or backward, if we are swaying side to side, or if we are stretched toward the sky. The somatic sensations that accompany these movements are different in nature. They inform us in unique ways about the world around us. Our movements through space determine the perceptions we process about the external world, and leave impressions in our psyche that build the basis of our worldview. The accumulation of these experiences comprises what we call personality. Within an anthroposophic perspective this formation of personality rests upon the physical body accessing certain experiences from the specific dimensions in space and the etheric body's capacity to remember these experiences in a kinesthetic way.

Once these sensations become feelings, we think about their meaning for us; that in turn provides motive for what we choose to do or not to do. This dynamic describes the nature of the astral body and eventually sets the predictable patterns of behaviors, feelings and thoughts that create a "persona," a personality for the soul to express its self. The self of the soul can be understood as the "I," the sense of what we often call the ego. The ego ("I") is dependent on the personality (astral body) for expressing its intentions. If the personality lacks healthy judgment, is fixated about certain ideas, limited in its range of emotions, and is undeveloped in the mastery of basic interpersonal skills, the ego may be thwarted in its primary intentions to find its true sense of destiny. If the assertions of the "I" are thwarted, there arises a kind of vacuum; the less developed astral body then dominates, thereby giving a baser version of the personality a more central role in the events of a person's biography than should be the case. Although the human being shares the astral world with the animal kingdom, it is not where the unique sovereignty of the "I" lives. When the "I" is not in command of the individual's life experiences, then the lower nature, akin to the animal, plays itself out in the person's life.

Despite the brevity of the few descriptions I have brought to augment our understanding of personality and personality disorders, I hope you will now be able to ground some of these anthroposophic concepts in the movement exercises we will do for each of the twelve types of personality. Before we move into our exercises I need to make one more important correspondence for our reconsideration of personality disorders. This is how the zodiac can be seen as the encircling container for astral forces. The ancient practitioners of astrology have distinguished these forces in an imaginative and qualitative way. Each sign of the zodiac is depicted by an animal image; etymologically the word zo-diac means the animal circle. Each sign was associated with the primal urge of the animal designated to represent the sign. The zodiac itself is organized in a fourfold way corresponding to the elements of fire, earth, air and water, expressive of the four temperaments. The zodiac is also organized in a threefold way corresponding to dynamic qualities of cardinal, fixed and mutable. These threefold qualities are phenomenologically perceived as movements in the astral organization impacting our senses: Cardinal is willing; fixed is feeling; and mutable is thinking. In spatial orientation we find the movements within the frontal plane are will-oriented, the movements within the horizontal plane are feeling-oriented, and the movements within the sagittal plane are thinking-oriented. In normal functioning, we move through all of these states rhythmically. Any fixation in movement will create an imbalance. As these movements imprint into our sense of being, they shape patterns of behaving and responding to the external world. They become, for better or worse, active forces embedded in our etheric body. These compelling forces become our habits.

The framework of threefold and fourfold might remain abstract concepts unless we begin to inhabit all the possibilities of spatial orientations consciously. Reflecting on our own sense experiences will allow us to grasp the qualitative nature of moving into certain spaces. We will need to develop a conscious awareness of our somatic experiences, allow them to resonate within us, and reflect on the relevancy of that resonance in relation to the context in which they arise. To go beyond the animal circle, the human being must discover the virtues inscribed into the zodiac by the spiritual beings that served as its architects in building the temple of the human being. The human being's uprightness as a column of light brings the moral into the earthly kingdom. Morality is not given to us in the same way as the laws of nature are given to us. Morality is the "not given" that we as human beings are destined to develop and offer to the Earth's evolution.

Let's begin with a chart of correspondences that unveil some of the twelvefold (threefold x fourfold) structures behind personality. We will soon ground this in more familiar somatic experiences.

Correspondences

Sign	Element	Dynamic	Urge	Sense	Virtues
Ram ♈	Fire	Cardinal	Waking	Speaking	Devotion becomes Power of Sacrifice
Bull ♉	Earth	Fixed	Digesting	Thinking	Integrity becomes Progress
Twins ♊	Air	Mutable	Playing	Ego	Perseverance becomes Faithfulness
Crab ♋	Water	Cardinal	Fleeing	Touch	Selflessness becomes Catharsis
Lion ♌	Fire	Fixed	Fighting	Well-being	Compassion becomes Freedom
Virgin ♍	Earth	Mutable	Protecting	Movement	Tactfulness of Heart becomes Grace
Scales ♎	Air	Cardinal	Resting	Balance	Equanimity becomes Peace
Scorpion ♏	Water	Fixed	Stalking	Smell	Humility becomes Insight
Archer ♐	Fire	Mutable	Hunting	Taste	Articulation of Speech becomes Feeling for Truth
Goat ♑	Earth	Cardinal	Exposing	Sight	Courage becomes Power of Redemption
Waterman ♒	Air	Fixed	Nourishing	Warmth	Discretion becomes Meditative Power
Fishes ♓	Water	Mutable	Propagating	Hearing	Generosity becomes Magnanimity

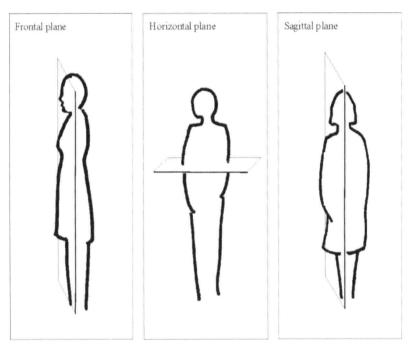

Figure I. *The three spatial planes.*

In exploring the three spatial planes, we shall emphasize one of four particular movements in a spatial plane. For example, concentrating on the frontal plane we can move with an emphasis 1.) on the forward motion, 2.) on the backward space, 3.) on a swinging or rocking movement of forward and backward, or 4.) on a movement that is non-perceptible because it is stuck between forward and backward space. In the horizontal plane we can emphasize 1.) the above space, 2.) the below space, 3.) the bouncing up and down movement, or 4.) the imperceptible frozen movement in the waist area. In the sagittal plane our movement can 1.) be rigid to one side, 2.) loose to one side, 3.) stuck in the midline, or 4.) disorganized moving side to side.

By moving into the spatial plane with these exaggerations, we will experience our selves, each other, and the world around us in an imbalanced way. These specific imbalances give rise to personality disorders. After a prolonged period of time, these movements leave an impression in our etheric body that becomes our physical bodily posture. Although subtle to discern, bodily postures indicate soul dispositions.

Discovering Personality Disorders Through Spatial Orientation: Fixations of Movement in the Frontal Plane

A tendency to be fixated in the front-space of the frontal plane
The frontal plane relates to our will. The primal gesture of the infant is to be propelled forward to experience the world through the senses. Most of our sense organs are oriented in the frontal plane. However, one can become stuck in always moving forward, thrusting the head and body forward, as the feet follow along, always falling and catching oneself, catching up to the head's leading. *A tendency to be fixated in forward movement in the frontal plane* can appear to make the head look and behave like a limb. The lack of peripheral vision adds to the feeling of being pulled into the forward space. In my research to ascertain phenomenological descriptions of fixations of forward movement into the frontal plane, I received feedback from seventy participants in eight specific areas. The descriptors listed below were selected because they were responses given by at least five or more participants.

- Physical motor activity = clumsy, felt like I was falling into the forward space, increased my speed, felt rushed, felt heavy, felt strained, stiff
- Physiological changes = breathing quickened, increased heart rate, back pain or stressed
- Sensorial changes = lost my balance, sight became like tunnel vision, my senses overall were diminished
- Emotional states = anxious, silly, joyous/happy
- Mental states = stressed, pre-occupied with self, confused
- Sense of self-image = foolish, attention seeking, not concerned, too busy
- Sense of inter-relatedness with others = too busy to seriously interact, did not feel connected to others, felt isolated and closed off from others
- Metaphors = "like a chicken running around on a farm,"

"running on all six cylinders," "a lost elephant ready to charge," "a glass spilling over."

The urge to wake others up to oneself, the excessive use of speech and the zealous devotion to one's self or one's causes are the problematic traits with which the person with Narcissistic Personality Disorder (NPD) struggles. A brief clinical descriptor of NPD is "a pervasive pattern of grandiosity (in fantasy or behavior), need for admiration, and lack of empathy..."

A tendency to be fixated in the backspace of the frontal plane shows itself as an incongruent movement where the body is moving forward and the head is being pulled along, but tends to lag behind. Inasmuch as the forward movement fixation tends to pull the head forward and down, the fixation of the backspace tends to push the head back and upward. There is the appearance of a reluctance to take the world in through the senses, as if to do so would cause pain. The sensory organs in the head are held back, resistant to the world. The descriptors from the original seventy participants to this fixated movement were as follows:

- Physical motor activity = restricted movement, lots of muscle tension, back ache
- Physiological changes = labored, slow breathing, taking shorter breathes, heart rate increased
- Sensorial changes = no peripheral vision, widened vision, hyper-vigilant vision
- Emotional states = distant and removed, suspicious, fearful, very stressed out
- Mental states = paranoid, inwardly focused, confused
- Sense of self-image = self consciously concerned about others' judgments, self-confident, puffed up, felt invisible
- Sense of inter-relatedness with others = held back from relating, stand-offish, fearful
- Metaphor = "Zombie"

The resistance to sensing the world, as well as the urge to expose everything in sight, the excessive need to see all hidden things, and the lack of courage to go forward are all typical traits of the Paranoid Personality Disorder (PPD). A brief clinical descriptor of PPD is "a pervasive distrust and suspiciousness of others such that their motives are interpreted as malevolent."

A tendency to habitually rock forward and backward as one walks into the frontal plane gives the impression of an infant in the process of self-soothing, or an adolescent be-bopping with swagger. One appears to be carried by the rocking movement in an unconscious rhythmic way. The descriptors from the original seventy participants to this fixated movement were as follows:

- Physical motor activity = rhythmic, fluid, spine opened up and popped
- Physiological changes = heavy breathing, heart rate increased, dizzy and nauseous
- Sensorial changes = a lot more tactile awareness, more self movement, not aware of anything below my waist
- Emotional states = fun, happy, unstable and anxious, silly
- Mental states = hard to find any clarity or hold a thought, indecisive, disoriented
- Sense of self-image = "I am cool," dramatic and expressive, wishy-washy
- Sense of inter-relatedness with others = a lot of interaction and connection, connected by foolish and silly behavior, hard to figure out where I am or others are coming from
- Metaphors = "like a boat in the ocean," "carelessly going through life as a happy-go-lucky," "dancing like a noodle," "The Fonz"

The urge to approach and flee, back and forth, in and out, the over sensitivity to touch, and the need to find a way to be centered in one's self are all aspects of the Histrionic Personality Disorder (HPD). A brief clinical descriptor of HPD is "a pervasive pattern of excessive emotionality and attention seeking."

A tendency to move into the frontal plane as a rigid column with little movement in feet and hands, neither moving ahead nor retreating back, nor moving back and forth, appears as a slow and arduous process, as if there were no sense of time. This movement provokes the mood of tentativeness, of sleepiness. The descriptors from the original seventy participants to this fixated still movement were as follows:

- Physical motor activity = stiff, slow movement, no flexibility in joints
- Physiological changes = shallow breathing, suffocating, light-headed
- Sensorial changes = Shut down senses, hyper-vigilant, static balance
- Emotional states = anxiety on verge of panic, depressed, afraid
- Mental states = self-absorbed, blank, terrified of the environment
- Sense of self-image = no awareness of self, low self esteem, lonely
- Sense of inter-relatedness with others = detached, can only take a little bit of connection, too shy to relate
- Metaphors = "like a mummy," "like a robot," "walking on eggshells"

The urge to sleep and become invisible, to rest in a state of balance, and to be at peace at all times characterizes the longing of the person with Avoidant Personality Disorder (APD). This idealized unrealistic goal of APD can be summarized as "a pervasive pattern of social inhibitions, feelings of inadequacy, and hypersensitivity to negative evaluation…"

Fixations of Movement in the Horizontal Plane

The horizontal plane is related to our feeling life. The above and below is not as sharply defined as front and back of the frontal plane. The dividing line of the above and below is not static but dynamic. It is constantly moving as the rhythmic system moves with pulse and breath.

*A **tendency to move upward into the above sphere of the horizontal plane*** will give the appearance of a body being stretched from above. The descriptors from the original seventy participants to this fixated movement towards the above in the horizontal plane were as follows:

- Physical motor activity = stiff, tension in neck and shoulders, walking on the balls of my feet
- Physiological changes = slow and controlled breathing,

shallow breathing, nausea
- Sensorial changes = hearing became acute, aware of my balance, sight focused on the below
- Emotional state = guarded and anxious, giddy, aloof
- Mental state = "I am in charge," embarrassingly self-conscious, withdrawn and disconnected
- Sense of self-image = arrogant, snob, living up to a high standard, pre-occupied
- Sense of inter-relatedness with others = detached, superior to others, difficult to make eye contact
- Metaphor = Giraffes, walking on air

The urge to cogitate, ruminate on thoughts over and over, the compelling need to think endlessly, and to be in the highest integrity captures the soul gesture of the Obsessive-Compulsive Personality Disorder (OCPD). From a clinical perspective OCPD is "a pervasive pattern of preoccupation with orderliness, perfectionism, and mental and interpersonal control, at the expense of flexibility, openness and efficacy..."

A tendency to move in such a way as to be bent toward the ground can convey the sense of weightiness as if gravity were pulling one into the earth. The movement tends to be ponderous and slow, yet the bended knees give the impression that one could spring up at any moment. The head hanging low and facing downward occludes the view of the face, the most distinguishing feature of the human being. The descriptors from the original seventy participants to this fixated movement towards the below in the horizontal plane were as follows:
- Physical motor activity = grounded through my feet, compressed, heaviness, tension in lower back
- Physiological changes = breathing increased, heart rate increased, breathing slowed down
- Sensorial changes = hyper-vigilant, greater vitality and strength in my body, sight was focused down and around
- Emotional state = aggressive, angry, oppressed
- Mental state = body focused, paranoid, agitated
- Sense of self-image = tough guy, low self-esteem, isolated
- Sense of inter-relatedness with others = with others yet

alone, did not want to connect with others, they are not important, hostile
- Metaphor = like an ape, like a caveman

The urge to stalk one's prey, to sense out vulnerability like a smell of the scent desired, and the lack of sensitivity for the other are elements that shape the Antisocial Personality Disorder (ASPD). The ASPD is high in anger, hostility, and excitement-seeking; low in straightforwardness, altruism, compliance, tender mindedness, dutifulness, self-discipline, and deliberation.

A tendency to move as if caught in a hula-hoop movement, going up and down and side to side appears both sensual and seductive. This is not an easy movement to inhabit, but once done the movement has the power to carry the body from the waist and hips almost effortlessly. The descriptors from the original seventy participants to this fixated movement of encircling the space of the body in the horizontal plane were as follows:
- Physical motor activity = uncoordinated and awkward, walk slowed, flexibility increased
- Physiological changes = breathing increased, heart rate increased, warmth increased
- Sensorial changes = sense of warmth increased, tactile awareness increased, unbalanced
- Emotional state = fun, happy, seeking sexual attention, frustrating
- Mental state = confused, easy going, relaxed, not grounded
- Sense of self-image = "I am a fool," self conscious, sexual and seductive
- Sense of inter-relatedness with others = sense of close connection, too self absorbed to connect, open to sharing
- Metaphor = doing the hula hoop, belly dancing, going to a party

The urge to fight as a way to stay connected, the sense of feeling life to the fullest, and the need to develop compassion characterize the themes of the Borderline Personality Disorder (BPD). The BPD is clinically considered a most difficult client. The BPD can be regarded as "a pervasive pattern of instability of interpersonal relationships, self-image and affects, and marked impulsivity...."

A tendency to move with intermittent moments of sustained in-breath alternating with explosive out breathing, moving up and down through the horizontal plane, gives the appearance of a hurkey-jerky movement. Sucking in air and blowing out air cannot replace the mobility of the feet and hands in movement, yet this irrational bodily movement dictates an unpredictability that accompanies the person caught in its grip. The swing between being embodied and expelled into a state of disembodiment is as disconcerting to the one who adopts this walk as to those who observe it. The descriptors from the original seventy participants to this fixated staccato movement above and below the horizontal plane were as follows:

- Physical motor activity = spastic, tension in the chest, limited movement
- Physiological changes = can't breathe, light headed and dizzy, irregular breathing
- Sensorial changes = senses shut down, sight and hearing magnified, fluctuating warmth and cold
- Emotional state = anxiety, fearful, angry and hostile feelings
- Mental state = unfocused, self concerned, withdrawn out of desperation
- Sense of self-image = "Who am I? I do not fit in," self consciously insecure, low self esteem
- Sense of inter-relatedness with others = not connected, yearning for some affirmation that I exist, unloading my hostility on others
- Metaphor = an exploding balloon, "Who am I?," Dr. Jekyll and Mr. Hyde

The urge to over nourish, to lose one's sense of self-regulation, and to struggle to find meditative spaces in the midst of hurriedness is a clear depiction of the soul of a persona harboring Multiple Personality Disorder (MPD). Although this disorder is now (in *DSM-5*) referred to as an Axis I Dissociative Identity Disorder, the inclusion as an Axis II disorder (along with other personality disorders, as in *DSM-IV*) is justified. MPD is "the existence within the person of two or more distinct personalities or personality states (each with its own relatively enduring pattern of perceiving, relating to and thinking about the environment and self), and at least two of these personalities or personality states recurrently take full control of the person's behavior..."

Fixations of Movement in the Sagittal Plane

The sagittal plane (left side and right side) is related to the thinking life. The mid-line dissects the body into a left and a right side. Although not visible from the exterior of the human being, the left and right hemisphere of the brain could be regarded as an archetypal expression of the significance of this plane's connection with the soul's capacity of thinking. What is most visible to us is the movement of the arms and feet—the limbs, which give us our mobility and flexibility in movement.

A tendency to move with muscle tightness on one side shows a spastic and uneven quality in movement. This movement mirrors a one-sidedness in the personality that is rigid and limiting. The descriptors from the original seventy participants to this fixated movement of rigid one-sidedness in the sagittal plane were as follows:

- Physical motor activities = strained and restrictive, movement slowed down, uncomfortable to move
- Physiological changes = breathing labored, sluggish, painful
- Sensorial changes = sight unfocused, senses went inward, hearing diminished
- Emotional state = depressed, sad, lonely, angry, agitated, frustrated
- Mental state = "I am not normal," pre-occupied with struggle, confused
- Sense of self-image = "I am deformed, crippled," low self-esteem, inept
- Sense of inter-relatedness with others = not open to meeting others, it hurts to try to connect with others, did not want others to look at me
- Metaphor = someone with a stroke, a person at war with himself, a person with a wooden leg

The urge to hunt and hit the mark, the sense of a strong taste for likes and not-likes, and the desire to speak the truth are all facets that make up and concern the person with Schizoid Personality Disorder. The clinical view of the Schizoid type is "a pervasive pattern of detachment from social relationships and a restricted range of expression of emotions in interpersonal settings..."

A tendency to move with looseness in one's muscles on one side, a kind of falling to one side, *suggest an unnatural need to lean on something or others to maintain one's stability.* This movement appears as though one cannot move straight nor maintain uprightness on one's own. The whole body cries out for support. The descriptors from the original seventy participants to this fixated movement falling to one side in the sagittal plane were as follows:

- Physical motor activity = needed a lot of strength to move, exhausting, slow movement
- Physiological changes = increased heart rate, increased breathing
- Sensorial changes = off balance, sight narrowed
- Emotional state = vulnerable, insecure, anxious, depressed, sad, frustrated, angry
- Mental state = "I need someone to help me," determined to make it somehow, self-doubting
- Sense of self-image = dependent, pathetic, handicapped
- Sense of inter-relatedness with others = mutual needs led to supportive connections, easily disengaged by need to find support, aggressive, feeling of resentment
- Metaphor = "Igor or Quasimodo," dragging a ball and chain, pirate with a wooden leg

The urge to propagate and solicit support, to hear others with needs and to offer and expect generosity from others is a primary concern of the Dependent Personality Disordered (DPD) person. The DPD type is clinically characterized as "a pervasive and excessive need to be taken care of that leads to submissive and clinging behavior and fears of separation..."

The tendency to move with disregard to the mid-line, moving arms, feet and head from side to side has a strong impact on *one's organization of perception.* The translation of percept to concept is interrupted leaving one to unique and unusual perspectives. Disorganization of the senses is likely to lead to disorganized thoughts. The descriptors from the original seventy participants to this fixated movement of crossing mid-line in the sagittal plane were as follows:

- Physical motor activities = swinging action, fluid, relaxed
- Physiological changes = increased heart rate, increased breathing, erratic breathing, dizzy
- Sensorial changes = off balance, less sight, more touching
- Emotional state = happy, having fun, giddy, anxious
- Mental state = scattered, confused and indecisive, self consciously focused, interested in watching what is going on
- Sense of self-image = goofy, silly, foolish, playful, no sense of self
- Sense of inter-relatedness with others = very connected and interactive with others, can't keep focused on others, having fun
- Metaphor = happy drunk, like doing the Charleston dance

The urge to play and sense the other "I" in play as a means to engender perseverance and faithfulness is a prominent motive for relating in the Schizotypal Personality Disordered type. From a clinical perspective the Schizotypal is a person "high in anxiety, self-consciousness, fantasy, actions, and ideas. Low in gregariousness, warmth, positive emotions, and trust."

The tendency to move deceptively by being open in gesture followed by being closed in gesture can suggest a need to be cautious toward others when approaching them. The changeableness can be understood as a purposeful chameleon-like tactic to obtain a goal. The descriptors from the original seventy participants to this fixated movement of open and closed gestures in a subtle deceptive manner in the sagittal plane were as follows:

- Physical motor activities = wrists, arms and shoulders tense, body locked up, disconnected from body
- Physiological changes = increased heart rate, heat in heart

area, increased breathing
- Sensorial changes = warmth increased, senses heightened, hearing increased
- Emotional state = high anxiety and stress, aggressive, exploitative, protective, guarded
- Mental changes = scheming, centered, grounded, ambivalent
- Sense of self-image = confident, defensive, self-conscious
- Sense of inter-relatedness with others = related from centered place, related directly, competitive
- Metaphor = a rock feels no pain, a con artist

The urge to protect one's assets and to move as the opportunities open and close with tact and grace is a major focus for the Passive Aggressive Personality Disordered (PAPD) type of person. From a clinical perspective the PAPD is high in anxiety, depression, self-consciousness, and vulnerability; low in gregariousness, assertiveness, and excitement seeking.

A comparison between the DSM–version IV–TR clinical criteria for Personality Disorders and participants' descriptors, based on their experiences gained from movement exercises derived from the Bento Body Behavior Battery (Bento, 2005), provides a reasonable basis to confirm the correspondences made between the historically given Personality Disorders and the twelve types of fixations found in relation to the three dimensions of space. This phenomenological correspondence also gives evidence to the significant role that the twelve signs of the zodiac play in determining personality dispositions.

Here is a summary of the personality disorders and their relation to the spatial dynamics that I studied. The criteria come from Theodore Millon and George Everly, *Personality and Its Disorders* (1985). These criteria on the left are compared with statements from people taking the posture described above.

Narcissistic/Frontal Forward

Narcissistic Personality Disorder	F1: Frontal Forward Fixation
1.) Has a grandiose sense of self-importance	
2.) Is preoccupied with fantasies of unlimited success, power, brilliance, beauty, or ideal love	Preoccupied with Self
3.) Believes that he or she is "special" and unique and can only be understood by, or should associate with, other special or high-status people	Did not feel connected, felt isolated and closed off from others
4.) Requires excessive admiration	Attention seeking
5.) Has a sense of entitlement	
6.) Is interpersonally exploitative	
7.) Lacks empathy	Not concerned, too busy
8.) Is often envious of others or believes that others are envious of him or her	
9.) Shows arrogant, haughty behaviors or attitudes	Too busy to seriously interact

Paranoid/Frontal Backward

Paranoid Personality Disorder	F2: Frontal Backward Fixation
1.) Suspects, without sufficient basis, that others are exploitative, harming, or deceiving him or her	Suspicious, fearful Very stressed out Paranoid
2.) Is preoccupied with unjustified doubts about the loyalty or trustworthiness of friends or associates	Distant, removed Inwardly focused
3.) Is reluctant to confide in others because of unwarranted fear that the information will be used maliciously against him or her	Self-consciously concerned about other's judgment

4.) Reads hidden demeaning or threatening meanings into benign remarks or events	Confused
5.) Persistently bears grudges, i.e., is unforgiving of insults, injuries, or slights	Held back from relating
6.) Perceives attacks on his or her character or reputation that are not apparent to others and is quick to react angrily or to counterattack	Stand-offish
7.) Has recurrent suspicions, without justification, regarding fidelity of spouse or sexual partner	

Histrionic/Frontal Moveable

Histrionic Personality Disorder	F3: Frontal Moveable Fixation
1.) Is uncomfortable in situations in which he or she is not the center of attention	Hard to figure out where I am or others are coming from
2.) Interaction with others is often characterized by inappropriate sexually seductive or provocative behavior	
3.) Displays rapidly shifting and shallow expression of emotions	Unstable and anxious
4.) Consistently uses physical appearance to draw attention to self	"I am Cool"
5.) Has a style of speech that is excessively impressionistic and lacking in detail	
6.) Shows self-dramatization, theatricality, and exaggerated expression of emotion	Fun, happy, silly Dramatic and expressive
7.) Is suggestible, i.e., easily influenced by others or circumstances	Indecisive Wishy-washy

8.) Considers relationships to be more intimate than they actually are	A lot of interaction and connections

Avoidant/Frontal Still

Avoidant Personality Disorder	*F4: Frontal Still Fixation*
1.) Avoids occupational activities that involve significant interpersonal contact, because of fears of criticism, disapproval, or rejection	Anxiety on verge of panic Terrified of the world
2.) Is unwilling to get involved with people unless certain of being liked	Afraid
3.) Shows restraint within intimate relationships because of the fear of being shamed or ridiculed	Detached Can only take a little bit of connection
4.) Is preoccupied with being criticized or rejected in social situations	Self absorbed Too shy to relate
5.) Is inhibited in new interpersonal situations because of feelings of inadequacy	Lonely
6.) Views self as socially inept, personally unappealing, or inferior to others	Low self esteem
7.) Is unusually reluctant to take personal risks or to engage in any new activities because they may prove embarrassing	

Antisocial/Horizontal Below

Antisocial Personality Disorder	*H1: Horizontal Below Fixation*
1.) Failure to conform to social norms; repeatedly performing acts that are grounds for arrest	Tough guy Isolated, with others, yet alone

2.) Deceitfulness, as indicated by repeated lying, use of aliases, or conning others for personal profit or pleasure	Did not want to connect with others, they are not important
3.) Impulsivity or failure to plan ahead	
4.) Irritability and aggressiveness, as indicated by repeated physical fights or assaults	Aggressive, angry Body focused Agitated, hostile
5.) Reckless disregard for safety of self or others	
6.) Consistent irresponsibility, as indicated by repeated failure to sustain consistent work behavior or honor financial obligations	
7.) Lack of remorse, as indicated by being indifferent to or rationalizing having hurt, mistreated, or stolen from another	Did not want to connect with others; they are not important

Obsessive-Compulsive/Horizontal Above

Obsessive-Compulsive Personality Disorder	H2: Horizontal Above Fixation
1.) Is preoccupied with details, rules, lists, order, organization, or schedules to the extent that the major point of the activity is lost	Preoccupied
2.) Shows perfection that interferes with task completion	Living up to high standards
3.) Is excessively devoted to work and productivity to the exclusion of leisure activities and friendships	Aloof, withdrawn, and disconnected
4.) Is over conscientious, scrupulous, and inflexible about matters of morality, ethics, or values	Arrogant, snob Superior to others Living up to high standards

5.) Is unable to discard worn-out or worthless objects even when they have no sentimental value	
6.) Is reluctant to delegate tasks or to work with others unless they submit to exactly his or her way of doing things	I am in charge, commanding Superior to others
7.) Adopts a miserly spending style toward both self and others; money is viewed as something to be hoarded for future catastrophes	Guarded and anxious
8.) Shows rigidity and stubbornness	

Borderline/Horizontal Moveable

Borderline Personality Disorder	H3: Horizontal Moveable Fixation
1.) Frantic efforts to avoid real or imagined abandonment	
2.) A pattern of unstable and intense interpersonal relationships characterized by alternating between extremes of idealization and devaluation	Self-conscious Too absorbed to connect Open to sharing
3.) Identity disturbance markedly and persistently unstable self-image or sense of self	Confused I am a fool
4.) Impulsivity in at least two areas that are potentially self-damaging (e.g., spending, sex, substance abuse, reckless driving, binge eating)	Seeking sexual attention Sexual and seductive

5.) Recurrent suicidal behavior, gestures, or threats, or self-mutilating behavior	
6.) Affective instability due to a marked reactivity of mood (e.g., intense episodic, dysphoria, irritability, or anxiety usually lasting a few hours and only rarely more than a few days	Frustrating
7.) Chronic feelings of emptiness	
8.) Inappropriate, intense anger or difficulty controlling anger	
9.) Transient, stress-related paranoid ideation or severe dissociative symptoms	Not grounded

Multiple/Horizontal Still

Multiple Personality Disorder (now termed Dissociative Identity Disorder)	H4: Horizontal Still Fixation
1.) The presence of two or more distinct identities or personality states	Self concerned
2.) At least two of these identities or personality states recurrently take control of the person's behavior	Who am I? Self consciously insecure Yearning for some affirmation that I exist
3.) Inability to recall important personal information that is too extensive to be explained by ordinary forgetfulness	Unfocused Withdrawn out of desperation Not connected
4.) The disturbance is not due to the direct physiological effects of a substance	Anxiety, fearful, angry, and hostile feelings Unloading my hostility on others

Schizotypal/Sagittal Moveable

Schizotypal Personality Disorder	*S1: Sagittal Moveable Fixation*
1.) Ideas of reference (excluding delusions)	Playful
2.) Odd beliefs or magical thinking that influences behavior and is inconsistent with cultural norms	Scattered, confused, and indecisive
3.) Unusual perceptual experiences, including bodily illusions	Interesting in watching what is going on
4.) Odd thinking and speech (e.g., vague, circumstantial, metaphorical, over elaborate, or stereotyped)	Goofy, silly, foolish
5.) Suspiciousness or paranoid ideation	
6.) Inappropriate or constricted affect	Goofy, silly, foolish
7.) Behavior or appearance that is odd, eccentric, or peculiar	
8.) Lack of close friends or confidants other than first-degree relatives	
9.) Excessive social anxiety that does not diminish with familiarity and tends to be associated with paranoid fears rather than negative judgments about self	Anxious Can not keep focused on others

Schizoid/Sagittal Tight

Schizoid Personality Disorder	*S2: Sagittal Tight Fixation*
1.) Neither desires nor enjoys close relationships, including part of a family	I am not normal Not open to meeting others

2.) Almost always chooses solitary activities	Preoccupied with struggle
3.) Has little, if any, interest in having sexual experiences with another person	It hurts to connect with others Did not want others to look at me
4.) Takes pleasure in few, if any, activities	Agitated, frustrated
5.) Lacks close friends or confidants other than first-degree relatives	Depressed, sad, lonely
6.) Appears indifferent to the praise or criticism of others	
7.) Shows emotional coldness, detachment, or flattened affectivity	

Dependent/Sagittal Loose

Dependent Personality Disorder	*S3: Sagittal Loose Fixation*
1.) Has difficulty making everyday decisions without an excessive amount of advice and reassurance from others	I need someone to help me
2.) Needs others to assume responsibility for most major areas of his or her life	Self doubting
3.) Has difficulty expressing disagreement with others because of fear of loss of support or approval	Easily disengaged by need to find support
4.) Has difficulty initiating projects or doing things on his or her own	Frustrated, angry
5.) Goes to excessive lengths to obtain nurturance and support from others, to the point of volunteering to do things that are unpleasant	

6.) Feels uncomfortable or helpless when alone because of exaggerated fears of being unable to care for himself or herself	Vulnerable, insecure, anxious
7.) Urgently seeks another relationship as a source of care and support when a close relationship ends	Mutual needs led to supportive connections
8.) Is unrealistically preoccupied with fears of being left to take care of himself or herself	Depressed, sad Determined to make it somehow

Passive-Aggressive/Sagittal Still

Passive-Aggressive Personality Disorder	*S4: Sagittal Still Fixation*
1.) Behavioral appearance: stubborn to contrary	
2.) Interpersonal conduct: ambivalent to uncooperative	Ambivalent, Competitive
3.) Cognitive style: inconsistent to disorienting	Scheming
4.) Affective expression: irritable to agitated	High anxiety and stress, aggressive, exploitive
5.) Self-perception: discontented to mistreated	
6.) Primary defense mechanism: displacement	Protected and guarded Defensive

Thus we see how movements are related to personality eccentricities—and even to dys-functional disorders. The movements may result from the disorder pattern, and they may cause those patterns. In either case, we can see the somatic component as very important to character, to individuality—and to disorder.

The correspondences between the twelve signs of the zodiac and the twelve personality disorders are archetypal, and by no means to be understood as a Sun sign designation to a personality disorder. (That is, where a person's Sun lies at his or her birth does not guarantee a character tendency or a personality disorder. An understanding of the imprint to the heavens at the dramatic moment of birth requires much more sensitivity.) The correspondence is yet another testimony to the maxim that asserts the human being is a microcosm of the macrocosm. Historically the term "persona," meaning mask, was first used to describe the nature of the zodiac signs and indicated how pervasive behaviors were associated with the signs.

The following table connects the correspondences between spatial fixations in movement, personality disorders, and the signs of the zodiac. This table is a helpful guide to keep the correspondences clear, but it does not replace the skill to make accurate somatic diagnostic assessments of personality disorders.

Spatial Orientation Fixations	Personality Disorders from the DSM-IV-TR	Signs of the Zodiac with Starry Image
Frontal Forward Fixation	Narcissistic Personality Disorder	Aries, the Ram
Frontal Backward Fixation	Paranoid Personality Disorder	Capricorn, the Goat
Frontal Moveable Fixation	Histrionic Personality Disorder	Cancer, the Crab
Frontal Still Fixation	Avoidant Personality Disorder	Libra, the Scales
Horizontal Below Fixation	Antisocial Personality Disorder	Scorpio, the Scorpion
Horizontal Above Fixation	Obsessive-Compulsive Personality Disorder	Taurus, the Bull
Horizontal Moveable Fixation	Borderline Personality Disorder	Leo, the Lion
Horizontal Still Fixation	Multiple Personality Disorder	Aquarius, the Waterman

Sagittal Moveable Fixation	Schizotypal Personality Disorder	Gemini, the Twins
Sagittal Tight Fixation	Schizoid Personality Disorder	Sagittarius, the Archer
Sagittal Loose Fixation	Dependent Personality Disorder	Pisces, the Fishes
Sagittal Still Fixation	Passive-Aggressive Personality Disorder	Virgo, the Virgin

Within the current view of personality disorders, there has been a conventional consensus that personality disorders can be divided into three clusters on the basis of common variables. These common variables are identified by behavior. Behaviors are categorized as eccentric (Cluster A), dramatic (Cluster B), or anxious (Cluster C). It gives a useful guide when making differential diagnosis from observations of a client's behavior.

Clusters Conventionally Conceived

Cluster A = Eccentric	Cluster B = Dramatic	Cluster C = Anxious
Schizoid	Borderline	Dependent
Schizotypal	Narcissistic	Obsessive-Compulsive
Paranoid	Antisocial	Avoidant
Multiple	Histrionic	Passive-Aggressive

However, this is just another example of how clinical psychology is driven by the notion of behaviorism. In an attempt to be empirical, psychological measures have weighted behaviors as central to making diagnosis. The factors that are often overlooked or marginalized are the inner experiences of the clients, their world outlook and core values. Instead, what has become common currency in psychology are theories explaining behaviors. Mental constructs are being created as an attempt to explain the mind and how it governs behavior or is governed by behaviors. The vacuum in psychological theories is the lack of an image of the human soul. In my view, the human soul lives in the realm of the dynamics of polarities, including the polarities implied by personality (and its disorders), as made much more clear when we see the one-sidedness of movement styles—implying the opposite movement. I have been compelled to reformulate the idea of personality clusters with the human soul, its three primary faculties of thinking, feeling and willing, and the four primary polarities of mind.

The Cluster that I have below designated as "A" has in its foreground the psychological issue of independence/dependence. The Narcissistic lives at the pole of independence and the Dependent lives at the pole of dependence, but the Antisocial disregards both poles. As a consequence, their lives are dictated by losses of both experiences. They have neither a healthy independence nor do they sustain a healthy dependence in their lives.

Cluster "B" is grouped around the psychological issues of detachment/engagement. The Paranoid is fixated at the pole of detachment and the Obsessive-Compulsive finds himself or herself fixated at the pole of engagement, whereas the Schizoid disregards both poles. As a consequence, the Schizoid finds no interest in being detached nor in being engaged.

Cluster "C" exhibits the psychological theme of containment/ freedom. The Borderline is preoccupied at the pole of containment, often urgently seeking for it, and the Schizotypal relishes in the unbounded pole of freedom, whereas the Histrionic disregards both poles. As a consequence these types are found rebounding from one pole to the other without rest.

Cluster "D" is oriented to the psychological theme of victimization/ambivalence. The Avoidant wishes to be socially involved but is more often caught in ambivalence, unable to make any true initiative. The Multiple tends to be identified with traumas entrapping this person on the pole of victimization. The Passive-Aggressive disregards both poles. As a result of this disregard, the Passive-Aggressive tends to wrestle with the unconscious roles of an ambivalent persecutor and a vulnerable victim.

It is my intuition that there is an important key to this formulation of clusters for the clinician, who desires to escape the one-sidedness and/or dualism implicit in conventional presentations of clinical dynamics. Adding the third dimension both gives a different view on the polarities, and may well hold a secret to the polarities' resolution. The clinician can see the value in regarding the polarities as important indicators for the need to strike a balance in one's life. Simply put, it is important to neither fixate upon nor to disregard the polarities in life, but rather to regard, respect, and balance them into your life.

The proposed newfound formulation of the personality disorder clusters is presented in a concise tabular format to follow. I offer it as a stimulus for provoking new thinking in the debate concerning personality clusters, not as a tested empirical orientation.

Personality Disorders Clinical Cluster Formulation

Clusters of Personality Disorders	Focused Soul Faculties	Psychological Themes
Cluster A		Independence/Dependence
F1: Narcissistic	Willing	Issues of independence
H1: Antisocial	Feeling	Disregard for both issues
S3: Dependent	Thinking	Issues of Dependence
Cluster B		Detachment/Engagement
F2: Paranoid	Willing	Issues of Detachment
H2: Obsessive-Compulsive	Feeling	Issues of Engagement
S2: Schizoid	Thinking	Disregard for both issues
Cluster C		Containment/Freedom

F3: Histrionic	Willing	Disregard of both issues
H3: Borderline	Feeling	Issues of containment
S1: Schizotypal	Thinking	Issues of freedom
Cluster D		Victimization/Ambivalence
F4: Avoidant	Willing	Issues of ambivalence
H4: Multiple	Feeling	Issues of victimization
S4: Passive-Aggressive	Thinking	Disregard of both issues

I emphasize that you must not accept what I have proposed, but rather test it with your own bodily experiences, and re-think every conceptual formulation given for the understanding of personality disorders.

Suggested References for Further Study

A much more exhaustive rendering of these propositions can be found in my doctoral dissertation, published by Lambert Academic Publishing entitled: *A Somatic Psycho-diagnostic Approach to Personality Disorders: An Understanding of Personality through Spatial Orientation (2009).*

Here are some other valuable references:

Benjamin, L. S. (2003). *Interpersonal Diagnosis and Treatment of Personality Disorders.* New York & London: The Guilford Press.

Cleckley, H. (1976 edition). *The Mask of Sanity: An Attempt to Clarify Some Issues about the So-Called Sociopathic Personality.* New York: C.V. Mosby Co.

Heatherton, T. & Weinberger, J. (Editors) (1997). *Can Personality Change?* Washington, D.C.: American Psychological Association.

Kernberg, O. (1984). *Severe Personality Disorders: Psychotherapeutic Strategies.* New Haven/London: Yale University Press.

Kretschmer, E. (1925). *Physique and Character: An Investigation of the Nature of Constitution and of the Theory of Temperament.* London: Paul, Trench & Trubner (out of print).

McWilliams, N. (1994). *Psychoanalytic Diagnosis: Understanding Personality Structure in the Clinical Process.* New York & London: The Guilford Press.

Millon, Theodore, and George Everly. (1985 and 2011) *Personality and Its Disorders.* New York, Wiley.

Robins, L. (1966). *Deviant Children Grow Up: A sociological and psychiatric study of sociopathic personality.* Baltimore, MD: Williams & Wilkins.

Stone, M. (1993). *Abnormalities of Personality: Within and Beyond the Realm of Treatment.* New York & London: W.W. Norton & Company.

CHAPTER 8

Depression

by William Bento, Ph.D. and
Edmund Knighton, Ph.D.

[*William Bento:*]

In previous chapters we addressed how the personality offers a vehicle through which the "I" can find expression in the world. The "I" bears our sense of destiny, our purpose for being. The sense of purpose has very much to do with what beats in our hearts. I am referring to something much more than the physical pulsing of blood flow, something more akin to what we can call the drive of the "I AM," the individuality—the ego drive—coming into this world.

In depression the ego drive is brought to a stand still. Movement into the world is obstructed and constrained. At the core of what we experience in depression is a loss of the fire that permeates soul life. In the book *Soulways* by Rudolf Treichler, we read an anthroposophical physician's perspective regarding the organs as interior spaces of consciousness. When we look at the liver, for example, we're looking at a particular quality of the etheric realm and the way in which the soul relates to the etheric dimension in a particular way. Because the etheric body is really a time organism, it has within itself all of the deepest perceptions, experiences, and memories. A key question for us is, "How does the soul live in time?"

In conventional psychology we often look for those deep images, events, and experiences at the edge of the realm of the unconscious. Unconsciously we are always accessing certain memories associated with present experience from our past. This fact has shaped the whole technique of psychology beginning with

Freud's focus on the unconscious. We tend to look to the past and attribute to the past the origin of all of our present problems and difficulties.

But in the anthroposophic approach, it's very important to realize that time does not move in just one linear stream; that is, time is not something that is only flowing from the past to the present and into the future. There is a stream of time that flows from the future to the present. When we are really awake and aware of this stream coming from the future into the present, we can then with our own awareness see the past differently. We can change the past. That has a lot to do with how you interpret the past, how you assign meaning to the past. In a counseling process, it is important to revisit and review and redefine the events of the past. How we attach meaning or do not attach meaning to our memories and experiences makes a lot of difference as to how we can feel the present and go forward in life. Even opening the possibility of feeling a particular stream of energy coming from the future—backwards, so to speak—can be liberating to this process.

Depression is a major clinical diagnosis. And yet we all use the term more widely to describe the blues, flatness, listlessness... I'm going to describe to you three types of clinical depressions that are related to the soul's capacity to relate to a particular aspect of time.

One form of depression is called the *agitated depression*, which does not look like depression. It looks like an angry negative person, always negative, always irritable, pessimistic and critical. Underlying every interchange is some tension. Persons with this affliction don't change. You're having a conversation and they make sure the whole mood is depressed because they cover everything with a quality of cynicism, a quality of disdain or discontent, that just doesn't seem to go away. A constant yet undefined agitation permeates all of their interchanges.

An agitated depression is based on the inability to let go of the past. When we are stuck in whatever kind of injustice, unfairness, or difficulty that has happened in the past, we feel that we can't change it. It has become stone. If you're living in that past injustice, you don't have the capacity to reformulate, rephrase, or change it. You're a victim of those memories that unconsciously set an undertone or a pervasive mood of discontent. It's very difficult for someone in an agitated depression to be in the present. They feel this in their gut. They sense an inner voice saying, "Why is it so difficult for me to be present?" That's because the client is not in the present. He or she is stuck in the past, repeatedly confirming the impossibility to change what has happened. What has happened has happened. Period. The difficulty to accept and forgive will hold such a person in whatever victimized postures they have been in, and that is a depressed position. Their position doesn't look like a typical depression because there is a continual foment of underlying anger that is not resolved. An agitated depression has this quality of anger in its expression connected to the past.

Another kind of clinical depression is called *dysthymia*. This is a depression that all of us know experientially. It is where we just seem to be in a rut day after day. We live in a constant sense of boredom. The present cannot sustain our interest. What is there to do? Dysthymia is a kind of prolonged, chronic feeling of despair and emptiness. Everything in life appears meaningless. Often people with dysthymia experience cycles where they come out of it. If situations draw them out and they need to be active, they can. Because they have some capacity to be functional for some situations and not others, it is difficult to see the underlying deep depression that is there. In dysthymia there is the sense that one's life is meaningless. Indeed that meaning itself cannot exist. If meaning can't exist, why even try to achieve any capacity of meaning? This depression has to do with an inability to be present.

The present cannot sustain their interests, so they're not present. Many people who have this particular kind of disposition spend most of their life living through osmosis, on the couch watching TV. That's some engagement, but it is not really an engagement that activates one's soul life. So it's a kind of soul life that is numb and dumbed down into its stillness, a kind of paralysis of being. Boredom becomes a way of life. With the agitated, anger is a way of life; with the dysthymics, boredom.

The classic form of depression is *melancholic depression*, typified by a pervasive anxiety about the future, and an incapacity to actually bring anything to meet the future. Although irrational from a cognitive point of view, melancholic depression is often sustained by catastrophic thinking. It becomes a way to forestall the future and to have no care to plan for the future. This pervasive anxiety spreads throughout all of one's affairs.

Popular opinion names the primary cause for a melancholic depression as events that were tainted with unexpected tragedy, failure, or disappointment. Tragedy can be found in the biographies of classically depressed people. However, the factor responsible for the sense of entrapment in a melancholic depression has more to do with being stuck in a future that hasn't happened yet. Because it hasn't happened experientially, it's always filled with assumptions of the worst kind. Do you know somebody who is depressed where all they're going to tell you is that everything is going to be worse and worse and worse? The symptoms cluster around the lack of hope. Anybody caught in a melancholic depression tends to use anything that is less than perfect to affirm his or her outlook that there is no hope for the future.

Anyone who has slipped into a depressive mood for a couple of days will be able to identify with these descriptions. Because we're talking about depression as a phenomenon that exists in time, we look at past, present, and future as a two-way continuum. We must guard against the natural tendency to look for the etiology of a depression only in the past. Depression is one of the most common forms of mental illness. Prior to any deep-seated clinical depression, there is usually a significant amount of stress. It need not even be of a particularly personal issue. Our times are full of stressors. The biggest over-arching stress has to do with living in what is indisputably "apocalyptic times." We are all being faced with the prospect of crossing the threshold into the spiritual world as described by anthroposophy. In doing so, we are being challenged by beasts arising within ourselves and in our world for which we may not be prepared.

A tabular format can help you compare and cross reference

the types of depression. However, keep in mind no one ever is a pure type. Distinctions between types of depression give us a capacity to assess the predominant type of depression. Think of one of your clients or maybe a friend you know struggling with depression.

Etiology and Progression of Depression

Responses to Stress	Anger	Apathy	Anxiety
Threshold Encounters	Hate	Doubt	Fear
Orientation to Streams of Time	Past	Present	Future
Type of Depression	Agitated	Dysthymic	Melancholic
Pathological Behaviors	Fight	Flight	Freeze
Extreme Consequences	Violence	Virtual Realities	Suicide
Treatment Interventions	Love Engendering Forgiveness	Faith in the Wisdom of Development	Hope Fostered by Gratitude in the Small Wonders of Life

[*Edmund Knighton:*]

William has the capacity to present in ten minutes what you could chew on for a lifetime. Let's acknowledge that, celebrate that, and give a little space to it rather than just jumping forward. Take a moment to write. William left you with a question: What approach would you take with each of these types of depression? This could be for the self; it could be for your client; it could be for a loved one—anything that comes to you, take this opportunity. He's warmed up the space into past, present, and future.

Now take a moment either to share a couple of words of a statement or a couple of words of a question, not that we're going to answer it or talk about it, simply to sound it and have the rest of us hear it. It's nice when you take in information also to express something, to put yourselves back into the room, before you hear more. Remember that it doesn't have to make any sense. It doesn't have to be logical. We're more concerned with your response to what you've heard. The soul process of your response can also be something that surprises you or mystifies you; we celebrate that and welcome that.

[Participant #1:] I'm thinking of a correlation with *anhedonia*, a kind of pervasive, almost national experience that we have in this country where our senses have been dulled. And then when there's a shock or a change or an event happens, sometimes that brings wakefulness to the present. I see economic challenges in the world, real stresses, and people now are waking up to things that perhaps had been a challenge in the past. Individuals too— they wake up to something—a crisis happens and it shocks them.

[David Tresemer:] Oftentimes you observe mixtures of the three types of depression. If someone comes into your consulting room and says he or she is overwhelmed, it could be from the past, or from the present, or from the future. It shows up in different ways. In terms of etiology, you have to look to all directions of time, streaming from the past, from the future....

[Participant #2:] If it's winter and then spring comes on, the first response to spring is actually a falling apart. Do you know what I'm saying with that? I see in that reaction a lot of resistance to change. When one would celebrate, what actually happens is a fear. It doesn't matter if it's because winter is coming or because spring is coming. That's just a cloud that's passing by in the sky and the sun is right here; naturally a continuity. In depression, there is a loss of continuity. And this brought me to a question: In terms of movement, what kind of movement would one do so that one can integrate shifts with a bit more flexibility?

[Edmund Knighton:]
You couldn't have said it better. You shared this image of how in spring something has to be in a way broken or crushed. How does new life come up through the soil? The soil is broken. Soil has to be rent asunder in order for something new to become of it. We have a blank slate like a pavement of soil, compact soil where nothing can grow in it. It's pounding down. We do that so we can put houses on it so nothing will grow underneath. Some-

thing does have to get broken up in order for new life to come, for the plant to come. It's a nice image.

Often when we hear the word depression, we have a pathological view of it, do we not? It's something to fear, to avoid, to run from, to hope like heck it never happens to me. And yet depression is a worthy and essential part of life that builds the capacity for depth. What enables you to carve out these deeper and deeper spaces through your own suffering is the capacity to embody more of the spiritual. In this way the nervous system is the most spiritual part of the body because it's empty. There's nothing in there; it's dark.

I'm going to give you a little poetic celebration of darkness. Invite the food of darkness around yourself as a celebration and in yourself. We'll begin with good friend, Wendell Berry.

> To go in the dark with a light is to know the light.
> To know the dark, go dark. Go without sight,
> and find that the dark, too, blooms and sings,
> and is traveled by dark feet and dark wings.

Wendell Berry knows darkness. So does Rainer Maria Rilke in his poem, "You, Darkness":

> You, darkness, that I come from
> I love you more than all the fires
> that fence in the world,
> for the fire makes a circle of light for everyone
> and then no one outside learns of you.
> But the darkness pulls in everything -
> shapes and fires, animals and myself,
> how easily it gathers them! -
> powers and people -
> and it is possible a great presence is moving near me.
> I have faith in nights.

David Whyte knows darkness and loves it:

> Put down the weight of your aloneness and ease into
> the conversation. The kettle is singing
> even as it pours you a drink. The cooking pots
> have left their arrogant aloofness and
> seen the good in you at last. All the birds
> and creatures of the world are unutterably
> themselves. Everything is waiting for you.

I would like to sing for you the epitaph of Galileo:

> Though my soul may set in darkness, it will rise in perfect light.

> I have loved the stars too fondly to be fearful of the night, fearful of the night.

In this moment celebrate darkness. Celebrate melancholy in you. Whatever word you choose for this state of darkness. Celebrate the deep humanness and the capacities that these can create in us. The energy that anger can give rise to when it doesn't turn to rage, the initiative that it brings into the world. The creativity that arises after a long period of boredom and apathy that can arise—the apathy so strong that suicide is an option. The immense sense of humor that can come on the other side of melancholia, along with the insistent possibility that nothing will ever work in my life.

Feel yourself stretched between these two poles, and yet always you have the capacity to be balanced in the center of them. If nothing else that you get from this time with me, I invite you, I exhort you, to celebrate depression. When someone comes to meet you who is depressed, you get excited, you come alive, and you practice these three gestures of past, present, and future depression. Allow yourself to move toward the capacity for rage. All of us have a murderer inside. Every one of us has this capacity. We're human beings. We are given it freely. Then this capacity for apathy—celebrate it, try it on like a cloak. If you do so, the person who comes to you who is practicing apathy will feel seen, heard, and met by you. Then the sense of melancholia, the world is never right.

You can bring these movements towards you and you don't have to inhabit them and lodge them inside your organs. Therein lies the difficulty where fixation occurs. We take these states and processes too close to us inside the body. The organ systems have their own constellation of movement which we should not be messing with. To the extent that we've placed these forces and movements inside of ourselves, we become ill. They are meant to come in close as visitors, and then let go.

The etheric surrounds the body primarily, so I invite you to bring these movements towards you and play with them outside of yourself, just beyond the body boundary, the skin. This gives you the ability to try on your patient's movements like a cloak, rather than to take them in, which causes burnout and illness in you. Try these things on, like a cloak. You can bring them toward you, but you don't have to bring them inside you.

At the same time you practice your own relationship of being balanced in the center and feeling the depth of agony, of despair, of distrust, without becoming identified with it. Just because you're feeling something doesn't mean that you are it. Just because you think something doesn't mean you have to believe it. Very, very different. People die when we start believing things strongly, when we kill each other. But if we are allowed to simply think them, we will see what unexpected developments unfold.

Concepts are so easily available in the world. All we have to do is click this button, and I have the world's concepts in this little screen in front of me, not just anthroposophic or Waldorf School, but the whole world; I can just click those up. But I'm inviting you to bring some activity, some active perception, to that, to bring it into movement.

Depression has different movements, and these are just three of them: restless depression, apathetic depression, or anxious depression. In this moment, ask yourself: "Which one of these do I feel the greatest resonance with? Which one of these can I celebrate in myself right now? Is it that sort of agitated restlessness of depression? Is it the apathetic, bored part of depression and my boredom? Or is this the anxious part of depression, the melancholic part?" The word anxiety literally means to narrow. So you're feeling a narrowing in, or a contraction. Anger is the opposite, an expansion. Do you feel a movement now? The boredom—how do you think boredom moves?

Feel bored for a moment. Right now—feel bored... Tell me how it moves. Exactly—nothing—it doesn't move. Boredom doesn't move. You see, it sits on the fulcrum of the crescent, in the center, unmoving. There's just really nothing going on. One time in my 20s, we had folks come around and just stop by. I always seem to live near people like this and so this fellow came up, this young black man and I opened the door and said "How're you doing?" He just looked at me. I said, "What's happening?" He said, "Nothing. Bored." So I walked outside and we had a little swinging porch and we sat down together for two hours and said nothing. And then we stood up and we took a walk together and said nothing. And then he left. And it was one of the most seminal moments of my life. Nothing took place except those words, and then we sat together silently, took a silent walk around the neighborhood. Bored. We could just hang out together and have nothing to talk about and not even know each other. We're just two human beings taking a walk in the world. I never saw him again.

It's that quality of nothing happening, yet it's OK. It's OK that there's nothing happening. Let's celebrate the fact there's nothing happening and sit here and swing into nothingness. Steiner described the Sun, that radiant being, as "less than nothing" in his *Karmic Relationships* lectures.

[Participant #3:] That is a good relationship with fear and the unknown.

[Edmund Knighton:] Steiner would say "All fear is useless; I must not let it take hold of me; I must think only of what must be done." All fear is useless. And he's someone who knows.

Regarding Steiner's lectures from 1912 to 1921 which can be located in a book entitled *Psychoanalysis and Spiritual Psychology*, you have, on the one hand, spirit and, on the other hand, psychology or psyche or soul. You have the spirit and you have the soul and they're moving together.

You can observe how the Christian Community, the renewed initiative begun by Steiner, starts with the aspect of spirit or priestliness and moves toward counseling and psychology. Perhaps in our field, we move from the side of counseling, the psyche, the soul—from that side to the spirit side.

Frank Lake was not trained in anthroposophy, and yet his work *Clinical Theology* relates very closely. Frank integrates theology with psychiatry; I find his work deeply helpful. Here is his understanding of what I call the reverent celebration of depression.

The Reverent Celebration of Depression

Repressed Activity and Passivity	Reaction Formation of Behavior
1. Touch. The infant seeks to touch the mother.	Abstinence: Denial of sexual interest. Prudery.
2. Attention-seeking fantasies	Humility: Excessive self-effacement
3. Rage and destructiveness	Openness: Compulsive compliant personality (predepressive)
4. Separation anxiety splits into "not me"	Equanimity: Brittle overconfidence
5. Fear of imminent death of the spirit	Fearlessness: Compulsive need to prove one is not afraid
6. Distrust of "bad universe" of mom and maybe dad	Positivity: Compulsive idealization of mother's perfect trustworthiness
7. Despair, no hope that mom will respond	Positivity: Compulsive optimism and persistence
8. Desolation when "I am with you always" is shattered	Intimacy: Compulsive clinging to family and friends
9. Weakness of will to go on living under such conditions	Fearlessness: Compulsive protestations of strength and courage
10. Apathy. Mom gives too little.	Compulsive show of keenness and doggedness
11. Weakness of the will to be good	Compulsive strong moral earnestness, tries too hard without joy
12. Feeling of worthlessness	Compulsive striving to achieve worth and value
13. Setting of life typified by denial, splitting off, repression	Openness: Obsessional person appears integrated open, honest, and uncomplicated (predepressive)

Frank Lake took a psychodynamic approach when he wrote about "the repressed activity." Lake's tabulation begins with the sense of touch, the first of the twelve senses that Rudolf Steiner enumerates. If the infant doesn't receive touch, if an animal, any animal, doesn't receive touch, what happens to the animal? It dies. Without touch there's death. The infant seeks to touch the mother. If this touch is somehow interrupted, the animal reacts with diminution of interest— in sex, in everything.

Instead there are attention-seeking fantasies (the second activity in Lake's chart). We all need attention; we all crave attention, the primary narcissism that William talked about. This might move into secondary narcissism, which is the narcissism to avoid—the narcissistic personality disorder. The primary narcissism is for survival and we all have to have that. What happens if this attention from the mother is not given? It could look like humility. It may look like a positive attribute. But when you see how it manifests, it's excessive self-effacement. This is an individual who is never willing to step into his or her own power. It looks like humility in the beginning. That's the reaction piece. They're trying to find something that will gain the attention of the mother, the caregiver. They translate the mother's behavior into: "Be more humble. If I don't cry as much, if I don't get angry, if I don't hit at things, then I'll get the attention I seek. If I deny my own sense of sexual interest and pleasure and wanting to touch my mom, then I'll get attention." How many babies stroke their mothers when they're nursing? It's the most beautiful thing on the planet.

Number three on Lake's chart: rage and destructiveness. Agitation turns into rage in relation to the past on the depressive scale. What does the individual do? He or she moves toward excessive openness, toward becoming a compliant personality. This is called a pre-depressive position. Your task as someone who works with individuals is to seek the pre-depressive position, ideally before they get into a depressive pathology, which means a fixated or stuck position. You're tracking the antecedents to the fixated or stuck position, and a compliant personality is one of them. You find this in the mature counselors and therapists who work with schizophrenia, particularly paranoid schizophrenia. The clients are often entirely willing to please if they have a compliant aspect, and they're very interested in who you are and making sure that you're comfortable—because they're dying inside. You need to be able to see that in your client.

Number four is the separation anxiety that splits into the "me" versus "not me." From Martin Buber's work, we can understand the I-It relationship as different from the I-Thou relationship. This can move to equanimity. Initially it looks equanimous, but then it turns into a brittle sense of overconfidence. The person says, "Nothing phases me, I'm cool. How ya doin'? I'm fine." Again, actually, the communication is, "I'm dying inside and I have no way to figure out how to express that."

Fifth: Here's where the theological aspect of Frank Lake's work comes in, the fear of the imminent death of the spirit. This is not something you'll find in traditional psychology books. What does this look like when you react against it?

It may appear as fearlessness and a compulsive need to prove I'm not afraid. Always fending off fear, and at the same time living in it. The client distrusts the bad universe of mom (now to number six), and reacts with excessive positivity. "I idealize mom. Mom is perfectly trustable, because if I act that way, maybe I'll get the care and attention I need." Thus the infant takes care of the mother.

Despair, number seven, no hope that mom will respond. Again, the client moves to positivity. "I become very optimistic and very persistent with my optimism." You can feel the level of fixation. Deep down, you feel the unconscious statement by the client is, "I'm fixated, I'm stuck in this position, and I don't know what to do about it."

Number eight: the desolation. Instead of "I am with you always," it's a feeling of abandonment. What way does the infant move? The reactive position is one of intimacy. I cling to family and friends. It looks like intimacy in the beginning, but the deeper statement is "I will never let go of your shirt—or skirt." The client's very existence hinges on the ability to hang on. The weakness of will to go on living under such conditions moves to fearlessness, and compulsively protesting one's strength. Feel the brittleness of clinging masquerading as intimacy.

Apathy (number 10): "If mom gives too little, then I become keen and dogged. I overcome her apathy with my initiative and maybe that will carry over into her. Maybe I can teach her initiative through my own doggedness." These are the frameworks of unspoken agreements deep within the client's psyche. Weakness of the will to be good turns into a kind of moral earnestness. "I try so hard in everything I do." It becomes a banner that the client waves. You know individuals like this, always trying so hard. But success eludes them. They're caught in the trying, over and over, again and again.

Worthlessness (number 12) turns into a compulsive striving to achieve worth and value, a sort of industriousness. You can tie all of these into Erik Erikson's life stages as well (chapters 4 and 5). Living by denial, splitting off and repressing, becomes openness. It's when an obsessional person appears to be integrated, open, honest, uncomplicated, sort of "it's all good," and then underneath they're preoccupied with needing to be in this position no matter what comes. That's the definition of neuroticism, always doing the same thing and expecting different results.

Now let's look at the last repressed activity (number 13). Regarding social media, one in three people on the planet is now on Facebook and there's a lot of research going on now with Facebook. What they're finding is that people present their best selves and a lot of times it's made up. 73% believe that people are lying about how good things are. But when you ask them about themselves and how often they lie, how many do you think it is? What do you think?

[Participant says 20%.]

Yes, it's the opposite: "I don't lie. Everybody else does. I'm telling the truth. This is how good my life is." Exaggerated. "It's all good." Then we compare. Someone else's kid is better playing tennis than our kid. Someone else's kid started talking before my kid did. And we walk away from a so-called social interaction feeling more hateful toward human beings. What is touted as "social" is actually anti-social.

In the reaction formation, some of the words that I've used like openness and positivity are part of the six basic exercises that Steiner offers us. There is a healthy position of openness, positivity, and equanimity. And there are fixated positions.

[Participant:] As I look at the chart, I see on the left side some of the primary injuries and the defenses. Each could be the defensive posture in the injury itself.

[Edmund Knighton:]

Yes, each one of these has a particular gesture or posture. Previously, I brought to you the molding, floating, flying, radiating exercise from Anton Chekov. Chekov uses what he calls psychological gesture. In a dramatic form for thespians, you're able to inhabit the movement of concepts. We need to move from concept to percept, from picture to primary experience. One way to do this is to take a concept into movement. It's the most simple way to do it, and to recognize how what you think can be translated into how you move. Take a concept that's a living concept for you—such as the concepts we've just explored in relation to depression. Then discover a gesture for that concept. Observe what comes up for you: What percept or primary experience arises out of that concept? You're completing this threefold cycle that Steiner often comes to with the body/soul/spirit—the concept being spirit, the soul part being the percept, and the sensate part being the body—a circular movement. (You can apply this exercise to the picture given in chapter 6, and discover more about spirit, soul, and body.)

The movement allows you to look at the concept objectively because movement is visible out in the world. You can film yourself doing it; you can have a loved one watch you; you can watch yourself moving. Moving puts the soul out in front of you, puts the spirit out in front of you. That's why movement is just such a wonderful approach and I think why we have bodies! Without them we don't have the capacity to move in gesture and posture. Without bodies we don't have the capacity to feel separation from the other, which is an illusion, and then find the resolution to that separation. Space is created only because we have bodies. Without bodies there is no concept of space. Space is probably not something disembodied beings discuss. Space offers the illusion of separation as well as the possibility to become interdependent, to link ... or to remain separate. The freedom available through this illusion offers an immense opportunity for humanness.

Back to the table from Frank Lake. That was a wonderful comment concerning the posture on the right-hand side, the injury on the left. On the left the injury, on the right the posture or gesture that arises as a result. Try to take the concept into embodiment in yourself; then move the concept. In my experience there are no concepts that cannot be moved. It can help you so, so much when you look at working with a client to take the client's injury into movement for yourself. It's creative; it's fun.

[William Bento:]

This is a format that can be used for almost any illness, constantly working with polarities. It comes back to the approach of salutogenesis (chapter 3) where we're looking for the harmony and the health which is always existent, even if dormant. While salutogenesis may appear to be all positive affect and without any negativity, to believe that would be an illusion. The middle ground is the task of good assessment. Edmund emphasized that one engage in assessment without becoming caught at either extreme. They both coexist, but what often happens is we only get to see a snapshot in time; we see someone caught in one of the extremes.

[Edmund Knighton:]

Recognizing the polarity we invite you in this work to say yes to both. It's not an either/or. We don't give you the *DSM-5* manual and say, "This summarizes all you need to know." You need to get familiar with this book; yet you hold it lightly in relation to these other aspects that we've talked about. And just as you hold diagnosis lightly, you also hold lightly the myriad moment to moment assessments that you make when sitting with another person. These are called formative assessments. The diagnosis is more like a summative assessment, which boils down thousands of formative assessments you have made. All are held lightly, with an awareness of what Goethe called metamorphosis. This suggests that in the very moment you are labeling another person, that label is merely a snapshot of him or her in that moment. The client has already moved on, metamorphosed, in the next moment. That is why we hold assessment lightly. It changes. And then it changes. And then it changes. Infinitely. But because we live in a world of polarity, we do need to work with both forms of assessment. Can you feel how you need both forms of assessment, and yet you need to be open to the reality that these assessments may only approach near to the living reality of any person?

You can't have one without the other. The roses rot on the ground without the trellis. Summative assessment is your trellis. Formative assessments are your roses unfolding moment to moment. They are always in motion, always growing. The moment you give a summative assessment called a diagnosis to a person, he or she has already moved on from it. As you're writing it down, they've already moved into something different. We accept the limitations of that and we do it nonetheless because it's required for growth.

[William Bento:]

One of the stigmas of diagnosis is that you become caught in the summative, caught in a conclusion. The process ends. As a clinician you must weave all the time. When you weave back to the diagnosis, you need to continue to reevaluate it. The client has already moved on. In the next session I'm likely to have a new perception, a formative one, not a summative one. Knowing that leaves us free to actually move with the process that a client may be going through rather than trying to move the client into a single summative box.

[Edmund Knighton:]

Back to what was given in chapter 6 by David, here is the "I" in the center. Your job as counselor and therapist is tracking. What are you tracking? Movement. You track the movement of thinking; you track the movement of feeling; you track the movement of the will, of the activity. Different psychological schools use different names for these things. They use cognition for thinking; they use affect for feeling; and they use volition for the will. They might use the term behavior for activity or for the working of the will. The archangel Michael, overseer of the cultural age of our modern world, needs to be redirected in the heavens rather than being overshadowed. You become this Michael or the countenance of Christ. You become a stand-in for Christ, a protector on behalf of the Christ in service of the other, your client. That's the best way to understand attachment and bonding with your client.

Someone asked about how you work with a client. The first thing you do is form a relationship with them. It's called rapport building. You have nothing if you don't have that rapport; all the research has shown that rapport is necessary. All the techniques in the world mean nothing without relationship. The person simply won't open up.

[William Bento:]

I would like to recall how Edmund brought this question of depression as something that could be celebrated in the darkness. In spiritual literature, those who have actually achieved something of what we might call the heights of equanimity have gone through a dark night of the soul. It is a crucial point in a path of initiation. Through this process they are able to hold at least something of the quality of the sacred even in the darkest time.

We set up an altar in the counseling session, either large or small or imagined, so that there is a possibility that this process spontaneously does become an enactment of something holy and sacred. With everyone who brings a story of depression in whatever way, as their personal gospel, can we offer the quality of listening that Roberta and Edmund talked about earlier? That's what you have to offer, the capacity to accept unconditionally and listen to that particular story. In that process there is something that moves between. We can call it transubstantiation, a communion that is not just myself with the client, but with the spirit element. This healing spirit fills our communion. There's something much higher than I or than my client. There is not I but the Christ in us.

There are many other issues with depression, including the

drugs that people use and their effects both physically and spiritually. However, for now, I'd like to close with a verse I wrote years ago that speaks to this question of how anthroposophic psychology can be perceived as movement towards a kind of pastoral practice, pastoral in the sense that one cares not only for the client in the session, but cares for the client as he or she journeys in his or her life. We become members of a secular priesthood. I think this idea of the sacred must not remain a concept, but should come into feeling and movement. What used to be in the confessional booth of the priest is now the space you create to meet with your clients.

> There is a priesthood of the 21st century
> wherein the sacraments are no longer held as in the days of old,
> but administered in the encounter from soul to soul.
> They are invested with a spiritual word and a light-filled gaze full of healing life.
> Out of them streams the force of goodness,
> the power of Christ working in the world as the substance of love.
> They will to do this as a sacrament of the Second Birth.

Suggested References for Further Study
(in addition to the references at the end of the book)

Berry, Wendell (1999). *The Selected Poems of Wendell Berry*. Berkeley, CA: Counterpoint.

Lake, Frank (2006). *Clinical Theology: A Theological and Psychiatric Basis to Clinical Pastoral Care*. Lexington, KY: Emeth Press.

Steiner, Rudolf (1990). *Psychoanalysis and Spiritual Psychology* (trans. M. Laird-Brown). Great Barrington, MA: Anthroposophic Press.

Treichler, Rudolf (1989). *Soulways: Development, Crises, and Illnesses of the Soul*. Stroud, UK: Hawthorn Press.

Whyte, David (2003). *Everything is Waiting for You*. Langley, WA: Many Rivers Press.

CHAPTER 9

Addiction

by Roberta Nelson, Ph.D. andWilliam Bento, Ph.D.

[*William Bento gives a succinct framework to understand addiction. Roberta Nelson follows with a valuable contribution based on her wide experience.*]

[*William Bento:*]

We come to addiction. Roberta Nelson deals with this subject day in and day out at a residential treatment facility, and will take up the main part of this presentation. I did my internship at the Salvation Army Addiction Rehabilitation Center in San Jose, California. I am presently working as a clinical psychologist at Folsom State Prison's Crisis Treatment Center. From this experience I will begin this presentation.

In my role of making brief diagnostic assessments, it is often difficult to determine what the inmate's primary mental illness is because so many of them have long histories of drug and alcohol addictions. Long standing addictions not only alter moods, but disrupt the whole biochemistry of a person's sense of self. We do not always see who the person is because addictions can mask mental illness and can diminish the gifts that a person might have to offer.

Let's begin with you, the counselor in training. I would like you to survey your own lifestyle habits and choose the addictions you have currently—the good ones too, like that cup of coffee that gets you started in the morning. Keep this self-appraisal in mind as this presentation unfolds. This topic will be all the more relevant if you admit that you are not exempt from habits.

Addictions run the gamut from working too long and too much, eating too much chocolate, consuming alcohol daily, dependency on a drug in order to function, and much more besides. Addiction can include acting out or indulging in certain substances. There are a wide variety of types of addiction. With addictions we are always faced with very obsessive-compulsive behaviors. The obsessive-compulsive behavior attempts to fill a particular void or gap in one's life. That sense of a void is pervasive to our whole culture and society.

In the beginning phase, what we call the *acquisition phase* of the addiction, the potential addict is driven by a compulsion to repeat an activity that is generating some form of sensation, usually a pleasurable sensation, a way to be happy. Of course, we all want pleasure and happiness. But, as the addict continues the activity, the consciousness surrounding the pursuit to feel a certain way diminishes and the somatic drive for the stimulation takes over. Biologically the human body is not just a machine where one can put in one thing to take out a pleasure without experiencing consequences. What the addict puts in his or her body starts to alter the body's chemistry. This starts to alter the synapses of their neurons to act in a way unusual to the normal healthy body. The substance alters mood and feeling and thinking. After a while, it alters the person's will, the capacity of volition, the ability to act on one's own.

After the acquisition stage, in the *maintenance stage*, when the person has become an addict, they no longer gain the same quality of pleasure from the experience. The repetitive activity gradually numbs their sense of despair and physical discomfort. Repeating the addictive behavior gives at best a very short-term symptom release. The addict relieves a symptom, an itch is scratched for a brief period of time. And then the itch comes back, strongly, insistently, because it has now become a part of the addict's psyche.

I will define three types of addictions, related in an anthroposophical frame of reference to the concept of threefoldness. The first type seeks arousal. There are many kinds of stimulating drugs available in the world, ranging from cocaine to caffeine.

The craving for a stimulating substance reveals a need for arous-al.

Arousal engenders a high state of expectation. We all experience it, a tremendous anticipation of lifting, which is precisely how the arousal stimulant functions. The addict is pursuing a particular feeling, you might call it a particular mood. It's the pursuit of a sense of invincibility, a sense of power and control. As illusory as that may be, that is one of the driving forces behind the seeking of arousal. This form of addiction attempts to enhance the will. The addiction gives a false sense of identification in the will with power and control. But there is no regulation, no control. That is the irony for the addict, who repeatedly arouses the body. Their will becomes detached from their thoughts and their feelings. And yet, as irrational as their thoughts are, as tragically consequential as the feelings may be in how the addiction interrupts relationships and possibilities for feeling, the raw instinctive will is boss and the craving persists.

A second type of addiction involves a pursuit of the experience of satiation. The addict seeks more of a sedative effect. This includes hashish, marijuana, Valium, pills of all sorts, where the real pursuit is relaxation. We all like to relax just as much as we like to be happy. With a substance aimed at arousal, the addict pursues a dynamic and exciting situation. With the pursuit of satiation, the sedative quality, the aim is pleasurable comfort. There is an unconscious desire to be asleep as long as possible. Avoiding stresses becomes the goal. One of the extreme drugs of this type is heroin. All over the world there are heroin or opiate clubs and cafés, with people comfortably lying about and drifting in and out of sleep. This mode of addiction emphasizes the feeling life. It becomes an all-consuming, self-absorbed feeling, which results in an isolation from the other. These addicts may shoot up together, but they don't interact with one another.

The third mode of addiction includes hallucinogens and psychedelics. Here fantasy becomes the pursuit. The addict seeks escape, not only to alter moods, but to alter perceptions. The addict pursues the mystical, seeking for something beyond the normal, something special, something truly "far out." These substances were often used in initiations in earlier cultures, to help people see the world from a very different point of view. In this mode, the primary emphasis is on the capacity of thinking. A kind of pseudo-imaginative cognition results from the dependence on hallucinogens. Although it conjures up different ways in which to perceive the world, tripping may not translate into practical participation in the world any differently. Repeated use may continue to stimulate the capacity of thinking, but undermines and numbs the will and feeling.

[David Tresemer:] This is a very useful way of understanding addictions. And one that sorts out some widespread confusions. Computers and televisions and iPhones, indeed screens of any sort, seem to stimulate thinking. But, because of the immensely compressed bandwidth in which they operate, there is actually a dulling of thinking. An increase of stimulation in such a small part of the full possibility of attention results in an overall dulling of thinking. Electronic media are not sources of stimulation. Images go jumping around, but the body becomes deathly still and the attention becomes focused in a tiny part of its range. These electronics are sought for their sedative effect, as you have outlined.

[William Bento:]
Yes. In all three types of addiction, whether you are taking a substance to be aroused, or sedated, or a hallucinogenic, addiction provides nothing but a trance. It's living in and through a trance state. One can easily be captured by the trance and that is the problem. When you are in a trance, there is nothing that is actually strengthening or supporting your "I." You are emphasizing one dimension of your soul at the exclusion of the others, and deluded within that favored dimension. Any drug addiction is going to lead to less than human behavior, whether it is a vegetable state, acting out of animal instincts or becoming a robot. But a true human being has to have an "I." With drugs, there is an attempt on the part of the adversaries to actually eliminate the "I." This is a grave danger.

There is another perspective one can take with this situation. Most people who have fallen into addiction are trying to escape deep pains. But it is not just an escape; they are searching for something. What the addict is actually searching for is a sense of Self as a spiritual being. They seek experiences that verify the Self and Spirit. For many who haven't had the education or the environmental support to accomplish this search in another or healthier way, drugs become a quick fix to get there, even if it provides only a momentary experience. This momentary verification comes at a great cost. It has long-term effects on the individual and on the community. That's our concern when we look at the increase of addictions going on in our society.

I have talked about substances, but addictions are not all about substances. We have people who are addicted to all kinds of activities. What are addictions to activities? They are rituals, rituals that in the end become devoid of true meaning and purpose. As human beings we long for rituals, we long for something that can connect us to something greater in ourselves, with each other, and with the dimensions of the spiritual world. Unfortunately addictions tend to disconnect us from each other and that is the sad tragedy about being addicted to anything. It overwhelms our ability to be free, conscious, attentive, and relational human beings.

[Roberta Nelson:]

I would like to begin by applying what Dr. Bento has outlined for us to a common clinical picture that I witness daily at the residential treatment facility where I work. Many philosophies and worldviews emphasize four elements: fire, air, water, and earth. In chapter 3, William has assimilated these elements forming a fourfold view of the human being that can help us unlock the mystery of common so-called pathologies seen through a spiritual lens: personality disorder, psychosis and posttraumatic stress disorder, depression, obsessions, and addictions.

Let us picture a frequent clinical situation. A client is diagnosed with addiction, which relates to the element of Earth. They also have depression, so they are now also struggling in the element of Water. In addition to that, they also will have issues of neglect and abuse or trauma, in the element of Air. And, as William has just finished stressing, their "I" or ego (I will interchange these two terms here, and mean the more developed organizing principle of the self) is no longer organizing their thinking, feeling and willing. This dysfunction of the "I" means that they are struggling in the element of Fire. We have disarray going on with all the four elements. This complex picture is a challenge of our time apparent in the statistics gathered at my site of employment. Over 80% of the two thousand clients that the facility serves have disturbances simultaneously happening in all four quadrants. *[These quadrants can be overlaid on those presented in chapter 3.]*

ELEMENT: FIRE **Principle of human nature:** **the "I" or Ego** **Affected bodily organ: heart**	ELEMENT: AIR **Principle of human nature:** **astral body** **Affected bodily organ: kidney**
• The "I" is displaced. Self-observation is impaired. • The client's capacity to organize his or her life is impaired. Often a client is homeless, unemployed, reporting: "I do not know who I am or what I want to do." He or she is disconnected from self and potential. • Client has identified the "I" with negative core beliefs perceiving the self as worthless, insignificant, and a failure. "I can't trust myself." • There is a disconnect between what is arising within and the external environments. They are powerless to bring into line coveted moral values with their actions in the world. • Thinking, feeling, and doing are not congruent, evident in inner discord and unwanted behaviors.	• Psychosis and/or post-traumatic stress disorder. • Thinking is dysfunctional. Delusions, hallucinations, flashbacks, nightmares, or night terrors might be present. • Client is unable to create meaningful long-lasting relationships yet yearns to do so. Co-dependency is a familiar feature along with social anxiety and guardedness. • Instead of being able to recognize and respectfully interact with others, the client is stuck in self-absorption.

ELEMENT: WATER	ELEMENT: EARTH
Principle of human nature: etheric body **Affected bodily organ: liver**	**Principle of human nature:** physical body **Affected bodily organ: lungs**
• Depression • Client has disconnected from the source of renewal in his or her life, evident in thoughts of uselessness, helplessness, hopelessness. • Interests have faded. Decision making and concentration is difficult. Shame, doubt, and guilt are reported. • The client has fallen into darkness. Suicidal ideation and attempts might surface.	• Obsessions and addictions. • Client has moved away from "I want to," apparent in impulsion, towards "I have to," evident in compulsion. • The client has re-wired his or her neurology, creating a schism between his or her bodily natures. • Drugs and alcohol have taken the place of wellness and self-care. • The 12 senses are disrupted: touch, self-movement, balance, smell, taste, sight, warmth, well-being, hearing, speech, thought, and the sense of the other. • With addiction the Self is usurped or exiled as long as usage continues. The fallen self inhabits the client's director's chair, in other words, the seat where the "I" should be.

In review, the downfall in the element of Earth is addiction, in Water depression, in Air the link with trauma, and in Fire loss of the "I." Incorporating the spiritual dimension in our four-fold model of the human being creates a multifaceted holistic image of a typical client seeking inpatient treatment in a residential facility. This composite picture is a byproduct of our time. Steiner explained an evolutionary phase that is currently unfolding, a state of being where unready human beings cross the threshold between the sensible world entering into the supersensible world ill-equipped. We are ill-equipped because we have not united our "I" with the Divine. We have not transformed our thinking, feeling, and doing. This happens with persons who are abusing drugs and alcohol. But they aren't alone. We too are crossing the threshold into spiritual realms—it is a sign of our times. In the past the Divine held our psychological forces together through the functions of the ego. Now, balance between thinking, feeling, and doing has been disrupted for all human beings. We all have the option of taking up the task of harmonizing our thinking, feeling, and doing, and of aligning our "I" with what is true, beautiful, and good within our nature.

Now to expand on what William just introduced us to, I would like to address the psychological functions of Will (what I usually call Doing), Feeling, and Thinking. Then we will take a look at demographic information on what's currently happening in a contemporary residential treatment center.

Function	Will or Doing	Feeling	Thinking
Drug	Stimulants	Sedatives	Hallucino-gens
Need or Pursuit	Arousal	Comfort and pleasantness	Pursuit of the mystical, the spiritual

The Will: Which drug do you think presently predominates in regard to the function of will? It is methamphetamine, a stimulant that produces astonishing illusions in the will. I often hear from methamphetamine users that this drug helped them to accomplish a lot. I remember a woman telling me that she was fixing the sink. This seemed like a successful stimulation of the will, until the full picture emerged. For weeks she was under her kitchen sink, "fixing" it, apparently in a will-oriented activity though she really wasn't getting anything done. Another time a client told me that she got a lot of cleaning done. When asked to explain, she described working with a toothbrush in the same corner of the room for days. The drug creates the illusion of industry. When telling their stories, the clients laugh at themselves and their various activities recalling how productive they thought they were.

Dopamine is a neurotransmitter linked with motivation and reward. Using a baseline control called percent of DA output, it has been determined that cocaine releases about 350 units whereas methamphetamine releases 1,000 units, with longer lasting effects in the blood than cocaine. Methamphetamine is a powerful stimulant and readily available in many places. Methamphetamine is preferred by addicts where I live. It is made from anhydrous ammonia. Anhydrous ammonia was used during World War II to create runways for airplanes to land. It hardens the soil. Imagine what it does in the human body. Following World War II there was a surplus supply of anhydrous ammonia; since it also is a source of nitrogen, it was marketed to farmers to increase soil fertility. Because anhydrous ammonia is readily available in farming country, persons who "cook" methamphetamine have access to one of its main ingredients. My clients tell me that methamphetamine is more available than cocaine and less costly.

In the realm of Feeling: Which drug predominates with clients entering the residential treatment facility with regard to feelings? The answer is: pain medications and marijuana. Dependency on heroin is also increasing. Of course there are others, but these predominate. This is the sedative class spoken of by William. Physicians are prolific in prescribing pain medications. I hear one story after another of how a client has secured on-going prescribed pain medication. Even though clients are required to let their physicians know that they are addicted to pain medications, they still come back to the center with oxycodone. On the other hand, chronic pain is an ongoing concern. How does a physician balance the need with the risk of addiction? Certainly there are physicians who are sensitive to this matter.

[William Bento:]

Prescribing strong and addictive substances has become conventional medicine's main paradigm for the relief of any symptoms of pain. They have many kinds of varieties of pain pills to offer the patient. And little understanding of other approaches to pain.

[Participant:] How does anthroposophy look at pain?

[Roberta Nelson:] Can you tackle your own question? What do you think?

[Participant:] Pain is one sure-fire method for the soul to awaken you.

[Roberta Nelson:] Yes!

[William Bento:]

The aim of circumventing pain does not take into account that pain is really there to awaken you, to bring consciousness to another level so that you can actually take hold of the situation, not sleep through it.

As Roberta has mentioned, if we continue to take any type of drugs without discerning what's good for us, we are actually inviting what we know as the *double*—the unresolved debris and sludge of our own shadow self—into the physical organism. There is actually a skeletal-shape taking place within us that is the inhabitation of the double. The whole and healthy human being becomes restricted and rigidified. The double or shadow uses our vitality in the body for its own purposes.

[Roberta Nelson:]

In the realm of thinking: How often do you think I see a client who is dependent on hallucinogens coming through the door? This may surprise you, but not very often. I will occasionally meet a client who has used Ecstasy (MDMA) or mushrooms. Technically marijuana is an hallucinogenic but it rarely produces hallucinations. Many clients have a history of marijuana abuse or dependency.

It is very rare that I see a client at the residential treatment facility that is addicted to only one substance. If there is only one dependency it is usually alcohol dependency. The usual picture is three dependencies such as methamphetamine, prescription pain pills or heroin, and cannabis. When there are four substances, which is frequent, alcohol is often the next one added to the list, since it may have been the first substance used and abused. Alcohol and marijuana seem to be the starter drugs adding methamphetamine and or pain pills in late adolescence or early adulthood. I.V. [intravenous injection] usage is fairly common particularly with methamphetamine.

[William Bento:] We should mention the addiction of sex. Pornography is a multi-billion dollar industry. The numbers are huge, yet pornography is only one form of sex addiction, one form of arousal. There are other activities involving sex such as sexual abuse, fetishism, cross-dressing, etc.

[Roberta Nelson:]

I worked with a woman educator who has a Master's degree. She is hooked on masturbation and has a difficulty getting out of the bathroom at school because of her compulsive need to masturbate. Sex addiction is all about arousal. It stimulates dopamine in the body.

All of these things and activities, whether it is sex addiction or whether it is an addiction to stimulants, take the place of Self, capital S Self, the higher self, the "I AM," our Holy of Holies. Our capacity to express what is good within our nature is set aside and instead we witness the false or fallen self take hold. The false or fallen self uses our thoughts, feelings, and will to express ill-will and self-destructive behaviors outward into the world. Addiction is a disease of estrangement. We become disconnected from our self, from others, and from what is Holy.

[Participant:] I see young people start with alcohol.

[William Bento:]

Alcohol can be used in all three modes of addictive behavior: thinking, feeling, and willing. Certain people drink because it is social; you drink to have a good time. If you drink too much, you slip into a comatose place where you have all kinds of imaginations and fantasies. So alcohol can slip into all three of the forms of addiction.

[Roberta Nelson:]

In the field of addiction, alcohol is considered one of the gateway drugs like marijuana; it leads to other substances. At our facility, with about 28% of our admissions, the primary drug is alcohol. As William stated, alcohol is both a stimulant and a sedative. A typical client perceives a diagnosis of addiction as negative and shameful. Most want to stop using. They are weary of a life centered on drugs and/or alcohol. Even those with unsuccessful discharges report to me a wish to stop.

Within twelve hours of admittance, each client goes through an extensive drug evaluation by a licensed addiction counselor. This generally takes from 2-3 hours. It is not unusual for a person to be admitted still high or in a state of withdrawal. Yet the assessment must be done. Drug evaluations include a list of questions related to seven areas: (1) chemical use history; (2) acute intoxication/withdrawal; (3) biomedical condition; (4) emotional, behavioral, and cognitive evaluation; (5) readiness to change; (6) relapse potential; and (7) recovery environment. Following a multidisciplinary staff meeting, treatment recommendations are formulated. If the recommendation is for high intensity care, a common recommendation, the client will participate in 25 hours of clinical services during the week as long as they remain at this level.

I hear from my clients that their chemical dependency treatment groups focus on consequences, on the havoc caused by their drug and/or alcohol usage. Lots of time is spent identifying and understanding triggers and cravings. Relapse prevention is also stressed. CBT (Cognitive Behavioral Therapy) is a familiar therapeutic approach. At the agency where I work, clients are required to take up the Twelve Step recovery program, work the steps, acquire a sponsor, and attend either an AA (Alcoholic Anonymous) or NA (Narcotics Anonymous) self-help meeting two times weekly. Rule infractions are addressed, resulting in "refocus." During "refocus," freedoms are restricted. For instance, a client might not be able to go to a grocery store by himself or herself. Instead they are transported by the organization. Although staff attempted to remove the punitive element, clients perceive "refocus" as punishment.

I'm hoping you are getting a picture of the complexity of addiction. This diagnosis rarely occurs as a single diagnostic impression. In other words, referring back to William's presentation (in chapter 3), a typical client does not only fall into the Earth element. Instead they present with other elements, in the form of depression or personality disorders, and so forth.

In chapter 3, we heard about salutogenesis—the process of healing, recovery, and repair. William has also talked about perceiving so-called pathologies as initiation pathways (chapter 13). Joseph Campbell, a renowned mythologist, called it the Hero's or Heroine's Journey. Because I too perceive addiction as a developmental opportunity, a blessing rather than a curse, I invite my clients to relook at their diagnoses in an exercise I call "Re-Imagine Addiction" (below).

Let's begin by imagining this: You have been given a diagnosis of addiction. Because you are a typical client, you feel guilt, shame. You are reminded of the consequences—of the harm—you have caused. You are a failure. You attend your NA (Narcotics Anonymous) meetings, introducing yourself as an addict. "My name is Susan and I am an addict." These reminders are perceived as what is needed to correct self-destructive behaviors, right? "I am an addict. I will never drink again. Never I.V. meth. Never again!" The treatment hinges on the power of those resolutions. In my view, that's not the main issue, and it is a set-up for failure.

[William Bento:]

In many agency trainings for alcohol and drug addiction counseling, you will be told to never trust an addict. This dictum is counter-effective. If there is no trust, how do you ever have a starting point with the client? The conventional approach is really saying, "Don't trust the 'I' of this individual."

[Roberta Nelson:]

Instead of mistrust, there is a place for acceptance, being more concerned and more compassionate towards the client, and most importantly encouraging them to access these qualities in relation to themselves. I agree with William, the overall perception of an addict is that they are deceitful and manipulative. Thus when a rule infraction occurs, the client becomes the culprit. Staff's judgments are rarely questioned. This is a challenge because when engaged in active addiction, behaviors often are deceitful. I am suggesting that caregivers become aware of issues related to transference and countertransference; that we become aware of and responsive to our own biases that silence the voice of judgment.

The learning activity that we are about to experience is used in my groups. It moves away from consequences and shame. After this exercise is completed, I often hear, "This session was so positive. I needed to hear this." I see expressions of surprise on the participants' faces. Or weeks later, maybe when a client is getting ready to discharge they will express gratitude for this "re-imagining" addiction exercise.

Exercise: "Re-imagine Addiction"

Step 1: Draw a line down the center of a white board or blackboard in front of the group. Write this question on one side of the board: "How have drugs and alcohol helped me?" (Needs motivate behaviors. Identifying an underlying need is essential in the process of moving towards wellness.)

In a group setting, I don't invite the client to verbally respond immediately to this question—"How have drugs and alcohol helped me?" I first ask them to be with their own experience. Remember, every little step you take, whether it be with a loved one, a friend, a client, or a colleague, every moment can be a moment to invite the "I" to enter. It is helpful to create time for each person to be within his or her personal self before hearing others. You ask them to ask themselves: "What do *I* think or feel?" Before you enter into a group exchange, you ask them to reflect on themselves. Prior to a group discussion, I usually ask clients to record their own insights and questions. If this isn't done, a person can lose his or her self during the discussion.

Step 2: Invite someone from the group to go to the board to record participants' responses. A person who is struggling with attention issues (as in ADHD) is often a good candidate for this job. It helps them to focus, to attend throughout the activity.

Step 3: Ask participants to float back into their lives reviewing what drugs and or alcohol did for them. Ask yourselves: "How did my drug of choice help me?"

Step 4: Speak out the answers to "How did my drug of choice help me?" And the recorder can put these statements on the board. [*The following responses are from the current conference.*]

o   A welcome distraction from life, from pain, from not fitting socially.

o   Reduction of pain; there was more pleasure in reducing consciousness.
o   Alcohol makes you more socially acceptable—you need to belong.
o   Ability to meet demands to achieve.
o   Feeling of being invincible.
o   Being invisible, not being judged or seen.
o   You nurture yourself, so you feel important.
o   Improves your reality so everything looks better.
o   You are doing something purposeful, important to yourself.
o   You lose inhibitions.

Some of your responses reflect a typical group of clients. Let's compare your answers to a typical list acquired during a group session.

Question One: How have drugs or alcohol helped me?	
• Numbing • Helped me forget • Pain control • Euphoria • Social, helped me get a date • Energy • Relaxation • Feel good • Calmed me down • Happiness • Slow my mind down. I can concentrate. • Coping • Peace • Better sex • Serenity • I'm okay • Manage stress • Invincible	

Step 5: When clients are through listing how drugs or alcohol helped them, comments are invited. "Are there any insights here? Do you all agree with this list? Are there any surprises?"

Step 6: If possible, I cover the left hand side of the board telling clients to imagine that their comments have disappeared. This sets up the next step in the activity. Then I write the next topic on the board in the form of a second question. Replies are recorded on the right-hand side of the board. Sample responses often include the following:

	Second Question: What words do you associate with spirituality? What characteristics does a spiritual person possess?
	• Religion • Serenity • God • Higher power • Calm • Kind • Unselfish • Love • Peaceful • Happy • What is good • Meditation • Euphoria

Step 7: Then I uncover the left side of the board. I step away. I ask this question: "What do you notice about these two lists?" It has never failed. Clients always say: "The lists are almost identical. It's the same stuff on both sides."

Step 8: Then I restate the obvious. Addiction is a suppressed yearning for spirituality. Addicts are persons who crave qualities associated with spirituality, with wholeness. Persons who have mistakenly disconnected from what is good, true, and beautiful within, in other words, their Spirit Self. The relationship to self, others, and the cosmos has been broken. Yet, the need to reconnect, evident in their responses to the first question, perseveres.

To end this segment of the exercise, I ask the group if characterizing addiction as "estrangement from the Divine" rings true for them. Clients report that the activity stimulated a new attitude on addiction. This newfound position fosters empowerment rather than dread. The diagnosis becomes a developmental stepping stone for becoming, rather than a doomsday prognosis.

The exercise, Re-Imagining Addiction, exemplifies a movement towards a salutogenesis approach to addiction rather than viewing addiction as a pathology. Change, which is really learning, arises when a person moves the issue, in this instance addiction, through the Seven Adult Learning Processes outlined in the Appendix to chapter 4.

Let us return to the exercise. Steps 1 through 8 have been completed. Now onto Steps 9 through 16.

(The Steps included in this exercise, 1 through 16, illustrate the application of the Seven Adult Learning Processes ending with a question related to the sixth process: What are you willing to do? If the person develops and implements a suitable action plan, the seventh process will be realized, that is, the experience of a new reality.)

Step 9: The name, Bill Wilson, is written on the board, asking participants: "Who is Bill Wilson?"

After they tell me that he is the founder of AA (Alcoholics Anonymous), I write another name on the board next to Bill Wilson's: Carl Jung. I ask if they know who Carl Jung is. Every once in a while a group participant will know who Jung is, but I have never had a group member link the two. I proceed with a brief lesson in the history of psychology in order to place Jung within a historical context stressing his role as a pioneer in the field of transpersonal or spiritual psychology.

Step 10: After the history lesson I go back to the connection between these two men, Wilson and Jung. I tell the clients that this pioneer in spiritual psychology played an instrumental role in founding the Twelve Step program.

Step 11: I pass out the letter that Bill Wilson wrote to Carl Jung in 1961. Wilson writes that this appreciation letter is long overdue. Nevertheless, Wilson wants Jung to know that his spiritual psychology played an instrumental role in putting together the Twelve Step recovery program.

Step 12: Carl Jung replied to Bill Wilson's letter. I then hand the reply out to the group.

Step 13: I write the Latin phrase on the board that Jung stated in his response to Wilson: "*Spiritus contra Spiritum.*"

Step 14: Jung's entire sentence is read aloud: "You see, 'alcohol' in Latin is 'spiritus' and you use the same word for the highest religious experience as well as for the most depraving poison. The helpful formula therefore is: spiritus contra spiritum." Spirit against spirit.

Step 15: We then explore an interpretation of the Latin phrase: *Spiritus contra spiritum.* Spirit against spirit. I then draw the clients' attention to a store in our town: In our community we have a store named the *Spirit Shop*. What do they sell? "Liquor." Have any of you noted what they have on the billboard outside the shop? "Get your spirits here." These examples highlight what Jung was in part addressing that the word used to describe lofty experiences is also used for a toxin—alcohol.

Step 16: The exercise is concluded by asking group members two questions: (1) What have you learned if anything? (2) What are you willing to do if anything?

In response to the second question a client might say, "Quit drinking." The client is encouraged to create an action plan that will promote the identified change. (The sixth of the Seven Adult Learning Processes. If an action plan is effectively carried out, the seventh of the Adult Learning Processes will be accomplished. Change or learning will occur. Something new will emerge.)

Step 17: Then as a group we brainstorm.

Rudolf Steiner and Marjorie Spock, and many outside of anthroposophy, have emphasized the extreme value of the human encounter. We too have emphasized the supreme importance of the human encounter, of talking and genuine listening. When a person can be seated in his or her "I," then he or she is connected to his or her true individuality. An "I-Thou" relationship becomes possible. They are connected to Love, to the Cosmic I AM. Thus in thoughtfully implemented group activity, human encounters are respected and experienced.

[William Bento:] What Roberta has described is a real confirmation to thc addicts of something no one has said to them before.

"Regard through merciful eyes,
Not what you are, nor what you have been,
But what you wish to be."
[Roberta Nelson:]

As Roberto Assagioli stated in his "Disidentification" exercise: "I have a body but I am not my body. I am an 'I,' a center of pure consciousness." In the four-fold map of the elements (chapter 3, echoed in this chapter), addictions were placed in the element of Earth, our bodies from the view of human nature. I tell a client: "I have addictions but I am more than my addictions. I am an 'I,' a center of pure consciousness." This statement counters the usual AA declaration, "I am an addict." The disidentification statement acknowledges that one has an addiction but is not the addiction. This liberates the "I" from its content of consciousness. Addiction is a false self; whereas the "I" is a conduit for the Divine to manifest in one's thinking, feeling, and doing.

You really want to build upon the clients' wish to change their lives by helping them to perceive their Selves anew. You can't coerce them to do it but you can awaken them to a different self-image. "I have an addiction but I am more than that." Judging blocks the healing process. Empathy opens the healing doorway. Labels and condescending attitudes objectify a person—make each into an object. Development is a choice. The spirits of goodwill respect our freedom to choose. The above exercise helps a client re-imagine who they are. It introduces a different way of looking at their addiction diagnosis. Instead of addiction as a plague, a death warrant, addiction becomes a journey towards what is good within them—a spiritual pathway. When we believe in a client or a friend, we support their capacity to become what they were created to be. The above exercise is an application of principles inherent in salutogenesis.

Now let us return to William's model by considering a contemporary metaphor. A three-headed dragon is a frequent mainstream metaphor for three dimensions of addiction, seen differently from how William presented a three-fold approach. It would be informative to compare this metaphor to the map that William has presented. The first head represents the body and the fact that addiction is defined as a chronic illness. The second head represents the mental, emotional, and behavioral aspects of the disease. The third head represents the spiritual dimension of addiction. From this point of view, the spiritual attests to the reality that the addict is undergoing an existential crisis separated from self, others, and the Divine. Instead of effective thinking, feeling, and willing, the client becomes a "soulless object," a phrase coming from John Firman and Ann Gila in their book titled, *The Primal Wound.*

The dragon as a metaphor is applied in another way. My clients sometimes talk about "chasing the dragon." They talk about continually trying to "grasp" the highs that they experienced early on in their usage. Tolerance increases. Insatiability sets in. The dragon is never caught. Never satisfied. Clients talk about merely existing, not ever living.

In anthroposophy, the dragon is a metaphor for the three soul functions of thinking, feeling, or doing that has become repetitive. In other words, the psychological forces have become self-destructive habits such as addiction to substances, things, or relationships. These habits share a common denominator: selfishness, reduction of the Self to the small-s self. It's still there, but diminished, and can be returned to its grandeur.

Exercise 2: Impulsion and Compulsion

To conclude this session on addiction, I want to invite you to take a look at your own compulsions. Let's examine two words that are sometimes confused. My clients frequently ask me, "What is the difference between impulsion and compulsion?" This is a useful question since the definition of both words helps us clarify addiction. So let's begin by experiencing the words.

This exercise will move you through the Seven Adult Learning Processes listed in the Appendix to chapter 4.

Step 1: Take out a piece of plain paper. Fold it in half. Now draw a line down the middle. You have two sides of the paper, each with a line drawn down the middle. On one side of your paper write: "I *want* to . . . ." List your responses to this phrase. For instance, "I want to go dancing." Or, "I want to go shopping." And so on.

Step 2: On the other side of the paper write "I have to . . . . " List things that you *have* to do.

Step 3: As you compare both sides of your paper, what is the difference between "I want to..." and "I have to.... "

"I want to..." is an impulsion; whereas "I have to ..." is a compulsion. A compulsion is another word for an addiction. You experience that you are compelled. Choice seems to disappear.

Step 4: Select one behavior from your "I have to..." list. One behavior that you would like to explore more thoroughly in the upcoming activity.

Step 5: You each have been given a box of soft pastels. Put them nearby and take another piece of unlined paper. Write the behavior that you experience as a compulsion on the top of the paper. (I prefer soft pastels because you can put down a little color and then use your portable paint brush—your finger—to smear it around to your liking. Having a color medium that you can expand and move around speaks more to the soul than pens. The only caution with pastel is not to put too much onto the paper, not to create too much pastel dust, because we don't want to breathe it in too much. A little bit of color and your fingers will give you the color effects that you need to express.)

Step 6: Put your pen down. Push your chair back away from the table. If you are comfortable with closing your eyes, close your eyes in order to shut out visual stimulation. I say this because sometimes persons who have been abused are not okay with closing their eyes. If this is the case, I suggest that they lower their eyes rather than close them. Continue by taking a slow deep breath. Take another breath. Bring the compulsion that you are focusing on into your field of consciousness. Take a moment to review it. Now, float back to a situation, maybe it is recent, when you were experiencing the compulsion, when you were experiencing "I have to..."

Step 7: With your eyes closed or lowered, began to review the situation. What is happening? Are others involved? What are you actually doing? Simply observe as if you are witness.

Step 8: How are you feeling?

Step 9: Become aware of what you are thinking.

Step 10: How do you perceive yourself when you are carrying out this action?

Step 11: How long has this behavior been in your life? You might actually visualize when it originated.

Step 12: Invite an image or symbol to appear in your consciousness that captures the essence of this behavior. Watch it. What is it? Give the image or symbol a voice. We can do this with our imaginations. If people don't seem to understand, ask them to notice what comes to their mind. Once identified, ask the essence or symbol: "How do you help me?" Listen. Ask it: "What do you really need?"

Step 13: Take a gentle breath opening your eyes when you are ready. On your new piece of paper, create a color gesture— a drawing or color gesture, whatever comes—that captures the essence of the compulsive behavior that you are focusing upon. This gesture can take a form. It can be an object or a movement of color. There is no wrong or right. Give yourself permission to play with color, and in this case, use color to display the behavior that you are stuck in. Use your fingers to move the color around, to get the color gesture onto the paper.

Step 14: Continue to work in color until you feel, "this is done." Fill up your paper expressing this behavior in color.

Step 15: When you are done working with color, on a new piece of paper, write your responses to the questions that I am writing on the board:

- What is the title of your color gesture?
- Describe in writing what it is.
- How does it relate to your compulsion? What is it capturing?
- Record your behaviors, feelings, and thoughts about this pattern.
- Do you have a sense of when the pattern emerged in your life? Was there an event that triggered it? How long has it been with you?
- How does the pattern help you?
- What does the compulsion really need?
- Were there any surprises or insights? If so, record these.

- o What did you learn, if anything?
- o What are you willing to do?

This material is invaluable to the client, to the therapist of that client, and—if the client is willing to share—to everyone in the room struggling with one of the many addictions affecting our modern world.

Exercise 3: The White Rose of Peace

I use storytelling to introduce concepts, telling my clients that stories, legends, and myths are like the time release capsules that we put on house plants: They release nourishment for our souls, slowly, over time. I talk about the value of hearing and telling stories, quoting Albert Einstein: "If you want your children to be intelligent, read them fairy tales. If you want them to be more intelligent, read them more fairy tales." I mention that there are different levels of interpretation possible. I emphasize that, as they listen to a story, they should try to relate all the characters to themselves. The male or female characters in a story dwell within each one of us irrespective of our gender.

In one of my favorite Native American legends called "The White Rose of Peace," there are two brothers who are twins. This legend is attributed to the Iroquois nation who dwelled on the East coast. Some mythologists believe that it was narrated as early as the year 800. Others place it around the 1500s. The version that I use is adopted from a book written by Jacob Needleman entitled *The American Soul*. It is a beautiful story that can deeply enrich us.

Here is the first part of the Iroquois legend:

The grandfathers and the grandmothers gathered in the sky, looking down upon the earth. "It is time for us to descend and to put before the twin brothers a test." The grandfathers and the grandmothers stood in front of the first brother and this is what they asked: "Where do you come from? And where will you go to when your allotted time is done upon the earth present here?"

This brother stood up and placed his hands upon the heavens, replying: "This is where I come from and this is where I will go when my allotted time upon the earth present here is through."

"Ah," said the grandfathers. "Ah," said the grandmothers. "From this time forward this brother shall be called, He-Who-Grasps-the-Sky-With-Both-Hands. For he has not forgotten from whence he comes or where he will go to when his allotted time is through. He is a creator god and all that flows from his hands will be good, true, and beautiful."

Then the grandfathers and the grandmothers stood in front of the second brother and this is what they asked: "Where will you go to when your allotted time is through upon the earth present here?"

The second brother looked annoyed. He waved his arms about and replied: "Look about me. There is much for my senses. Is it not enough that I have arrived upon the earth present here? I am not worried about where I come from or where I will to go when my allotted time is through."

"Ah," said the grandfathers. "Ah," said the grandmothers. "This brother has forgotten from whence he comes and where he will go to when his allotted time is through upon the earth. From this time forth he shall be called Flint or Crystal Ice. From his hands ill will flow."

The grandfathers and the grandmothers ascended and from on high they watched the twin brothers to see what they would do. Given who he was, He-Who-Grasps-the-Sky-With-Both-Hands began to create. Sunflowers sprang up from the earth. Birds filled the skies. Fruit hung from the boughs.

Now being who he was, Flint watched his brother from afar and decided that he too would create things. He begin to imitate what he had observed. But when he tried to create a sunflower, thistle sprang up from the earth. And when he tried to create birds, everything that stung and bit came from his hands.

And being who he was, he turned to fetch his brother so that He-Who-Grasps-the-Sky-With-Both-Hands could see what Flint had made. He-Who-Grasps-the-Sky-With-Both-Hands had already arrived at his brother's lodge. He viewed what his twin had created and said, "These too will be used for good."

He-Who-Grasps-the-Sky-With-Both-Hands noticed that much chaos flowed out of his brother's lodge. So he decided to pick his own lodge up, moving it away from Flint's. As soon as he began to move his lodge away from Flint's, the chaos increased. He-Who-Grasps-the-Sky-With-Both-Hands knew that he would need to stay near Flint so he moved his lodge back where he could keep an eye on his brother.

Time passed and He-Who-Grasps-the-Sky-With-Both-Hands decided that it was time to bring forth human beings upon the earth present here. Carefully he gathered the foam on top of the waters. He created two forms. He placed a portion of his mind into the two forms. He placed a portion of his voice into the forms. He placed a portion of his heart into the forms. Lastly, he blew breath into them. From this, She and He stood up. They walked and talked upon the earth present here.

Being who he was, Flint had watched this from afar and began to copy what his twin brother had done. He gathered the foam on top of the waters. He created a form. He put a portion of his mind, his voice, and his heart into the form that he had created. Lastly he blew breath into the form. He watched and waited. The form cried and leapt into the water. "This is not a human being," Flint announced. "I will try again."

Once again Flint gathered the foam on top of the water and created another form. He put a portion of his mind, his voice, and his heart into the form. Lastly he blew breath into the form that he had created. He watched. He waited. It cried and ran up into a tree. "This too is not a human being. I will try again."

This time Flint slowed down. He gathered the foam from on top of the water. He created a form. He put a portion of his mind, his voice, his heart into the form. Lastly he blew breath into the form. It stood. It walked upon the earth. "Aha. I too have created a human being."

Flint ran to fetch his brother, who had already arrived at his lodge, to show him what he had created. He-Who-Grasps-the-Sky-With-Both-Hands knelt. He watched. He listened to the voice of the first form that Flint had made. After some time, He-Who-Grasps-the-Sky-With-Both-Hands turned to his brother saying, "This is not a human being, Flint. We shall call it frog."

Then he went to the second form that Flint had created. He

watched. He listened to its voice. Then he turned back to his brother saying: "This too is not a human being. We shall call it squirrel."

Then he went to the third form that Flint had created. He watched. He listened to its voice. Then he turned back to his brother saying: "This too is not a human being. We shall call it grizzly bear."

Flint pleaded with his brother: "Help me to make a human being." He-Who-Grasps-the-Sky-With-Both-Hands thought for a while and then replied: "Yes, this too is to be. I will help you make human beings."

Flint listened closely to his brother's directions. Then he gathered the foam on top of the waters. He carefully shaped two forms. Then he placed a portion of his mind into the forms. He put a portion of his voice into the forms. He put a portion of his heart into the forms. Lastly he blew breath into the forms. He watched. He waited. They did not stand or walk upon the earth present here.

He-Who-Grasps-the-Sky-With-Both-Hands came forward. He placed a portion of his mind into the forms. He put a portion of his voice into the forms. He put a portion of his heart into the forms. Lastly he blew breath into the forms. From this, She and He stood. They walked and talked upon the earth present here.

He-Who-Grasps-the-Sky-With-Both-Hands turned to his brother saying: "The human beings that we have created together shall be called The Hatchet Makers for they will forget from whence they come and where they are going to. They will bring much ill-will to the earth present here."

Then he turned to the human beings who had already begun to multiply saying, "Many times I will send you great teachers. Each time they will tell you that there are two lodges, two minds upon the earth present here: my brother's lodge and my lodge. If you choose to dwell in Flint's lodge, there will be strife and chaos. Fear, hate, and doubt will thrive for you and your children's children. But if you choose to dwell in my lodge, then there will be plenty. Love will flourish for you and your children's children."

He-Who-Grasps-the-Sky-With-Both-Hands began to ascend

towards the heavens. He turned towards the humans saying: "The choice is yours. Which lodge will you dwell in?"

How do I use this beautiful legend in group counseling? I use it to introduce a picture of human nature to my clients, emphasizing that we humans have all experienced in our foundations a sacred wound. This wound has led to the experience of two egos, sometimes referred to in the literature as the Higher or True Self, with a capital "S," and a Lower or Fallen self, with a small "s."

Following the story, I put the two brothers' names on the board asking the clients to list qualities associated with both brothers. The following map facilitates comprehension of human nature.

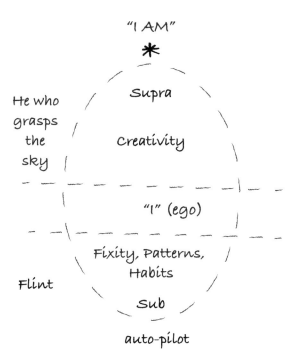

I emphasize the displacement of the ego. Clients become identified with being an addict: "I am an addict; I think, I feel, I act as an addict." End of story! The identification seems complete to them. With the help of this Native American tale, clients can learn to dis-identify from their label. Instead of saying, "I am an addict," another way of perceiving their selves—large S and small s—is introduced. They learn to say, "I have an addiction but I am more than this."

The story presents a picture of two levels of consciousness or principles of human nature. Flint is a picture of the subconscious, possessing fixed patterns and habits. It is experienced as a state of auto-pilot, evident in reactivity, impulsions, and compulsions. Flint represents this state of being. He-Who-Grasps-the-Sky-With-Both-Hands represents supra-consciousness, the realm of creativity, abilities, and the capacities demonstrated by He-Who-Grasps-the-Sky-With-Both-Hands. The "I"—where consciousness resides in our daytime awareness—resides in between. Choice is introduced, the possibility of freedom. Living in picture language has great value. Instead of a fixed way of approaching their diagnoses, clients are invited to re-vision who they are. The picture language of the legend opens up that possibility.

[William Bento:] At AA [Alcoholics Anonymous] meetings, everyone stands and says, "I am an alcoholic." They don't say, "I struggle with alcoholism." They "are" an alcoholic—they have defined themselves in that way. That identification, and the certainty of it, undermines the capacity to be independent of the dependency that the disease forms.

[Roberta Nelson:]

In his book, *Lifting the Veil of Mental Illness*, William Bento has described a fourfold process for looking at symptoms, diagnosis, prognosis, and prescription. I am today presenting how a story can plant a seed to help clients begin to think differently about their diagnoses and who they really are. The rest—prognosis, prescription—follows. Given our time constraints, I am unable to outline the different activities that are used with this tale, such as the "Who Am I?" exercise.

I emphasize today the facilitation of identification with who you really are, your True Self. This is decisive in the healing process. Whether it is addiction or depression, we *have* those states of being, yet we are more than those states. Clients understandably lose sight of this. Addiction, depression, or anxiety can become overwhelming and incontrollable. Storytelling, as well as many other activities, support the re-connection with what is good, true, and beautiful, with who we really are. The client begins to distance his or her Self from the symptoms, from the phenomena, from the labels. "I set the disorder apart from my 'Holy of Holies,' my 'I Am,' my most intimate and true sense of my Self." That could almost be a chant or mantram, though most clients would be overwhelmed by the concepts in that statement. For them, a story about two brothers may be a more potent method to come to this realization. However, an anthroposophic counselor could come to such a statement, and may need to do so regularly.

What are those two words in anthroposophy, the "I Am?" They are the Christ or the Being of Love. It is important for me to know this; however, I seldom use the phrase, "The Christ." Why? Many clients are alienated from Christianity because of the way they were raised or what they have endured under the name of Christianity. Trust or faith in the divine is dubious to them. Instead I will use with my clients universal phrases, such as, "what is good, true, and beautiful within your nature," when referencing what I experience to be The Christ. Alienation can readily occur if certain words are used. The clinician's task is to be helpful, not to alienate with concepts, even if true.

Part of what we're after here with ourselves and with others, is to create distance between the symptoms, or labels, and our true Selves. We are trying to awaken the Observer Self—the capacity to witness one's thoughts, emotions, and behaviors from an objective standpoint. Much can be done to activate the Observer Self. Doing so supports a movement towards organizing and managing our thinking, feeling, and doing. Rather than the familiar auto-pilot state portrayed by Flint in the Native American tale, we move towards a proactive state demonstrated by He-Who-Grasps-the-Sky-With-Both-Hands. We become creators of our destiny instead of reactive agents.

Color Gesture Exercise: Two Brothers & Me

To deepen clients' understanding of human nature, I invite clients to relate the story to their own lives. This is done through a color gesture exercise that asks: "Where are these brothers in my life? Which brother am I mirroring, He-Who-Grasps-the-Sky-With-Both-Hands or Flint? What thoughts, emotions, and behaviors do I exhibit?" Since clients have been introduced to an imaginative picture of human nature and consciousness, they quickly respond to this exercise.

Step One: After reviewing the map of consciousness that I gave above, I ask clients: "Which brother do you identify with when you are in active addiction?" The group participants always say, "Flint."

Step Two: "You will need three pieces of paper, a pen or pencil to write with and your soft pastels. Using a clean piece of paper, record your thoughts, emotions, and behaviors when you are Flint."

Step Three: "Move your chairs around in the room so that you can create your own space, your own bubble supporting your inward movement. (Wait for participants to get settled.) If comfortable close your eyes in order to shut out outside stimulation. Take a gentle deep breath beginning to quiet your thoughts. Take another gentle breath. Notice if you are comfortable at this moment; if not, adjust your situation. Continue to gently breathe, creating an inward receptive space."

Step Four: "Bring into your field of consciousness the words and phrases that you wrote on your paper describing how you think, feel, and act when you are mirroring Flint. You might even begin to see yourself doing certain actions, feeling certain emotions, and/or thinking certain thoughts."

Step Five: "Invite an image, a symbol, or a color movement that depicts the essence of who you are when you are behaving as Flint. There are no right or wrong images. I encourage you to accept whatever emerges in your field of consciousness at this time. If it does not fit, you can discard it later in the activity. For now simply observe whatever arose. Observe without the voice of judgment. Simply notice. What is it?"

Step Six: "When you are ready, open your eyes and begin to create the image, symbol or movement in color that arose. Continue to work until it feels complete."

Step Seven: "On a separate piece of paper, write a title for your color gesture. A title, like a movie title, tells you with a word or two what the show is about. Find your title and record it."

Step Eight: "Write responses to the following: (1) Describe what you drew. (2) How does your drawing relate to Flint as a metaphor for the subconscious? (3) What did you learn, if anything? (4) What, if anything, are you willing to do?"

Client Example 1: Client is 26 years old. Substance abuse started at age 14. Drugs of choice: cannabis; methamphetamine; alcohol. Here is her drawing.

Title: Life Sucks

Identified Behaviors: Isolate. Don't call family. Depressed. Alone. Lie. Don't want to live.

Identified Emotions:
Hate myself. Lonely. Ugly. Sick. Lost.

Description of Color Gesture: Blinding darkness. Looks like fun and draws me into the darkness. Inviting. Lost fun. A smile on my darkness. Happiness in the dark not the light. My Addict is happy when I'm suffering.

What am I willing to do?: Wipe a smile off my addict's face.

Relating color gesture to Native American tale: My addict self is like one house. It is able to teach me and be used for good but there is another house within me. Where do I choose to reside? All things can be used for good. Do not forget from where I came from.

Client Example 2: Client is 20 years old. Drug usage began at age 9 with cannabis adding methamphetamine at age 19.

Title: The Point of Life.

Emotions & Behaviors: Angry. Obsessive. Unhealthy. Uncaring. Self-centered. Crazy. Manipulator. Numb. Judgmental. Content. Sad. Depressed. Pissed Off!

Description of Color Gesture and Response to Exercise Questions:

I can't live without using. No reason to quit using. Can't find happiness without using. When I was using I was a horrible self-centered person. The point of life, the most important thing in life. My only concern. Sad.

What did I learn and what am I willing to do?: The fact that Flint and his brother represented good and evil. How if you forget where you have come from and where you will end up after life, you will be lost on earth. That if you choose the wrong lodge.

When I was using I was a horrible person and self-centered. I need to stay away from the people and places where I used to use. Keep my family and sisters at the top of my mind. Always. I have come a long way. And if I hadn't or gotten or wanted to be sober I would be in the same or worse situation than I was in before. And all that I have accomplished since I've been sober would go to waste.

You see how useful a story can be, especially when followed by artistic expression. At all levels—of thinking, feeling, and willing—we have made progress in the client's encounter with addiction. The exercises incorporate the Seven Adult Learning Processes (chapter 4), which I use frequently to guide my approach to the addiction process.

Suggested References for Further Study
(in addition to the references at the end of the book)

Assagioli, Roberto (1980). *Psychosynthesis: a Collection of Basic Writings.* New York: Penguin Books.

Bento, William (2004). *Lifting the Veil of Mental Illness: An Approach to Anthroposophical Psychology.* PA: Camphill Publications.

Dunselman, Ron (1993). *In Place of the Self: How Drugs Work.* United Kingdom: Hawthorn Press.

Firman, John, & Ann Gila (1997). *The Primal Wound: A Transpersonal View of Trauma, Addiction, and Growth.* New York: University of New York Press.

Needleman, Jacob (2003). *The American Soul: Rediscovering the Wisdom of the Founders.* New York: Tarcher.

CHAPTER 10

Trauma and Post-Traumatic Stress

by Roberta Nelson, Ph.D.

and William Bento, Ph.D.

[This presentation begins with William Bento setting the stage, then goes into Roberta Nelson's exercises in relation to trauma.]

[William Bento:]

In chapter 3, I promised that we would take you through the fourfold assessment of the deeper pathologies. I had placed post-traumatic stress disorder in the realm of the kidney, the realm in which we process sight, the realm in which we take our possibilities of sight into reality. When that system is disrupted, we can end up with psychosis. Anthroposophical medical approaches concur with this understanding. I have tested it, and then asked Roberta about her clinical view. She has had much experience with this disorder.

The term post-traumatic stress disorder, PTSD, has been in use for around fifty years. It was used quite often in relationship to the Viet Nam War. Prior to that, in WWI and WWII, it was given the name "shell shock," or "soldier's wound." You can even find these terms used in the American Civil War in the 19th century.

This pathology arises out of the human being's experience with war, where we see brother against brother. In a certain way, we have revisited the archetypal genocide of Cain against Abel. By archetypal, I mean fundamental; by genocide, I mean that one line kills another line.

PTSD is an acute stress disorder. There are many types of stress disorder. We have all experienced what one could call mini-traumatic stresses. These can accumulate over time and erode the capacity for us to find a sense of our True Self in anything other than hyper-vigilant states. Any traumatic stress, large or small, kicks in a survival instinct. In that state a tremendous amount of cortisol is being dumped into the body. The amygdala picks up an alarm from the limbic brain that there is a threat. The limbic brain, which gives us our sense of reality and how to make meaning of it, senses threat and danger. When the limbic brain sends a message to the amygdala, chemicals are excreted Into the body in a cascade, an overflow. The autonomic nervous system starts a process that doesn't want to stop—much like pulling the fire alarm in a school hallway. Once the alert happens, processes are put into motion that can't be stopped. The fire department has to come. Even if it turns out to be a small event, the process must unfold. The key element here is that cortisol continues to dump. When that happens, the heart races, the breath quickens; your body and all of its physiological functions feel as if taken over by some kind of fear or terror.

Though the following is long, I feel it is very important that you hear how clinicians have defined PTSD, what they are seeing, and what they are saying about this disorder.

In the Diagnostic Statistical Manual (version IV here, though similar in version 5), we have the consensus definition of PTSD. In PTSD, the person has been exposed to a traumatic event in which both of the following have been present:

1. The person experienced, witnessed, or was confronted with an event or events that involved actual or threatened death or serious injury, or threat to physical integrity of self and others.
2. The person's response involved intense fear, helplessness, or horror.

The traumatic event is persistently re-experienced in one or more of the following ways:

1. Reoccurring and intrusive distressing recollections of the event including images, thoughts, or perceptions.
2. Reoccurring distressing dreams of the events.

3. Acting or feeling as if the traumatic event were reoccurring here and now. Flashback episodes.
4. Intense psychological distress at exposure to external or internal keys that symbolize or resemble an aspect of the traumatic event.
5. Physiological reactivity on exposure to internal or external cues that resemble or symbolize the traumatic event.

Another category of awareness around this issue is the persistent avoidance of stimuli associated with the trauma, and numbing of general responsiveness, as indicated in three or more of the following:

1. Efforts to avoid thoughts, feelings or conversations associated with the trauma.
2. Efforts to avoid activities, places or people that arouse recollections of the trauma.
3. Inability to recall an important aspect of the trauma.
4. Markedly diminished interest or participation in significant activities.
5. Feeling of detachment or estrangement from others.
6. Restricted range of affect, unable to have love feelings.
7. Sense of a short future, does not expect to have a career, marriage, children, or any sense of a normal lifestyle.

The persistent symptoms of increased arousal to the trauma are indicated by:

1. Difficulty falling or staying asleep.
2. Irritability or outbursts of anger.
3. Difficulty concentrating.
4. Hyper-vigilance.
5. Exaggerated startle responses.

Duration of these disturbances is usually more than one month.

When you see a list of all of these particular symptoms, you begin to dismantle any image you may have of the normal human being. You're then talking about something that is almost like an animal in survival mode. You observe an inability to have love feelings; an inability to plan or execute, to be more than just being in the present; an inability to go into the future. The person is stuck in the past, and the present is just one big abyss. It's really a terrifying situation. Recall, this comes from exposure to those situations in which there is real and severe threat to one's existence such as abuse by those in power over you ... or such as war.

What is happening to the human being as a whole, to the wholeness of the human being? Let's focus our anthroposophical lens and ask what's happening here.

The sentient body can be seen as the "skin" of the soul life, the healthy ability to perceive the sense world and take it in. The sentient body is the first of seven soul stages. Steiner's seven soul stages begin with the senses. In the next stage, this becomes a sensation; the sensation marks an unconscious stream of feeling life that begins to emerge. We try to visualize it so that we have some way to keep it in our grasp when we are no longer perceiving it. This is a mental representation of an object or an event. Because we can visualize it, we can now begin to reflect upon it. Reflecting upon it is something that the "I" does, like judging "what is the significance and value of that which I have taken in?"

When the seven soul stages are not navigated healthily, we will see various types of pathology.

One antidote for problems with the sentient body that I discovered is something that was transacted in a conversation between the Christ being and Mary Magdalene. This conversation is found in the *Pistis Sophia*. The Christ being was telling many stories about his mission on Earth including the mission to penetrate to the interior of the earth where many forms of demons held the Sophia in chains. His task was a task of liberation. But Mary Magdalene thought that these demons might be everywhere and not just in the interior of the Earth. She asked him, "How are we meeting these demons? What can we do?" He then gave the "prescription" for encountering this kind of evil, which puts us back into the Consciousness Soul age, the level of maturity of the soul in our time. How did he suggest that we discern and confront those demons?

The first thing he said was: peace; One would have to find within one's self the capacity to engender a state of peace. PTSD has its historical origin in war, not in peace. We don't need to be in a formally declared war to have the experiences that involve trauma. When I watched the event of September 11, 2001, I saw war. That event exceeded my imagination. It was not in my consciousness that something like this terror could ever happen. But we all have had those kinds of situations in our lives. And war, that terrible assault on human dignity, typifies them all. Does the Christ mean that we must have peace in the world? No. Peace for the sentient body is an inner activity. It's not an outer event; we're not going to transact peace ever in our lifetime in today's world. I don't say that with any glee; it's not a prophecy I would like to stand on. But it's a sobering reality. The only peace that we can find is within. When veterans come home from war with the naive expectation that they are leaving war for peace, they find a more subtle form of war at home. They don't even find significant others who can care for them.

There has been a rupture. The skin of the soul, the sentient body, has been ruptured. Holes and wounds have occurred in the sentient body, which means that the whole sentient organism no longer functions in the same way it once functioned. The quality of the intense hyper-vigilance accompanied with moods and feelings of fear and terror distort the most simple forms of sensory processing. You find your client with PTSD under the table looking for their gun. They don't even have the ability to clearly distinguish sights and sounds.

We observe these ruptures in the body and soul of the client. The first thing we can think of is the importance of repairing the senses. Learning how to trust touching, distinguishing between hard and soft. Coming into touch with the reality of the sense world again without trepidation. Veterans come back with these wounds, having every right to be righteous and angry. The ones who return have offered their lives for us, having left behind others who actually did give their lives for their country—for us. One finds anger expressed in many different ways in a traumatized person. Someone under PTSD wonders whether he or she can trust anybody again, or trust the true nature of the human being, or its potential. For veterans it is very difficult to overcome the trauma, especially as they have been victimized by lies. Truth becomes extremely important to them.

To repair the senses, we also have to understand how to bring meaning and roles of significant responsibility back so they can have their vitality directed, rather than dammed up and going through intermittent, explosive episodes. The best Socratic dialogue you can muster is well worth the effort with people who are traumatized. By asking questions you not only bypass the trap of reaction to authority, you also prompt the client to move from the amygdala to the frontal cortex, thereby igniting temporal thinking. They have to rediscover the true meaning of life again because it has been ripped apart. As we have holes in the body and soul, it's hard to feel the virtue of the human being. We are hoping that, out of grace, the tremendous terror can actually be transformed and, out of grace, the "I" can return. Because what we have now—what takes over the senses—are memories of the traumatic event, fixed and lodged in the etheric body. Normal human beings are able to forget. Those who have been traumatized cannot forget. You could say that their memories have become compulsive with images that won't go away, day or night. The etheric body is in a fixated state, a hypnotic trans-like state only being able to see, feel, and react to those images that resurface day in and day out.

Since the traumatic event, the person with PTSD has had no biography. No biography means homelessness, not geographically, rather a homelessness of the soul. Every traumatized person has left behind major parts of his or her sense of identity. Their biography has, in a certain psychological way, ended. And yet a new life is there to begin. New life occurs for all of us, for our biographies are constantly changing. As the soul develops, the person matures. In a normal person, this means going from home to home. To the one who suffers PTSD, the homes have been lost, and they are in the transition place, not able to leave the past behind, and not able to embrace a new present.

The repairing work is huge, and involves working on all seven soul processes (chapter 4, appendix), beginning with retraining the senses. Hopefully this process brings about healing through the seven adult learning methods. That allows them to move through all the damaged areas, and begin self-development based on the fact that they have gained some meaning from the traumatizing event. Learning to see something positive in any relationship is an important part of the self-development forward.

Not everyone comes back from war with PTSD, though there are many for whom PTSD is undetected and can remain undetected for years. The capacity for resilience in a life is based on initial conditions in the life. If these conditions were not there, then it requires a re-training later in life. There are seven elements involved in the establishment of resilience, gleaned from the literature on resilience. I take these elements as a way to approach re-training of victims of trauma.

Seven Aspects of Resilience

The first element of a healthy sense of resilience involves the quality of early home life. These individuals have had important, attentive primary care givers in life when their senses were being developed. They had a sense of love from a significant other.

The second element that was discovered is that, as children, they were able to have an understanding of an important authority figure that allowed them to be children. Parental authority figures set the boundaries and containers for children to play. The children are protected as children; they do not have to perform like adults to meet an adult expectation. Healthy protection of play is usually found in the early years where the child has good teachers who know that play is important. A wise authority figure allows children to play. Primary care givers allow children to experience love.

The third element has to do with being able to have someone to look up to. The child has a man or woman as an ideal role model. This ideal role model sets up a picture of what it means to be human, adult, responsible, grown-up.

The fourth element involves the ability to experience time not in a linear fashion, as quantity, but rather time as a phenomenon of quality. When at bedtime I got on my knees to pray, I experienced a qualitative time for my mother and father and me. When we went to the dinner table to eat together and sing a song of praise for the foods we were given, that was a quality time, not a quantity time. This kind of time is experienced as qualities through festivals, through acknowledging the rhythms of time rather than time being an abstraction, or being something we are rushing to get through. It involves living in rhythms. Living rhythm is a quality of time.

The fifth element pictures the individual having the ability to look towards something higher than himself or herself. This may be through an established religion or simply the awareness of a high power. Spirituality was a part of one's youth. An alignment to something greater is one of our core needs.

The sixth element discovered, in the meta-analysis of resilience literature, was that the person was able to draw on a surplus of positivity toward life.

The seventh element necessary, from the studies for establishing resilience, is a great interest in participating in creative, artistic projects such as music or painting. This was emphasized in Sarajevo when bombs had fallen, buildings had fallen, lives had been lost or damaged: Many clinicians from around the world were sent to help the tormented, traumatized people who had experienced these bombs and the devastation of their homes. The clinicians were inside having groups and counseling individuals. Outside, the children were creating forts and houses out of bricks and bottles, creating living sculptures out of the destruction. They were creating even in the most difficult of devastations.

These seven stages of resilience give us a map of how to proceed with treatment for those who have PTSD, because those who were victimized by severe trauma had most likely a weakness in one or more of these elements. People who have deficiencies in any of these seven areas risk a greater possibility of impact of trauma and a reaction to trauma. Therefore, we strive to build up these people who have no biography any longer, build them up from where they began as a child and all the way up.

We work directly with a quality of time. Not "are you on time?," but "are you flowing in the stream of time, both into the past and into the future?"

These seven principles can be understood as principles of wholeness. They lead to resilience.

[Roberta Nelson:]

In the context of the concepts that William presented, I'm going to put up two collages that female clients constructed in a trauma group that I facilitated. Before we look at the pictures a bit of information about why collages are utilized in groups that are gathering to process trauma.

Trauma is often the topic that clients sidestep during treatment. Why is that? It's painful. Who wants to go into something that is painful? Plus, we are often told, or say to ourselves, "It's past. Get over it." Approaching the topic of trauma requires thoughtful procedures that create safety, warmth, and empowerment. Collages can help us to create sacred space, a space where the eluded topic can be taken up. They also provide an effective prologue towards imaginative thinking — a goal of anthroposophic psychology.

Clients are used to looking through magazines. It's a familiar mode. It does not intimidate them. It is important to select methods in early treatment stages that are not threatening and in this case the collage assignment asks group participants to clip out pictures from magazines that depict their journeys through trauma, a scary task for some. This assignment applies a routine process — looking at magazine pictures — to stimulate primary aspects of memory, to elicit images, to express positive and negative core beliefs. Lastly, the collage activity is a steppingstone easing the clients towards color gesture work which can follow.

Here are two examples I have with me of women's collages. The women were given a variety of magazines, a piece of cardboard, and glue. The assignment was to look through the magazines cutting out pictures that illustrate the effects of trauma in their lives.

[William Bento:]

These are very vivid images. This shows a kind of fragmentation of consciousness, both in messages that are deeply imprinted in the sense of her identity now, a snapshot of something she is experiencing now. It's not her fragmentation, but the world being fragmented. It's chaotic. You can internalize what's shown here and see for yourself, what visualizations are there. How can you think about yourself when your thoughts are not in an overlay of what you are?

[Roberta Nelson:] Here is another one. *[See next page.]*

[William Bento:] This one looks like a broken heart. You see a trail of abuse in it.

[Participant:] You have to admire the level of self-knowledge to be able to identify the issues and these questions in this collage. This is someone involved in a process of self-discovery. I feel very positive about this.

[William Bento:] Yes. This person is thinking in such a way that they are willing to begin to express the "I" and to begin self-reflection.

[Participant:] I look for a movement in the words. It shows you the past sometimes.

[Roberta Nelson:]

More often than not, the clients I see at the residential treatment facility have a history of abuse and/or neglect. Yet they fall outside of the DSM criteria for a Post-traumatic Stress Disorder (PTSD) diagnosis. Dr. Bento has coined a useful phrase: "pervasive stress disorder." I like it. It fits what I witness with the women and men that I work with. If you are schooled in trauma, abuse, and neglect, you can spot trauma's footprints but the tracks often do not fit the specific PTSD criteria. Sadly, most of us aren't adequately trained, or we rely on the DSM standpoint. If we miss the cues, then trauma can remain the untreated issue underlying the client's assessment and treatment. My clients frequently say, "I never told anyone this. It didn't seem to really matter." This is extremely important. They may not have been in a war, but they have been through one war, maybe more wars, as they grew up, wars that no one knows about. Or, a client will announce during a mental health evaluation, after they have declared that this is their fourth or seventh treatment, that *they* know that they have some "stuff" that needs to be dealt with. "Stuff" that wasn't life threatening but, as I recall one client stating, "It is always in my head." Listen for these cues of stress and trauma.

I have had the opportunity to be trained in EMDR (Eye Movement Desensitization Reprocessing), a protocol developed by Dr. Francine Shapiro. She defines trauma as anything that has had a lasting negative effect in our lives. Wow! This definition expanded the way I perceived trauma. It also takes into account William's phrase "pervasive stress disorder."

I would like to describe a two-step process that might reveal prolonged stress manifest in lasting negative effects in a person's life. I begin by asking clients to float back into their adolescence or childhood in order to gain access to positive affect and memories. It's not unusual to hear, "I can't find any positive memories." Another scenario is more common. A client will search for a positive memory, finally landing on one. They will identify the event, the affect, and the core beliefs associated with the memory. I will ask them to float back again, and then again, in order to discover additional positive memories. The usual picture is that my clients can find four or six positive memories but seldom ten. When this activity is completed, I ask them what they learned. The usual response is surprise that there are positive memories at all. This is sad but it is also a possible warning signal. Not always but sometimes. It requires additional exploration.

Please do not make the mistake of assuming that such scenarios belong to a particular socio-economic status or that these clients are uneducated. Prolonged stress is widespread. Trauma, like addiction (chapter 9), is inclusive of everyone. It does not just happen to those who are poor and uneducated. It is a symptom of our time.

I appreciate that Francine Shapiro's model differentiates two types of trauma: little "t" trauma and big "T" Trauma. Big "T" events include rape, abuse, assaults, being shot at, and natural disasters, life-threatening events that were experienced, or witnessed. Big "T" events might meet DSM criteria for PTSD, whereas little "t" events usually do not fit into the DSM criteria for a PTSD diagnosis. Little "t" trauma takes in childhood neglect or emotional abuse, bullying, constantly being told or shown that you are somehow not important, situations of being shamed or put down, moving from one school to another, from one primary caregiver to another, hearing mom and dad fight, or mom coming home periodically with a different date. These scenarios have an accumulative effect and might lead to little "t" trauma, acknowledged in the EMDR model.

William used the phrase "mini-traumatic stresses" to describe a situation that disconnects us from our True Self. Little "t" trauma demonstrates this disconnection. Our True Self, from an anthroposophical viewpoint, points towards what is good, true, and beautiful within us. It takes in creativity, capacity and potential. It is our blue print: our *raison d'être,* or purpose for existence. Ann Gila and John Firman begin their book titled, *The Primal Wound*, with a noteworthy quote from Charles Whitfield:

> When our True Self goes into hiding,
> in order to please its parent figure and to survive,
> a false, co-dependent self emerges to take its place.
> We thus lose our awareness of our True Self
> to such an extent
> that we actually lose
> awareness of its existence.
> We lose contact with who we really are.
> Gradually, we begin to think we are the false self—
> so that it becomes a habit,
> and finally an addiction.

The false self is what my clients experience over and over again. It is evident in dysfunctional patterns or habits. The false self is a fixed state of being, often declared in the following manner, "I am stuck." Clients know that there is something else; they know that they are not becoming all that they were created to be. "I am lost. I do not know who I am." To lose connection with one's purpose for existence is a major existential crisis of a spiritual nature.

Little "t" trauma is pervasive—inescapable, even though our primary caregivers are well intended. We can have experiences in childhood that are scary, moments of helplessness, despite loving protective parents. Over and over again I experience that an accumulation of little "t" traumas erodes a client's self-image. I use the analogy of a layer cake with my clients, explaining that actual events, such as neglect, shaming, attending a new school, an intense storm that scared you to death, and a host of other experiences can create negative core beliefs. Beliefs such as: "I am unimportant, insignificant." "I should have done something." "I can't trust myself or others." The foundation for disconnection from the True Self has been put into place by little "t" traumas.

As development continues to unfold, let us say around ages of 12 or 13, a person with an accumulation of little "t" traumas can begin to behave in ways that are destructive, such as fighting with parents, skipping class, smoking weed off the school property, and so on. Or we might experience events that reinforce a negative self-perception. "I can't wear designer jeans because I'm too fat." Or "I can't afford them—no one cares about me." Or, "Peers tease me, saying mean things." "My parents are divorced or they are too busy to show up at my school events." Now my own actions and experiences began to reinforce the unconscious core beliefs established at an early age. I might not have a memory of that frightening storm, the car accident, or the kids that consistently picked on me in kindergarten calling me "stupid" or "fatty." Yet those memories are there and they break down who I perceive myself to be. Instead of using "I" statements that reflect what is good or beautiful about me, I start making statements such as, "I am worthless, a failure." The identification with a false self has been established and I begin to think, feel, and act accordingly.

Activity: Core Beliefs

The following activity is one way to quickly reveal prolonged stress, which can be caused by big "T" or little "t" trauma. In either case the counselor has seen that there is evidence of lingering negative effects from earlier experiences, again either big ones or an accumulation of little ones. Before moving into the activity itself, I would like to describe the scene of a typical first session in a women's trauma group.

Women who participate in such groups are referred to me

by their primary counselors. This might be the first time I meet the female client. They often know little, if anything about the group other than the fact that it addresses trauma. Seven to ten women have been told to attend a trauma group that meets in room number 115. They come in the door often dragging their feet, looking at me with questions on their faces that are quickly voiced. "I don't know why I'm here; I don't belong in this group."

The women are asking a reasonable question. Why are they here? Right away there is an educational opportunity. And, an opening to engage group participants in an experiential learning activity—one of the principles emphasized in anthroposophic psychology. I do not answer their question. Instead participants are led through an activity that aids self-discovery and empowerment. Their question is addressed through an experiential activity that facilitates self-discovery rather than me telling them why they are here.

Step One: I pass out a handout (see the following page) that includes a listing of negative and positive core beliefs. I say, "The one that I am passing out is taken from the EMDR literature."

Step Two: "Fold the handout in half. Put half of the paper with the title 'negative cognitions' upright facing you."

Step Three: "Take a moment to look at the listing. Notice that each sentence begins with an 'I.' 'I'-statements are self-perceptions or self-images. This list represents who I think I am."

Step Four: "Read through the list of self-perceptions, underlining the ones that are familiar. In other words, underline statements you know that you say to yourself—your self-talk. Underline only the ones that you frequently say to yourself, that are triggered often in your head."

Step Five: "How many did you underline?" Invite the group to share how many "I" statements they underlined. Record the range on the blackboard or whiteboard. Then ask, "Were there any surprises?"

Step Six: "Now, go back to your list of 'I' statements. As you read through the ones you underlined, place an age by the statement. At what approximate age do you think you started to perceive yourself in this manner? For instance, take the statement, 'I

NEGATIVE COGNITIONS

Responsibility (I am defective)
I don't deserve love
I am a bad person
I am terrible
I am worthless (inadequate)
I am shameful
I am not lovable
I am not good enough
I deserve only bad things
I am permanently damaged
I am ugly (my body is hateful)
I do not deserve...
I am stupid (not smart enough)
I am insignificant (unimportant)
I am a disapointment
I deserve to die
I deserve to be miserable
I am different (don't belong)

Responsibilty (I did something wrong)
I should have done something*
I did something wrong*
I should have known better*
 *What does this say about you? (e.g.,
  does it make you feel: I am shameful/I
  am stupid/I am a bad person).

Safety/Vulnerability
I cannot be trusted
I cannot trust myself
I cannot trust my judgement
I cannot trust anyone
I cannot protect myself
I am in danger
It's not OK to feel (show) my emotions
I cannot stand up for myself
I cannot let it out

Control/Choices
I am not in control
I am powerless (helpless)
I am weak
I cannot get what I want
I am a failure (will fail)
I cannot succeed
I have to be perfect (please everyone)/ I
can't handle it/I am inadequate/ I can-
not trust anyone

POSITIVE COGNITIONS

Responsibility
I deserve love; I can have love
I am a good (loving) person
I am fine as I am
I am worthy; I am worthwhile
I am honorable
I am lovable
I am good enough
I deserve good things
I am (can be) healthy
I am fine (attractive/lovable)
I can have (deserve)
I am intelligent (able to learn)
I am significant (important)
I am OK just the way I am
I deserve to live
I deserve to be happy
I am OK as I am

Responsibilty
I did the best I could
I learned (can learn) from it
I do the best I can (I can learn)

Safety/Vulnerability
I can be trusted
I can (learn to) trust myself
I can trust my judgement
I can choose whom to trust
I can (learn to) take care of myself
It's over; I am safe now
I can safely feel (show) my emotions
I can make my needs known
I can choose to let it out

Control/Choices
I am now in control
I now have choices
I am strong
I can get what I want
I can succeed
I can be myself (make mistakes)
I can handle it
I am capable/ I can choose whom to
trust

Handout: *Examples of Cognitions*

don't deserve love.' If you underlined it, at what age do you think you were saying this to yourself, believing that it was true?"

Step Seven: Then you ask each participant, going around the room, "What age range do you have on your paper? What is the earliest age?" Record the earliest ages on the board. "Were there any surprises? What did you learn?"

I use the Core Belief activity to introduce little "t" and big "T" traumas as well as definitions of trauma. In the trauma groups the earliest age is usually around the age of four. Following the Core Belief activity, I invite the group participants to discuss what they have discovered and whether they are candidates for the trauma group. I do not tell them. I respect their capacity to self-assess. The women recognize that they may not meet DSM criteria for a PSTD diagnosis; nevertheless, they are experiencing the prolonged effects of little "t" trauma in their lives, evident in problematic or negative self-perceptions. This is an empowerment activity rooted in self-discovery.

[David Tresemer:] The challenge of group work is that everyone in the room is in a process. You can have people going off in various directions, popping open their traumas all at once, each one needing your full attention. However, when handled gently and with the mastery that Roberta shows, it's possible that you can heal twenty people at the same time.

[Roberta Nelson:] And that often happens. Great steps forward can be made in a group setting with an exercise such as this. As for the right-hand side of the piece of paper that you folded in half, "Examples of Cognitions," we can do many things in the group. A second session parallels the first. I ask the clients to recall which of the beliefs on the right side that they held or hold, and at what age these started. Then I connect the two sides. You might ask, "Why do you hand out the positive beliefs at the first session, when the first session concentrates only on the negative core beliefs and the little 't' traumas underlying them?" You probably have answered your own question—at all times underlying the difficult and negative beliefs are the positive ones, even if we don't look at them in the first session.

Recommended Resources for Further Study

The Pistis Sophia can be found in several versions, the best known is translated and edited by G.R.S. Mead. A version by Desiree Hurtak and J. J. Hurtak is a modern interpretation and very helpful.

Firman, John, and Ann Gila (1997). *The Primal Wound: A Transpersonal View of Trauma, Addiction, and Growth.* State University of New York.

Shapiro, Francine (2013). *Getting Past your Past: Take Control of your Life with Self-Help Techniques from EMDR.* Rodale Books.

Innner Development of the Counselor

INTRODUCTION TO INNER DEVELOPMENT
by David Tresemer, Ph.D.

Insurance companies and employers—and now the general public—have become quite interested in the criteria for diagnosis of disturbance. OCD has become a common adjective that labels you obsessive-compulsive or not, no matter if you have four or more of the eight criteria named in the DSM. It's thrown about: About a woman with a sparkly clean kitchen, "Oh, she's way too OCD!"

Similarly, PTSD has now become a "thing" that you might have: "Did I startle you? Do you think you might have PTSD?" We are all becoming experts (and hypochondriacs), labeling ourselves and others with technical terms.

Absent from this emphasis on disturbance and "what to do about it," is the emphasis on health in general, and especially the health of the helper—the counselor. This section of the book introduces some of the many ways of understanding the healthy human being, the healthy human being's destiny, and the way of keeping the counselor sane and on a pathway of growing and maturing. We call this general view, from which we begin our inquiry for counselor and client, salutogenesis.

Chapter 11 gives several approaches to self-care. This is not a list of the five things you need to do today. Several magazine editors have told me that these lists of "five things to do today to improve your sex life" are a proven method for selling magazines. These lists offer a promise that if I buy the magazine and do those five things then my sex life will, perhaps, be better.

Rather than a list, we give here some perspectives from each of the authors of this book in order to engage you in the conversation about your own self-care. We may not have said the following adequately: Institutional and economic forces do not have your best interests in mind. As a counselor, you may feel pressured to sit in your consulting chair more hours a day, talk on the phone or work your computer more hours in the day— more hours than exist in the day. You have to take self-care quite seriously, making it a part of your day, your weekly schedule, and the rhythm of your year.

Chapter 12 presents information on meditation and mindfulness, both buzzwords in recent psychology. Quite beyond the studies— for example, the display from MRI images of the brain to demonstrate that, yes, something amazing is happening—are the experiences of practitioners of meditation and mindfulness. These techniques pertain to what you might use with clients as well. Most important is how you can use these tools for yourself. Chapter 12 has varied contributions intended to provide different entryways into meditation and mindfulness.

Chapter 13 enters the territory of pathos (from chapter 1) as part of the counselor's path. You must understand in yourself and others that what is labeled pathology provides a path for initiation into greater maturity. We have heard the ancient dictum, "Doctor, heal thyself!" This chapter goes further: "Doctor— healer, counselor—do not cover over your pathos—rather seek it out and live it out—thereby you will find a pathway through darkness into a greater light!"

In the final chapter of the book, we hear other experiences shared with the students of anthroposophic psychology concerning the extraordinary—or should we say "ordinary"?—realms in which we must learn to move. To come to know the spirit of healing, and to invoke its help in ourselves and in our practices, we must awaken to greater possibilities than those that are usually invoked.

Self-Care

Here's a Homeric simile: JUST AS in an airplane, when the oxygen masks fall from the ceiling, you are directed to put yours on first, before assisting others near you, JUST SO you must, in counseling others, care for yourself first, before extending yourself to others. In this chapter the various authors of this book give their perspectives on self-care based on their years of experience.

This chapter does not give a succinct recipe for self-care, as our experience is that each person in the present time of heightened individualism—the Consciousness Soul Age—must pick and choose his or her own program.

A. The Counselor's Chair
by David Tresemer

A counselor assists clients to find their way in the world, to find ways to meet their needs, to provide the caring that all human beings need. The counselor needs all these things too. The level of attention required when seeing a client in crisis, or a series of clients, can tax your systems. These systems need replenishment. Otherwise, you will discover that burn-out can happen not only to your clients but to you also—an accumulated wounding that may go under the radar of your awareness into your autonomic nervous system, a debilitation that goes right into the roots of your soul.

What to do? Some days I wake up and long for the time in the monastery, when my every minute was planned. I suspect it's a memory. That was appropriate then; yet here I am now, in a very different world. I know that I would last only a short time with the monastery's schedule, until my individuality would rise up and begin to push against those old stone walls. I suspect that you also might rebel at a strict schedule. After all, it's the era of the consciousness soul, where individuality reigns! It wouldn't do to give you a list of things you ought to do each day. You might even agree with every good idea. But we both know that this is not how life works. You will make a change in your life for the better, or take up a new practice, only when the idea strikes you in some special way—and then you might give it a try.

Therefore we have gathered some of our best thoughts on self-care for this chapter, and will give them as topics, not as a schedule for your day.

In each of the chapters of this book, there are hints about the particular approach of anthroposophic psychology. When you perceive the workings of soul (and spirit, mediated by the "I AM"), the counseling room grows in size. Even if the chairs are old and plastic, and the lighting is fluorescent, knowing "soul" dissolves the furniture, the lighting, and the walls. One stands comfortably amongst stars and elemental beings—in relation to another soul.

The Will in Counseling

Too often we see training programs for counseling or psychology, at the master's level or Ph.D. level, where the full emphasis focuses on thinking—on concepts, reading, protocols, reading, reports, paper-work, more reading, moving clients through a system or through The System. This emphasis continues in subsequent job placements. The consequence is a sedentary life for the counselor. Metaphorically, it is a kind of crucifixion—one feels nailed to one's chair. Clients come and go, but there you are, nailed to your chair. The comparison may be shocking, but is intentional, and we can take it further. The way in which crucifixion was used by the Romans was intended to neutralize the will forces by tying or nailing the victim's limbs to a cross.

As the body sagged under its own weight, the feeling centers of the body—heart and lungs—were increasingly constricted. The body died from suffocation, stopping of heart and lungs. This strangulation of the feeling life is indeed the risk of the counselor's life style, unless a fresh approach is taken towards the will.

The will forces move, unceasingly move, to action, to deeds. In larger movements, we walk, we run, we dance, we hike, we turn cartwheels. In smaller movements, we gesture, we smile, we grimace, we wink. Every movement assists fluids to move, to wash our interior and deliver the soul substance of the blood to every cell. We don't think the deeds of will, or if we do, it sounds silly: Listen to how an exercise physiologist describes a movement. Language shows its poverty when trying to describe the deeds of the will. Movements arise, especially the poetical and graceful ones, not from following a protocol or description of that movement but rather from its own internal arising.

Or is it only internal? An exercise very helpful to the counselor is called The Statue: One person stands in the center, as one or more people move the body parts of that central person. The central person's job is to yield to the guiding hands of the sculptor(s), and then hold the position into which he or she has been set. The positions taken can arouse associative thoughts—"This looks like the Charioteer sculpture from Delphi," "This is just like Botticelli's Venus arising from the sea." But the postures do not arise from those thoughts. They have their own sources of inspiration.

Perhaps one can think of the will arising from external promptings as well as from internal. This begins a new relationship to the will. It is a fundamental idea in anthroposophy, mentioned before in this book, though one struggles to come to terms with it, that thinking streams from the past, and willing streams from the future. To many this sounds ridiculous, but stay with it, as it is a key to freeing you from the pain of being stuck in the counselor's chair, with the degeneration of muscles, skeleton, and feeling that often results from years as a counselor.

Thinking understands the world in terms of the past, applying categories of the known world to what the person experiences in the present. Everything is compared to the past. Thinking even thinks that time moves as thinking does, from the past to the present. However, willing streams from the future. It does not come with concepts and categories and associations, because the future hasn't been appraised by thinking yet. Thus thinking rejects future-streaming as impossible. Yet everyone has a sense of what's-coming, not a worked-out thinking-sense but an impression of the destiny of the self and of the world. Sometimes this pops through as premonition, which is a future-fact dipping enough into the past that thinking can grasp it and claim it as its own.

In our thinking culture, the will is suppressed. In indigenous cultures, you can find much more will-force in evidence—in spontaneous ceremonies, in healing work, or in the activity of heading out into the forest or jungle, without a reason but because something draws one on. For Australian aborigines, they call this "gone bush," because even before someone has stepped into the bush, it has already happened, thus "gone" bush: "He's gone bush."

In modern times, we sometimes name these unexplained and inexplicable actions as intuition, sometimes as "trust your gut."

In the center is the realm of feeling, of heart and lung, the feeling in the present for what is happening relationally between those who take this expedition of life together. When the will is functioning and in balance with the thinking function, then the heart sings. You will know that your will is not balanced with your thinking, and your feeling is suffocating, when you dread the next client coming in, or find yourself staring at a protocol rather than at a person, running through the steps of a treatment, repeatedly looking at the clock. When your feeling is active, your only reason to look at the clock is to acknowledge that, even though you are fascinated and interested and engaged, unfortunately the session has run out. If your feeling is inactive, it may be because your will has been inactivated and you are dying the slow death of the crucified.

We suggest that an important way to liberate your feeling is to change your relation to your will. You have to find ways to change that feeling of suffering—of crucifixion—to something active. As I've used the crucifixion word, let me explain further. I feel that the end of Christ Jesus's life should only be revealed to Christians after they've learned the other parts of Christianity—admiration of the soul life of self and other, interconnection with divinity, the importance of helping others in their development, the golden rule and its esoteric underpinnings... After a few years, then one can learn about the end of Jesus's life. Then one can experience that Christ Jesus lived through in some hours what we all live through though spread out over lifetimes. Indeed, seen accumulatively, each human soul lives through far worse than Christ Jesus's crucifixion. Christ Jesus demonstrates a summary of our situation, and shows where it leads—to the release of the Resurrection Body into spirit, followed by the choice to enter into this world again in order to assist others. Then one can understand that Christ Jesus does not promise immortality of you in your present state, a common misconception. Rather he encourages you to improve yourself, a natural process of unfolding and purification that may involve suffering, blood, sweat, and tears. You don't try to create suffering for its own sake. The suffering is not the goal, rather the improvement of soul developing toward spirit. But don't be afraid of suffering should it occur along the way. We have all found that suffering can happen along the way. The model of Christ Jesus leads you to the power of relationship for improvement. You work in relation to others, who can assist you beyond your own capacities, and who can hurt you. Through these encounters, you learn love.

It can sometimes help to see the client across from you as another human being in the same training as you, who has lost his or her way on the path of improvement. In the process of helping, you learn love. And you know the process is working when you feel the love from the client's soul, assisting in your own improvement.

What practical steps can you take to alleviate the feeling of being nailed to your chair? This is important. You have to find other times in your day where you activate the will in large movements, through walking (where has that gone in our culture?!), dancing, hiking, free spontaneous movement when the situation permits. Eurythmy is an anthroposophical answer, learning to move through yourself the impulses arising from within and from without—the internal and external that I spoke about before. Viewing eurythmy gives only a taste; you have to move it yourself. Find a good teacher or join a class to open up these pathways for the will moving through you, with feeling.

Eurythmy also acquaints you with the power of small gesture. And that is key to someone in a chair. You can learn large movements using the whole floor and as high as you can reach into the air. Then find the gestures' essence in smaller and smaller versions of those movements, taking what you've found into micro-movements. This can involve your upper body, which is still presumably available for gestures, unless you've taken away one arm with a telephone or both arms with a computer. Most important are the parts stuck in the chair, your legs, torso, and especially your pelvis. In the modern world, the pelvis has become stagnant and crippled through inaction. You can learn to move your pelvis, either in dance, or free movements, or in eurythmy. Watch native peoples from any indigenous culture; follow them as they walk, and mimic their bodily movements. Then continue that movement in your counseling sessions or in any of your sitting. As I have an interest in theatre, I have taken classes over the years from dancers who work in theatre, and been amazed that during rest periods from activity, their legs and torsos, their pelvises, their toes, are always in movement.

When you have mastered bringing will-force alive even though limited by the chair in range of movement, you will experience something holy in this. Crucifixion is not something to endure in order to ascend to spirit away from the body. Rather, crucifixion is an aspect of our daily lives. We must learn to live with it. When we do so, the heart and lungs open again, and the feeling realm awards us with depth of insight into ourselves and our clients. Then the chair becomes one's personal throne wherein all the functions and senses of the soul are alive.

Practically speaking, there are many sitting postures: Discover them all.

Perhaps you have a workout routine in the gym that you like. I have two suggestions. First, try to do something in each of several categories, including balance, strength, flexibility, and cardio-vascular engagement. There are so many programs.

My second suggestion for the gym: Don't plug in headphones or television. A person spinning a bicycle while listening to rock music—or to a lecture on anthroposophic counseling psychology—is going backwards a little bit. The thinking has been divorced further from the body and from the will.

B. Credo

by Roberta Nelson

[*The request came from a student: "But what do you do for self-care!? How can you deal with a day full of challenging clients?" When Roberta spoke the following words, they cascaded out as in a waterfall, with confidence and power, without pause. The details of what she said are explained by David Tresemer in the next section. Here they are given as presented.*]

You asked what I do for self-care. I work with the subsidiary exercises; I work with the virtues; I work with the Foundation Stone Meditation; I work with the eight-fold path. I speak a meditation three times a day. I do the Hallelujah when I walk into my office and close the door. I work with my heart energy all the time. I work and develop that while in session. I continually let things go. I let my clients go before I sleep. I walk through my evening review. I celebrate the festivals. I put the armor of God on every day and often. I do the color gesture. When I don't do one of those activities, I can't help but notice the difference.

I don't relate to the symptoms as one typically would. I am joyful when I find something new, some breakthrough. I share my feeling with my client when I experience it. I also say, "This is so sad," when I hear their story and feel their circumstances.

Remember, most traumatic events have never been acknowledged. If I am listening to a horrific story of neglect and abuse, if I want to cry, I let my tears come and it wakes them up. If I want to blow my nose, I do so, and tell them how sorry I am. Many times I have clients that thank me for feeling them, for showing the sadness for them. As all of my clients, I am human, and as human I accompany them.

They dump their story thousands of times. They do that constantly. But to have somebody accompany them and respond from my authenticity is very important and real for them.

I don't do a fifty-minute hour. I don't have my day where I get ten minutes in between each session and "dump" my energy, dump my feelings. You are always working on yourself; you are doing your work; you are working on developing; you are working on your heart center. I call on the Spiritual Beings when I am taxed and have more clients to go.

C. About Roberta Nelson's Credo
by David Tresemer

I would like to explain the details of Roberta Nelson's response to the question: "What do you do about self-care?" The flow of what she said was so immediate and strong, that the thing of first import was not the details, but rather in the clear sense of knowing-oneself, knowing one's capacities, knowing one's tools. This is the master craftsman laying out her tools.

Explaining the details of Roberta's self-care do not imply that you should be using the same practices; more important, they tell you the kinds of things that sustain this extraordinary counselor. She concluded this list with, "When I don't do one of those activities, I can't help but notice the difference." Meditative practices make a difference.

  o   "I work with the subsidiary exercises." Rudolf Steiner taught what he called "subsidiary exercises" to his meditation students. To learn these takes time. As with other meditative techniques, you start with part one for a few days or a week, then add part 2 for a week, etc. 1.) The first exercise involves "control of one's thought," with the most humorous preliminary: "We should find at least five free minutes every day and contemplate a thought which is as insignificant as possible, which does not hold any interest for us whatsoever." (from a 1907 lecture by Steiner) That's where you begin. You use your five minutes each day to contemplate that simple thought in its fullness and in its extensions. The point of choosing something uninteresting is that you are there to observe the thought, not the complex of reactions to something useful or worthwhile. Simply the process of thinking a thought. 2.) Then you add to the first exercise a meaningless gesture to work with the forces of will (quite similar to an exercise given by Roberto Assagioli). 3.) Then you master joy and sorrow through practicing equanimity in relation to imagined scenes. 4.) The fourth step is to practice positivity toward anything and everything. 5.) The fifth is the practice of "lack of prejudice" or complete openness; you open to all possibilities. As Steiner said, someone could tell you that the local cathedral has overnight turned upside down and sits on its steeple, and you would respond, "That's interesting," and imagine that as true. 6.) The final sixth step is to practice the integration of all of these steps. This can take months to build up, but then you have it. There are other hints, locations in the body in which to imagine this work being done, and colors to use, but the main point here is that you begin small with such a contemplation and build each of these into powers of soul.

o "I work with the virtues." Steiner named twelve major virtues or character traits, associating them with the twelve zodiacal signs, such as "compassion becomes freedom" and "contentment becomes composure." One can follow each zodiacal month with an emphasis on that metamorphosis of virtues. I find these challenging because they are so general, though a closer relation to them does come with time. My way into these has come from Playback Theatre where you work on exercises such as, "Find anger—feel anger— now transform that into joy." You have to find a way to make that shift in your feeling life and in the gestures of your body. Then you recognize that you've traveled this path— from anger to joy—before. The "virtues" from Steiner are much more complicated and nuanced, yet the process can be the same. "Find compassion—feel compassion—now transform it into freedom."

○ "I work with the Foundation Stone Meditation." In the Christmas period at the end of 1923 and the beginning of 1924, Rudolf Steiner gave a set of four interlocking verses that he said would be the foundation for a new understanding of the cosmos, and what it meant to be human in it. People take years to master the implications of these verses. Some people pronounce the Foundation Stone Meditation daily, giving the speaker an outline for all of creation whenever they do. The fourth and final verse reads (putting together parts of three translations):

> At the Turning-point of Time
> The light of the Spirit of the Cosmos
> Entered the earthly stream of being.
> Deep darkness had lost its efficacy;
> Sun-radiant light streamed into human souls;
> A Light,
> That enwarms the simple shepherds' hearts,
> A Light,
> that enlightens the wise heads of kings.
> Godly Light
> Christ-Sun
> Warm our hearts
> Enlighten our heads
> That good may become
> What we from our hearts found
> What we from our heads direct
> With single will.

This excerpt from the Foundation Stone Meditation illustrates that a powerful verse can take one out of the immediate and pressing demands of the counseling setting. One is reminded that far vaster forces are at work, always.

○ "I work with the eight-fold path." The Buddha gave an eight-fold path, including such reminders as "Right Action," "Right Speech," and "Right Concentration." After months of contemplation, each can become a code-word for a deep understanding of eight aspects of human behavior—its challenges, and the path to integrity through those challenges. This is the kind of thing that the Buddhists meditate on for long periods, to find the essence of each of the eight paths.

o "I speak a meditation three times a day." There are hundreds of meditations to choose from. They all assist you to focus your attention during your day. You find that a well-crafted meditation remains infinitely interesting, no matter how many times you say it. When you do this rhythmically during the day, as in morning, noon, and night, then you affirm your cooperation with the beings who govern the patterns of the day. We have given a few verses and meditations in this book, and they are places to start. Here is one of my favorites:

> In purest outpoured light
> shimmers the Divinity of the world.
> In purest love for all that lives
> outpours the Divinity of my soul.
> I rest within the Divinity of the world.
> There shall I find my Self, within the Divinity of the world.

This verse from Rudolf Steiner has kept my attention, feeling into the subtleties of its words and phrases, for many years. I have changed Gottheit to Divinity. Making such changes is acceptable if it helps your comprehension and complete agreement. This verse is supremely optimistic. This is a "with seed" meditation, that asks for quiet silence afterwards to let these focuses of my attention work within me. The point here is that a verse can be quite powerful. Here is one from chapter 14:

> More radiant than the sun,
> purer than snow,
> finer than ether,
> is the Self,
> the spirit of my heart.
> I am this Self.
> This Self am I.

Other sources for verses are cited in the references at the end of this chapter.

o "I do the Hallelujah when I walk into my office and close the door." In eurythmy, there are movements combining both gesture and footwork that are suggested for various moods and challenges. The Hallelujah is one such choreography, and can be performed by one person or a whole group. It makes awe of creation into a choreography. Once you have learned it in hand gestures for all of the sounds, and movements of the feet, you can essentialize it with small gestures, even when seated. Having a movement form in the body can be very helpful to you in many situations where engaging the body engages your will forces in consonance with greater powers moving in the cosmos.

o   "I work with my heart energy all the time." The heart mediates the forces of thinking and willing, which are often in battle, especially so for the clinician seeing clients in life crisis. Roberta also described above how she lets her feelings flow with her clients, as this affirms her—and therefore, their—humanity.

o   "I continually let things go. I let my clients go before I sleep." A memory too rigid can impede your client's development, both their memory and yours. Sleep is a great leveler, as we all go, possessionless, into realms of spirit. Perhaps you have an impression of the client that you've seen this day. Lest this image—or diagnosis—become enchaining to the client, you let it go, and greet the client afresh in the next meeting.

o   "I walk through my evening review." Rudolf Steiner emphasized this technique above many others. Essentially, before resting at night—either just before sleeping or in a few minutes late in the evening—you walk yourself through the main features of your day. The key is to do this without judgment, without emotional attachment, without adding something to your next day. Simply observe and move on. It's an unwinding of the day rather than a relegation of the precious experiences of the day to forgetfulness (because you never really forget anything). When you unwind the day through simple observation, it releases the energies bound up in your impressions, emotional knots, and unfinished business—releases them to be enjoyed by your own higher powers as well as by angelic beings. These reviews provide a kind of nourishment for the angels. The notion of unwinding makes it more understandable why it is suggested that you walk through the day backwards, beginning with the most recent occurrence, and ending with what happened in the day's morning. You unwind. (See more about this technique in the next section, D.)

o "I celebrate the festivals." We have the rhythm of the day (as in the evening review), and the rhythm of the year. Anthroposophy has identified certain festivals relating to the seasons that give important opportunities to experience the breathing of the whole earth is it goes through a great out-breath in summer and an in-breath in the winter—and the response of the plant and animal world to these rhythms. Steiner counseled repeatedly to observe and participate in the festivals that mark the seasons of the year, as you can thus participate in the breathing rhythms of the earth herself. When you resonate with the powers of earth, rather than ignore them, it can bring great support to your counseling.

o "I put the armor of God on every day and often." The term "armor of God" comes from passages in Ephesians 6:10-18 and 2 Corinthians 6:7, illustrating that Dr. Nelson draws from many sources for her daily practices. Divinity has the capacity to inspire, and the capacity to protect. On a daily basis, a counselor is in the presence of other people's demons. Protection is warranted. Communication with spiritual beings is available and wise—all emanating from God, and summarized here by the term "God." The particular names of God matter far less than the personal experience of divinity streaming through you and through everyone and everything around you.

o "Color gesture." Dr. Nelson relates in chapters 9 and 10 her work with artistic media with clients. She also works these media for herself, regularly. Her favorite mode is with soft pastels—soft because you can soften them and move them around with your fingers after they're applied to the paper.

As she says, "Why would you want to make art that couldn't change?" Holding the question, "Who am I today?," one lets the colors flow, and in so doing finds a direct communication of the soul life to the personality.

○　"Call on the Spiritual Beings." Anthroposophy distinguishes many kinds of spiritual beings. Over time one can come to know them. One begins with one's personal angel, then other angels, then archangels, and so on. An anthroposophic counselor does not advertise this connection because it may be completely foreign to a client. However, for the self-care of the counselor, knowing that you thrive within a living matrix of spirit and spirits can be very helpful.

D. The Evening and Morning Review

by David Tresemer

One compendium of Steiner's lectures contains excerpts of the many times that he recommended the evening review, as a way of emphasizing the importance of this technique. Evening review relates also to Dr. Nelson's point about letting clients go—at day's end, you bring them back to awareness, briefly, without re-entering the turbulence of the session. You simply notice what occurred, and move on. You can begin such a practice by noticing the two or three strong points of the day. That's enough, and is helpful too if you're running yourself hard through long days. Review two or three impressions or events from the day. You can add in more on subsequent evenings as you become comfortable with this process. A full evening review can unravel the entire harvest of the day, backwards, in five or ten minutes. When you gather this harvest, it acts as nutrition for the helpful beings around us, who accompany and support us through our maturation.

One way to use the evening review and its follow-up in the morning is this exercise:

Evening Meditation

Note for the following something that comes to you. Do not take too long with it, though note the experiences in their fullness.

This is not for chewing over, or imagining "I could have done it differently." Here you simply notice what comes to you or what happened.

1. Attention. Some thing comes to your senses toward the end of the day, something that you see, hear, touch... Note that thing and write down a few keywords to tag it.

2. Interest. To whom did you relate this day with warm interest? Note that person; write down the name and a couple of words about the quality of your experience.

3. Meaning and purpose. Find this connection to your day through questions, "Why here?," "Why now?," Why me?" An answer may arise in the form of a moment in your day. Note the occasion and its quality.

Morning Meditation

What arises at the beginning of your day—from night-school or from early morning experiences in these three areas:

1. Attention. A sensory experience.
2. Interest. A human in whom you find warm interest.
3. Meaning. Insights or questions that arise. Note a few words for each of these.

Interrelationship

Pair the Attention experiences, the Interests, and the encounters with Meaning. How has this gifted you from other realms? Note that the physical and etheric bodies are excited through sensory attention; the astral body and soul through interest; and the spirit (or "I AM") through meaning.

E. Self-Care through the Senses

by Edmund Knighton

[*Here, Dr. Knighton approaches his self-care regimen by going through the twelve senses posited by anthroposophy—to which he adds a few more. Some of these are enigmas; many demand further explication; all have the feeling of alignment with a truth discovered through living life to the full.*]

As to the first sense, *Touch*: Caress my son Liam's limbs at nighttime, daily hugs and kisses. Tactilely experience the natural world: boulders, plants.

As to the second sense, *Life* (Well-being): Humor. Experience Breath. Before breakfast, find one thing I am grateful for. Asleep by 9 to meet my midnight angel. Drink lots of water. Vacations with family. And I schedule vacations with friends away from family (annual backpacking trip).

Movement: Embodied mindfulness body scan meditation upon awakening, five minutes. Open to movement that is subtle and unsensed-on-the-way-to-sensing. Dowsing. Walks in Lithia Park with my family. Twenty minute daily run. Asanas. Sit on floor or stand ... avoid a chair. Spatial practices during therapy with self and other. Model self-care practices to demonstrate for client and influence client self-care.

Balance: Boundaries. Clarifying questions. Check-ins.

Smell: Sandalwood in hair, lavender: rub on torso while paying attention to which areas need it most and which direction I need to move my hands for efficacious healing. Pillow potion. Cedar pine forests, roses. Flowers and weeds one wouldn't ordinarily smell. Incense aroma in bedroom reinvigorates meditative mood.

Taste: I eat mindfully, slowly, mostly plant-based, greens every meal. I fast weekly, monthly enemas. New recipes, gardening. Small dinner. Limit processed foods.

Warmth: Increase self-awareness, development, and maturation through personal therapy. Interest in other. Privilege and prioritize right brain implicit sharing (express feelings, movement-communication).

Sight: Observe client movement at point of origin. Show a complementary movement.

Hearing: Meditation. Listen to others while empty in myself. Mindful Conversation/Dialog.

Speaking: Recite heart-learned poems aloud to create a sacred mood and dwell there (as in poems from Rumi). Recite Steiner mantras from my heart. Chant "I Am." Dictation Journaling. External processing. Vulnerability, disclosure of fears and failures. Share the "nonshare." Fill myself with love for my child as we sing daily. Prayer of Protection.

Thinking: Set realistic, specific, and measurable self-care goals. Spiritual study. Enneagram. Self-education. Writing spiritual reality. Professional development and support, includes work-related activities. Enjoy a variety of work outlets (offer seminars, teaching, admin, therapist, writing, journal reviewing, consulting). Case consultation, daily breaks, continuing education seminars, realistic expectations at work, monitoring manageable caseload size and types of cases. Practice "non" (nonattitude, nonpathologizing, nonjudgment...). Research, e.g., learning I only get it right 30% of the time but it is how I repair that deepens relationships.

"I" of Other: Interpersonal realm. Ask for help, say sorry. Call friends/family weekly. Erase all that I think I know about a person to enable freedom when apart and keep the space clear. Emptiness for freedom when together. Once a client is out of sight, cut all ties and erase client from being. I cut myself off from my clients between sessions so they and I can be free to grow, and I practice meeting them as if for the first time when I see them again so I don't hold them in old patterns. Upon seeing them again, I engage beginner's mind and open myself to them fully. Initiating contact and intimate distance. Model self-care. Embrace/celebrate conflict as a valued part of relationship. Joyful connection with my wife and child. Maintain 5 close relationships where we could share anything. I like and respect the people I work with. Opponents Meditation, Loving Kindness. Realize limitations, e.g., I can't help everyone so I refer out. I let clients be responsible for their own lives. Share feelings, motivations, countertransference with colleagues. Seek counsel from wise ones. Visualize difficult clients during a positive moment before sleep; chakra work.

A thirteenth sense, *Imagination*: I use creativity, humor, and playfulness in therapy. I pay attention to emotion in my dreams. Remain mindful of my fantasy life. Play "The Transformation Game®."

A fourteenth sense, *Inspiration*: Prayer for inspiration, well-being, and guidance. Knowing I have a spiritual purpose, destiny. I reflect on joys and meaning in my work. My family is supportive of my work. Look for something I can love and be nourished by in my clients.

A fifteenth sense, *Intuition*: Meditative Mantras while engendering sacred mood and practicing subtle threefold movements of each line, lesson 10. *[Here, Dr. Knighton references the tenth lesson of the First Class of the School of Spiritual Science. See references at chapter's end.]* I recite lesson 10 by heart and feel its movement through my thought, heart, and limb. I connect with spiritual beings. I listen to intuition, that still small voice within. Transformation Game. Six basic exercises. Sitting practice with body scan.

And for all the senses: Each season I share time with loved ones in the wilderness. I also take a break from all senses occasionally, space out, have space to do nothing, be spontaneous.

F. Elaborations

[William Bento:]
Being an Anthroposophic Counselor is not a job. It is a way of life, it doesn't stop in between sessions. To deal with this intensity requires an intuitive sense of knowing. You don't have to be anything, you just have to *Be*, open and alive.

After many years of accompanying people through times of distress I have developed an intuitive sense of knowing when to speak and when to be silent. In doing psychotherapy you don't have to be anything, you just have to *Be*, open and alive. This quality of open-ness and alive-ness can be fructified by Rudolf Steiner's "Six Basic Exercises" given in *How to Know Higher Worlds* and in *An Outline of Esoteric Science*. These exercises strengthen our capacity to open the heart chakra and allow it to become the organ of perception for the subtle and supersensible realities that surround us at all times.

It may sound paradoxical but my best days of self-care while doing psychotherapy are days when I do not put emphasis on my own issues. These are times where I am totally dedicated to being in the flow with my clients. It is being in the flow that nourishes my own soul.

The principle, "To thine own self be true," is one to which I not only attempt to live, but attempt to transmit to my clients. It is far more pertinent to the psychotherapeutic process than any adherence to best practice methods. Any specific technique will become simply just that, a technique. If you aren't able to be present in the meeting with another, the process and opportunity for therapeutic efficacy will become dead.

Here is my poem to strengthen the counselor, "There is a Friendship."

> There is a friendship...
> ...among men and women who dare to open
> their heart's secrets to one another,
> there lives the *Hope* and promise of friendship.
> In the deepening silence they will bear with *Love*
> the knowing of what one has and has not done.
> And in this understanding, friendship shall bring
> to each of them the light of the Spirit Sun.
> *Faith* in this experience of true friendship
> will be the foundation of the World to come.

[Edmund Knighton, picking up on Roberta Nelson's comment about authenticity with the client:] In graduate schools throughout the country, students are taught not to be authentic. Students are taught, "Protect yourself; it's all laid out in the book, symptoms, treatment, it's all there. So mechanize it. Diagnose and treat by the book."

[David Tresemer:]

Sometimes a training program, such as a master's degree program, will require twenty hours of some kind of therapy as a means of gaining personal experience in counseling or therapy. In this the designers of the training consider that they've broadened your experience. That's absurd. You have to keep learning. When filling your Continuing Education requirements, branch out into new territory. Learn some new aspect of counseling that you've never known about.

Find a mentor. Find a supervisor, no matter how many years you've been counseling others. Everyone needs someone with whom he or she can speak, someone with more experience. It needn't be someone experienced in anthroposophic counseling psychology. It does need to be someone who has had life experience, and knows about what is unseen behind the veils of the consensual.

An experience of the "I" in full consciousness—an experience of grace—comes as an accident—unexpected. However, through fully embracing your inner life and your relational life—through self-care—you can become accident-prone.

Suggested Resources for Further Study
(in addition to the references at the end of the book)

Hughes, Gertrude Reif (2011). *More Radiant than the Sun: A Handbook for Working with Steiner's Meditations and Exercises.* Great Barrington, MA: SteinerBooks.

Lowndes, Florin (2000). *Enlivening the Chakra of the Heart.* Rudolf Steiner Press, second edition. This gives a more modern version of the six exercises from Steiner.

Romero, Lisa (2014). *The Inner Work Path: A Foundation for Meditative Practice in the Light of Anthroposophy.* Great Barrington, MA: Steiner-Books.

Steiner, Rudolf (2013). *The Constitution of the School of Spiritual Science: An Introductory Guide.* London: Rudolf Steiner Press.

Steiner, Rudolf (1998). *Guidance in Esoteric Training.* London: Rudolf Steiner Press. Includes a section on the six basic exercises.

CHAPTER 12

Meditation and Mindfulness

by Edmund Knighton, Ph.D.

and David Tresemer, Ph.D.

What is meditation? There is not one answer, nor one form, nor one technique. Recently the term mindfulness has arisen to define a form of meditation. Anthroposophy encourages meditation in various forms. How does mindfulness integrate with anthroposophy? To address these issues, this chapter comes in several parts. Though useful to clients, the counselor must learn about these realms and techniques first.

A. Meditation—What It Is

by David Tresemer

What is your most precious asset? Ponder this: "My most precious asset is my attention." None of the other candidates for "most precious" matter without my attention, my awareness, my consciousness. Therefore, does it not make sense to care for my most precious asset—to feed it, keep it clean, train it further?

One sees immediately that my relationship to my attention/ consciousness depends heavily on what state of soul I've developed (what level of Spiritus, referring to the diagram from chapter 1). If it is sentient soul, then I direct my awareness to sensations, and can mature my senses—to hear the signature sound of a pine tree in a breeze, to appreciate the taste of a Bosc pear.... If I have developed an intellectual or mind soul, then I hone my awareness in ideas, in inventions, in games of chess, and in the dynamics of poetry. If I have developed a consciousness soul (or spiritual soul), my attention goes to perceiving and cooperating with the spiritual beings moving and creating (and destroying) in my midst.

I happen to have a personal love of compost. From the sentient soul level, I can meditate on the smells of good compost, on the wondrous earthworms who crawl through and eat it all up; I get my hands into it. From the intellectual soul level, I can revel in the interactions of the billions of micro-organisms of many species, and the details of the chemical processes that take place there. From a consciousness soul level, I can marvel at the activity of gnomes and sylphs, and the spirits that overlight and direct them, in the processes of creating a stable source of fertility. I can enjoy the addition of the bio-dynamic preparations as invitations to particular spiritual beings to attend the process. (The intellectual soul has great difficulty understanding the bio-dynamic preparations!)

The point is that each of these approaches to compost can include activity that fosters my precious attention, that can be labeled meditative, though each kind of meditation is different.

Life for many is simply waking-business punctuated by collapse into dreamless sleep. If there isn't stimulation and things-to-do, then the mind turns off. However, there is always a little gap between waking and sleeping. The task of meditation is to broaden that gap, where there is neither stimulation and restlessness nor sound sleep. Over time, the gap becomes a space large enough that one can navigate in what turns out to be great landscapes and territories of wonder.

Meditation can begin with a minute of silence. Indeed, Wellesley Tudor Pole, the man who set up the Chalice Well Trust at the base of the Glastonbury Tor, initiated, in 1940 during the bombing of London, a Silent Minute as a prayer for peace and freedom. At nine o'clock each evening the great bells of Big Ben would toll and all of England, joined by others around the world, would become silent for one minute. After the war, a top German official credited that unified field of meditative power as a "secret weapon" that prevented their attack on England. Meditation can begin that way, as a single minute of silence.

One can enter meditation "with seed" or "without seed."

"With seed" means that you use a poem or a verse or a mantram or an image to calm your mind and alert it to the meditative state. Nikola Tesla would design a machine in his mind and set it running, checking in every so often to see that it was functioning properly. Or a "seed" could be a wise or provocative saying, such as "More radiant than the sun is my 'I'."

"Without seed" means that you simply find a posture that is not distracting—and it need not be a particular posture, seated or standing—and you become quiet. For some, becoming quiet for a few minutes is enough. Others await the flood of images, colors, and voices that rush into the vacuum.

Most important is to make space for "the still small voice within," the one that Elijah heard, and that many others hear. You learn over time to distinguish the still small voice from the voice of your inner critic (superego); you learn to distinguish it from lyrics of your latest favorite singer.

The foundation of meditation is the ability to find that quiet, so that the small voice can speak. This begins with creating space in your environment where you can be calm. Even if you can turn off your electronics, don't underestimate the power of other stimuli in your environment to grab you—the books on the bookshelves in your office for instance. If you can't find a physical space and a portion of time in which you can be free from disturbance, you are not alone in that conundrum. You must try. Eckhart Tolle found a park bench. Roberto Assagioli found the greatest calm when he was incarcerated as a political prisoner. You can find that space and time to widen the gap between sleep and waking.

Then begin to work the different levels of soul development. Meditating on your clients before your sessions is claimed by many to be the most effective preparation. With ho'oponopono, Joe Vitale takes this as far as it goes, taking on the client's dynamic, in what Edmund Knighton calls (in the next section) the first space. Way before that, you can find the one minute before the session where you meet your client, soul-to-soul. The session between counselor and client then unfolds from there.

Consciousness as a Strange Attractor

The field called chaos theory (less dramatically and more accurately called complexity theory or dynamical systems theory) has given us some pictures that are very helpful to understanding consciousness. In particular, the Lorenz attractor traces the path of a point moving in space under the direction of a formula, through millions of repetitions of that formula. Here is a version of a Lorenz "strange attractor":

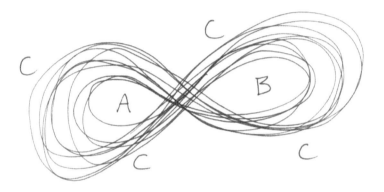

This provides a picture of consciousness, if we imagine that our consciousness moves like the point in this pattern:

- Our awareness or consciousness is always active, scanning our environment, both inner and outer. Everyone can recognize that feeling of restless sensory awareness, sensitive to any and all phenomena.
- Our attention never ceases its activity. Scanning—always scanning, often subliminal, sometimes restless.
- The roving point of consciousness travels near to familiar paths, but never the same path twice. Everything is a little bit new and thus interests our awareness. It is very important that we realize that every breath and every heartbeat are slightly different from the ones that happened before. We repeat but not exactly. Thus the secret of rhythm without boredom.
- The path of consciousness circles about two attractive centers that it never comes to know fully. One can think of

A as the center of one's Soul and B as the center of one's "I" (framing the diagrams in chapter 6 differently). These centers are mysteries that we assess and orbit, though may never come to know consciously. The zone of C can then represent the undiscovered territories of spirit.

o   We strive for balance, in a system that is never static, with ever-new circulation between body, soul, and spirit.

o   If we add the perspective of quantum physics, we can imagine a point moving swiftly in ever new pathways becoming a wave form. The quantum is sometimes a "thing" and sometimes a wave. We are more accurate in understanding ourselves as wave forms in constant motion, resonating with some aspects of our environment, both internal environment and external, and sometimes not resonating.

o   The brilliance of a figure-8 or lemniscate is that it changes direction. We don't have a circle or curve going round and round, balancing centripetal and centrifugal motion. Consciousness circles round one end, then yields to centrifugal motion, opening up, and for a short time at the crossing-point experiences neither centripetal nor centrifugal motion. At that point a will force must come in, to turn the path in a new way: If it had been rounding clockwise, it now rounds counter-clockwise. This spike of will force taking consciousness in a new direction wakes us up, repeatedly.

If the constant scanning, the circling, is too tight, you may feel chained, like a hamster in a cage.

You obsess; you repeat; you perseverate, you worry; you check that you turned the lights out in the garage again and again. Or you arrange all your vegetables in rows, moving them slightly to make it all perfect, and then start over again.... This is a picture of perseverance, endless repetition, "*déjà vu* all over again," the inability to think or behave or feel outside of a rut.

Anthroposophists love this picture of the lemniscate ("figure-eight") but must understand that a simple 8-shape is a distillation or special case of the non-exact repetition of this form (pictured by the Lorenz attractor). The slight newness of the trajectory over the same territory keeps the soul interested. Obsession is a matter of degree of tightness of the constantly moving consciousness. When it's this tight, you feel "what's in the way is the way." The path has become too constrained.

We all need to obsess to some extent to stay awake to our immediate surroundings. The alternative is flying out and away into completely new and unfamiliar territory.

A consciousness that is always in new territory is one that has entirely new percepts that are not understood by pre-existing concepts—we are more in schizoid territory in this diagram. Lacking any referents, we are unable to speak about our experiences. A pioneer changes surroundings slowly and can integrate those new experiences. Change the context too quickly and you become utterly lost.

The healthy purpose of meditation is to investigate the territories of A, B, and C, moving into those new realms and learning about them, and bringing their fruits into your present awareness. You then can move slowly into new realms.

You can use this propensity to repeat in your spiritual work. Many traditions use repetition in the form of japa or chanting, orienting your mind and heart to transcendent experiences through repetition. Active japa becomes an exercise of the will, and opens you to other possibilities: Not only is meditation an exercise in "stilling one's thoughts," that is, the "without-seed" condition in the realm of thinking. It also includes directing thought (the "with-seed" condition), working actively with feelings, and working with the qualities of will. Indeed, some claim that meditation is simply a churning of half-formed thoughts unless there is a deed of will that is sought and enacted either during or after the meditation.

In meditation, one comes to know the three functions of the soul more intimately. One comes to know one's thoughts better. One observes the monkey chatter or "discursive thought," the repetitions too tight and too loud. Thinking streams from the past, based on past experiences formulated into concepts. One can learn to discern the difference between regurgitated thoughts and true thinking, which is creative and new, and infused with soul and spirit.

In an addiction treatment center that I know, "morning meditation" consists of reading aloud a paragraph from a self-help book on addiction, and talking about it for a few minutes. This may be inspirational, but this is not meditation. The path of consciousness does not expand much or at all, but continues its whirr closely around the familiar.

In meditation, one observes one's deeds, the impulses to move, to jiggle, to jitter restlessly. Immature will forces show as habits, repetitions of movements—some of which we are thankful for, as these include heartbeat and breathing. However, new will forces stream from the future and we know them as intuitions of destiny, and our sense of a personal calling in simple deeds and in life direction.

One observes one's feelings, the immature ones that arise spontaneously when one is still. Feeling is understood in anthroposophy to mediate thinking from the past and willing from the future—and to exercise this mediation in the present. In every tradition, teachers of meditation emphasize "this moment," the present, which in a mature person is full of a quality of feeling unlike the irritations of the immature. "This moment" has a fullness, openness, a quality of acceptance, and a quality of love that shows the maturation of feeling. Equanimity does not mean numbness to experience, but rather a fullness of experience that can include every possible emotion, as the flow through your being.

These matured versions of thinking, willing, and feeling permit one to engage in whole-soul conversation with another.

B. Exercise in Meditation: Movement Memory

by Edmund Knighton

[This is a text with notes from one of Edmund's brilliant exercises relating to meditation and mindfulness, in relation to oneself and to others. Edmund began standing in the middle of a circle of participants.]

The first thing you are going to do is watch me as I make a simple movement, and then I'll ask you to do something with your observation. Let me know when you are ready.

[Participants signal they are ready. Edmund demonstrates a simple movement as participants observe it: His arms rise to the sides and then overhead and then return to resting by his sides.]

Just observing, movement. *[Silence.]* That's the movement. I'd like you now to remember the movement to yourself. How many of you remember the movement, here? *[Edmund points to his head, indicating a possible location of memory.]* Two of you. Where are you sensing it? Where did you experience that in space? How many of you experienced my movement around your whole body? Seven of you. How many of you experienced the movement where it took place, here in the center of the circle? *[Edmund gestures to the limb system of his body.]*

Three places exist where you can experience movement. The first space is inside the body, usually the head, particularly the forehead, as if you are viewing the image shrunken into a two-inch viewing screen.

The second space of experience is around the observer's body, often as a whole, although some may experience more sensation localized to a particular area of the body, for example, heart or knees. Utilizing the second space, the therapist can try on a client's movement like a cloak. The therapist can then remove the client's movement from their personal field.

The third space to experience movement is where it occurred. In this case just now, it occurred around my body in the center of the circle. I raised my arms and lowered them. We know from muscular experiments that when one part of the body moves, then the whole body moves. It is not possible to move a part of the body in isolation. All parts of the body are affected. We also know that when you watch me move, you are moved too, via mirror neurons. And sometimes, if my movement resonates with you, you are moved to physically repeat it, or you are moved to initiate a different movement in response to my movement. This is akin to what is sometimes called somesthetic or kinesthetic resonance.

Children often experience both their own and others' movement in the location it occurred, rather than around or inside their bodies. For example, a child is running through a meadow and trips over a stone. She comes to you in tears. You ask her, "Sweetie, where did you hurt yourself?" You expect that she will point to a part of her body. Instead, she points to the stone. Her movement memory lives strongly in the location of activity. As adults, we benefit from cultivating this situation-movement-memory. When we understand that memory is stored not in the head but around the body and in the world, our memory strengthens. Shrinking memory into the body, especially the head, can tend toward contraction and result in headache and migraine production. On the path of development, we strengthen world-memory, and then we are invited to release it for body-free memory.

This innate childlike ability to experience movement where it occurs is what we want. With clients, allow the movements that your client brings you to remain around themselves. A misunderstanding occurs when we bring these movements toward us and shrink these movements into our heads or bodies. Burnout for the counselor can occur as a result of absorbing unhealthy or unrhythmical movement from clients into our own bodies, especially when these movements flow disharmoniously and disrupt our own tonal rhythm.

Therapists may think they are being helpful in "visualizing" the movement. However, if by visualization we mean we take the movements of another into ourselves, be they physical, emotional, or energetic, we can make ourselves sick as a consequence. Some therapists contend that they are able to transmute the client's movement. Others believe they must be able to take in the client's movement in order to understand it. I invite you to consider that you are best able to comprehend movement when you observe it from its point of origin, rather than inserting it into your body. It is also possible to allow the client's movement to flow toward and around you without taking it inside your bodily boundary, but this takes a second space of awareness.

Instead of "visualization," I suggest the word "spatialization." I hope this helps you to remember to allow the activity to take place where it takes place in the third space. I mentioned that you can move it toward you like a cloak, which is second space movement. You watch the movement take place and then bring it around your body.

I invite you to let go of shrinking space, adulterating it from its present form and contracting it into your body, into the first space or second space.

Let's practice this again. I will raise my arms. Enjoy leaving my movement where it is, in the third space. [Edmund makes a movement.] Now bring it toward you like a cloak, in the second space. But please leave your intimate space, your organs' space or your head, free. Don't bring this movement there to the first space. [Quiet while Edmund enacts the movement again.]

Notice where in space you remember it. Notice what you feel when you sense it in the center. Notice it as a wave. Experience it, and let it go. I hope you experience it around the sheath of the body. [Participant says she is picking it up as tingling in her fingers.]

The hands and especially the palms are exquisitely sensitive. This sensitization reaches a critical mass just before puberty. That is why it is so important in sixth grade to start juggling with children. Children pick up things all the time in their environment. They draw things strongly to themselves. It is akin to working with magnets. The palms are very sensitive; thus, in a good curriculum, the teacher begins the first physics lesson. Cause and effect become conscious experience. Props are introduced, both to protect the palms and block outside influences that may disrupt or distract, and because props are lawful cause-and-effect teachers. The prop becomes the teacher, and the teacher takes a step back in the teaching process.

There's an exception. I described warding off negative or destructive movement. In contrast, for intimate movements of love, times in nature, when listening to exquisitely divine music, etc., persons often choose to allow these movements inside their bodily boundary. Love, nature, and inspired music contain intelligent rhythm that nourishes the soul and organizes organ and nervous systems. You want to take them into the first space, intimately into yourselves. However, these experiences manifest sparingly within a therapeutic setting.

When I moved and you observed, I attempted to do something which would be beautiful, that would be harmonious, something that would be pleasing, a movement you would like to imitate. This can occur when the physical body follows lawful etheric movement. The opposite would occur if I moved by initiating the movement from within my body with physical thrust only, mechanically. To overcome this way of moving, we allow ourselves to feel moved in a mood, to follow something greater than ourselves, originating from the periphery. Thus something archetypal is introduced. Before we speak, think, or move, we summon up an accompanying inner mood. For instance, if you were listening to your favorite singer, someone you feel is connected to something universal in origin, you might choose to say to yourself consciously, "I will take this into my organ space because this sound is divine. My organs recognize it and I will respond to this downbeat because this organ movement and that singer's voice sound from the same source." Do you feel that? When you take this in, there is a certain listening you took in because you recognized it as a part of yourself.

What do you do when an individual is presenting something that is in complete disarray in the etheric body? How is it that you can see the presence of that individual and not feel so connected to them that you want to absorb everything that made them feel that way? Naive realism comes with such an incredible sense of warm heartedness. Let's practice an exercise together.

In dyads, we will discuss something, anything that is going on in your life. Choose something that is midlevel, not so close that it is fully active in your life, and not so far that it has passed. Something that has enough energy in it to maintain your interest, but not so much energy that you may get carried away emotionally by bringing it up. The other person's job is to find something in that individual's story that nourishes them. As a therapist, look for something, a feeling, a voice, something that nourishes you as a therapist as you listen to the other.

You as a therapist allow yourself to be nourished. Where spatially is the nourishment? Where is the world, the body, etc. nourished in an outward way, nourished in an inward way?

Find a way in movement to effect movement and be nourished by them to stay healthy. *[Dr. Knighton continued with this exercise, demonstrating that bodily movements can be taken into first space, second space, and third space—and that another's stories can be worked with in the same way.]*

C. Brief Introduction to Mindfulness
by David Tresemer

There are now dozens of books describing mindfulness (some excellent ones referenced at the end of this chapter). I will remark briefly on its history. Buddhism came to the West along with the counter-cultural impulses of the 1960s. It brought along lessons on consciousness and how to interact with the world. At first the strongest influence was from Zen Buddhism, through such pioneers as Shunryu Suzuki (*Zen Mind, Beginner's Mind*) and Alan Watts (author of many books, and speaker at many conferences). Chogyam Trungpa, a refugee from Tibet, lectured, wrote books, and founded Naropa University; he predicted in 1974 that "Buddhism will come to the West as psychology." The

Mind & Life Institute, founded in 1990, began actively to connect Buddhism with science, including the monitoring of meditators using western brain technology. The Dalai Lama became particularly active in the last two decades in the West, specifically supporting the connection between Buddhism and mind-science. Though William James used Buddhist terms in his work a hundred years ago (as in "stream of consciousness" in *The Varieties of Religious Experience*), it has only happened recently that Buddhist psychology has been recognized by mainstream science and scientific psychology.

A pillar of Buddhist psychology is mindfulness. Across the many varieties of Buddhism, this feature is constant—a way of focusing the mind, stilling rampant emotions, and observing that-which-arises in consciousness.

Buddhism and anthroposophy share many understandings of the nature of reality.

o   An admiration of freedom, and engaging in practices that increase freedom.

o   A recognition of infinite states of consciousness—or bardos or fields of glory.

o   A recognition of repeated lifetimes, though in anthroposophy this is seen as the return of the "I" to different circumstances on a road of improvement. The concept of karma is shared (though understood differently—in Buddhism as a burden and in Anthroposophy as an opportunity).

o   The cessation of suffering through corrections to oneself, through right knowledge, right intention, right speech.... There are eight aspects of this noble path of development.

o   Recognition of the existence and interplay of spirit in our lives.

o   Recognition of the energy-structure of the human body, especially in the form of chakras or energy-centers through the body.

o   Certain sayings, mantras, and verses have particular power in assisting development.

There are also differences:

o   Buddhism speaks about escaping the cycle of death and rebirth. Anthroposophy understands the goal of human life as greater improvement of the soul and the "I," in relation to Sophia and Anthropos, as described in chapter 6.

o   Buddhism imagines that the highest attainment is emptiness. Anthroposophy agrees that emptiness is an important stage in development—what is called the achievement of Spirit-Self (or manas), the purification of the astral body—yet the individuality is meant to grow further. Mindfulness as often practiced leads to emptiness, which is valuable yet incomplete.

o   In Buddhism, importance is put on emptiness. Whatever "arises" afterwards is seen as a kind of natural behavior. There is not the same sense of what we find in Anthroposophy as sacred vocation, nor the active working of the will realm. (Indeed, Buddhism can tend toward a cool intellectualization ... though Anthroposophy can easily err in this direction as well.)

o   Though Spirit is recognized in Buddhism, Spirits (referring to the description of anthroposophic psychology in chapter 1) are seen by some sects as fantasy.

o   What we call in anthroposophic psychology the "soul," or "Self," or "I," are, in many branches of Buddhism, rejected as illusory. The self does not exist. Emptiness is seen as the true nature of reality. I have had several conversations with Buddhists who speak in terms of "soul"or "higher Self," and then say, "Of course, those don't really exist."

This is an incomplete list, and Buddhist sects differ from one another on nearly every point, but it is adequate for an initial understanding of similarities and differences between Buddhism and anthroposophic psychology. The point is that there are many similarities between anthroposophy and Buddhism, and yet there are many differences as well.

Mindfulness is akin to meditation in that it works in that gap between sleeping and active-waking to help us observe the incessant workings of our minds, as pictured by the Lorenz attractor in part A. Mindfulness increases one's awareness of the present moment, and thereby insights into the true nature of reality beyond the labels of what we perceive, what we feel, and what we do.

As a young man, Rudolf Steiner was chosen to edit Goethe's scientific works. Steiner uncovered a method of thinking in Goethe that he championed. Some people today speak of "Goethean conversation" or "Goethean thinking," but it was Steiner who revealed what Goethe was writing about. Steiner elaborated and developed that approach into something that is anthroposophic (meaning the connection of Anthropos and Sophia) and that is as sophisticated as Buddhist meditation and mindfulness.

We must get used to the term mindfulness appearing everywhere, just as we see the terms quantum or love in many places, some appropriate and some where they don't belong. We must discern what is valuable and what is not. We can use techniques of mindfulness—demonstrated in parts B and D of this chapter—and we can utilize the many studies on mindfulness as support for anthroposophic psychological meditative approaches. However, we should always remember some of the assumptions underlying mindfulness. In anthroposophic psychology, we utilize with gratitude the work done on mindfulness, and then seek to expand our understanding of spirit, spirits, bodies, soul, destiny, and the stars.

D. Mindful Conversation
by Edmund Knighton

[*Here Dr. Knighton illustrates how to use mindfulness in relation to conversation, between one and another (dyadic), and in groups. This expands upon the exploration in part B of first space, second space, and third space.*]

Mindful conversation initially involves being with oneself intimately when in the presence of another or others. At root, such self-intimacy involves a threefold self-listening: (a) when the room is silent, (b) when I am speaking, and (c) when I am listening to another person communicate. Communication occurs in some form or another throughout the encounter, even when the room is silent. I follow subtle inward cues during this practice, such as how and where to listen spatially, both in my body and in the room. I can practice making my whole being like an ear, or listening into my backspace between the shoulder blades, or listening with the backs of my knees. The body differentiates myriad tone qualities depending upon where listening takes place. My listening ability receives instruction at this time. I am listening to others communicate in such a way that I grow silent around any form of response or reaction, in body, soul, or spirit. This inner quiet entails that I do not think, feel, or sense into the content and process of the sharer. I provide a sounding board so that the other person can come to understand herself and hear her expression in a completely new way.

The effect is much like the principle of sympathetic resonance. In a room full of pianos, if a key is played on one piano, then all the other pianos will echo and vibrate to that note. This occurs of course only if all of the pianos are silent and not being played. A similar reality occurs when we listen to another person deeply and completely. We are silent enough to resonate with whatever note is played by the other. We do not have thoughts ahead of time to obstruct the resonance of the speaker's note.

Once a listener forms thoughts, the larynx begins to vibrate with the force of this thought; the room swells with two notes, perhaps two chords, often slightly discordant. As a result, the speaker may be deprived of the possibility of hearing herself in a new way. Instead, she may experience the old way of ordinary intellectual conversation, where we prepare responses before the speaker finishes, and the room is full of cacophony.

At times we even finish other's sentences or interrupt them and cut them off. Rarely is a pregnant pause left between one speaker and the next. This filling up of the space is a misunderstanding of the purpose of listening in mindful conversation.

We do not listen in order to speak. We listen in order to listen. No response is required. The speaker comes to know that when she comes to an end with her words, no one will enter this space. The speaker comes to know that the silence following her sharing will allow her to feel the power and insight of what she has shared. This silence also allows her to see the portions of the sharing that did not clearly convey what she wished to share. This understanding grows into an intention to communicate more clearly in the future.

If we are able, even for a moment, to come to quiet, then resonance can occur. Accompanying resonance is reverence, which involves the capacity to experience the other as a Self, as sacred, even if what they happen to be sharing isn't particularly special or new at the moment. This quiet is much like what occurs when in the presence of ancient beings, such as virgin forests of redwood evergreens in the seaboard of the American West, or the Allegheny's "Hearts Content" old-growth forest in northwestern Pennsylvania. At the bodily level, this resonance is termed kinesthetic resonance, at the soul level, sympathetic resonance. At the thought level, where the reflective apparatus of the brain mirrors the other, it is called limbic resonance.

Preparation

Requisites to a mindful conversation include: (a) daily practice; (b) holding the topic meditatively; (c) dyad/group consistency; (d) trust; (e) an ongoing agreement that members work out conflicts directly and immediately whenever feasible, knowing that there is no good time to address conflict, hence anytime is a good time; and (f) confidentiality, that is, "What is said in here stays in here."

Unlike in a dyad, confidentiality in a group setting cannot be required, only requested. You can suggest that members don't discuss outside what other members shared, and if they discuss what they shared, do it privately rather than at Starbucks. You never know who is sitting at the next table.

Daily Practice

Members of the group deepen the experience through a daily meditative practice of their own. The practice can be for as little as a few minutes, and can be focused on an attention-based practice such as training the mind to follow one thought along a course. That is a concentrative practice, devoted to an object; in this case, the thought is the object. Alternately, a mindfulness awareness practice complements the attention-based practice.

Before individuals come together to partake of mindful conversation, it is helpful if they have a daily solitary practice that involves the deepening of listening. Even a few minutes of wholly devoted listening is enough. Emptying oneself forms the heart of this practice, such that we do not form inner pictures of any outer worldly mental representations. After a time, glimpses of spaciousness open, and these experiences become cherished. Paradoxically, such moments cannot be sought, only prepared for. We construct an inner cathedral with enough space to allow spaciousness.

Seeding the Conversation

Choose a topic at least three days before you sit together for the mindful conversation and encourage each member to carry the topic into his or her meditation. If holding does not occur, then it often happens that speakers are not prepared for the topic. At these times, speakers sometimes speak off topic and fail to connect with the heart of the topic. In contrast, creating space to plant the topic within our consciousness allows for meditation and times during sleep to incubate it and receive imaginations, inspirations, and intuitions regarding the topic that may only manifest when in the presence of the other group members. When possible, choose topics that are nourishing for the group.

Physical Space

Before beginning a mindful conversation, the physical space preparation helps to create the intended mood of reverence. Choose an aesthetically pleasing room with natural light or incandescent lamps. Arrange a circle of chairs with no desks in front of them. Desks or tables could be behind or to the side if participants need space for papers and food for later after the mindful conversation is over. A candle, flowers, silks, or anything simple and aesthetically pleasing helps set a mood and suggest that "now we are going to practice communicating in this very special way." The candle is blown out by the facilitator after she recites the closing verse.

Silence

Creating a quiet space can be hard to find in the city. Close windows and doors to prevent background noise and interruptions. Is the sunlight going to shine into someone's face or be too hot on them? If so, close curtains. All these preparations demonstrate care for the members and attention to detail.

Drinking or eating during the conversation usually creates a distraction. If you need to unwrap a cough drop from cellophane, do it beforehand. Use the bathroom beforehand. Try not to have papers in front of you if the information written on them might tend to distract you. At rare times it may be helpful to have the question written on a half sheet of paper, particularly if the question is long and has several clarifying characteristics. If possible leave cell phones out of the room, or at the very least turn them completely off, so no vibrating, bells, or whistles distract the process.

Movement

Make sure you are comfortable in your seat. Move occasionally as necessary in order to be able to sustain the listening mood without being distracted by physical discomfort. Shift your body position so that you can come back into presence. Stillness is a movement. Just don't lean forward as a direct response or to seek the attention of the speaker. Don't choose to insert yourself through movement as a direct response to what gets spoken by another member.

Verse

Choose a verse and learn it together by heart. This creates a mood of listening attention. The rotating facilitator speaks the verse to begin the conversation. A facilitator can be stipulated to lead for one time, or for the number of meetings that the topic is explored, such as three times. Say this verse to remind everyone what you are about to do. The facilitator will speak the same verse to close. Learning the verse by heart brings a special quality into the room, versus reading the verse. Practice speaking the verse together outside of the mindful conversation time, so that all vowels and consonants are clearly articulated, and so that each person brings a similar inflection to the room when it comes to be their time to facilitate.

Time

Fifteen minutes is a good amount of time to apportion when first practicing mindful conversation. Participants can work up to a full thirty minute session. However, for persons who have no relationship to practicing listening in silence, begin with a few moments. Exercises can be developed in pairs whereby one person speaks about any topic and the other listens for sixty seconds. Then both speaker and listener share their experience.

Don't use the full time allotted if the topic is done. End early. "We said what we needed to say." The facilitator's job is to listen for when the conversation feels complete for the session. Sometimes the topic won't be particularly fruitful, and another topic needs to be chosen for next time. Sometimes a last comment may fuel the next week's topic. Immediately following the conversation, close it with the same verse, spoken by the facilitator again, and then choose the next week's topic using dialog, yet still trying to maintain lack of reaction.

Entering/Leaving

Coming in late and leaving early can be disruptive to a group. Most often, it is agreed upon that no one enters or leaves during a mindful conversation. Tell the group leader ahead of time when possible if you will not attend. If you cannot attend the whole conversation it is better to skip it. The group leader shares which members will be absent on a given day. Other group members mention anyone else who needs to be absent. Start on time with whoever is present.

Populations

Mindful conversation can occur in a myriad of contexts, including alone, in dyads, and in groups. An example of working alone would be in working with dearly departed friends and family members. This working can occur seasonally when the veil between the worlds grows thinner during the day of the dead (All Hallows Eve), weekly on Saturdays when many persons in the Anthroposophical community read spiritual texts aloud to those across the threshold, or anytime you choose to sit and establish your presence with an intention to communicate to unseen loved ones.

Patient

Mindful conversation in dyads can occur with colleagues, family members, friends, and in therapeutic settings. This space can be cultivated when one person, who has been practicing mindful listening in herself, brings the practice as an invitation to a partner. Until this is brought overtly, a subtle or covert process takes place between the two persons.

Care is needed here in order not to adversely affect the relationship. If you begin to practice non-reaction when listening to someone close to you, yet you do not tell them what you are practicing, they may feel or interpret the opposite of your intention to connect deeply with them; they may assume you are not listening at all, not engaged, aloof, or just being odd or manipulative. This practice bears no resemblance to the tabula rasa or blank slate that psychoanalysis is often ridiculed for, although to be fair to psychoanalysts, this ridicule is unsubstantiated, except in loudspoken rarities. Far more often, psychoanalytic listening is dynamic and approaches the method articulated here.

Why is it so important to explicitly share what you seek to accomplish? Facial expressions, gestures, verbal responses, nodding, touching, and other outward forms that demonstrate affection will not be present to your friend or patient. She may assume you do not want to be with her, even though quite the opposite is the case. Discretion, common sense, and sound judgment are needed when introducing this practice with a patient, friend, or colleague. Failing this, the reversal of intention is likely.

In fact, before you begin working in this way, it is essential that you have built a solid relationship on the niceties of ordinary connection, including humor, being real, enjoying each other's company, admitting to screwing up and committing to fixing it, etc. Mindful conversation is an extension of a working worldly relationship, not a replacement for it. Spiritual bypass plays no part in this work.

Group

An example of mindful conversation in groups can be practiced with any number of support groups in communities (e.g., schools, hospitals, prisons, and mental health centers). It is helpful if members have developed trust, and practices around listening and speaking as elucidated above. If not, modeling the method to the group and then practicing in triads, where the members—who in life were least exposed to solid communication skills or unable to understand what you are suggesting—get to observe the other two practicing in the triad. Biography work also supports members to get to know each other and to share and be vulnerable at increasing levels of depth. For example, create a space and allow group members to share for five minutes on a biographical topic specifically related to the conversation you intend to have together. Again, build on success and reduce anxiety by asking them to meet in pairs first and try out the activity before speaking in the group.

If a member shares something that you would like to discuss with them, either because it stirred something in you that you want to share and ask their advice about, or because you want to inquire further about their comment, wait until the meeting is over and ask the person for permission to discuss the topic before launching in. Remember they have the right to decline.

The Process

The term "mindful" in mindful conversation is not used in the traditional sense of mindfulness meditation which is awareness without an object. "Mindful" is meant as a concentration activity, an activity with an object, in this case a topic, from the root "topos" which means a space. We refrain from any trace of bodily, emotional, and mental reaction outwardly and inwardly. We will define conversation as distinct from discussion which takes place in ordinary consciousness, which is sometimes called mindlessness or intellect. We don't fill ourselves with a thought in response to whatever is brought from another person. We open to something greater than ourselves in order to possibly learn something new. This may be a challenge for those who want to nod or smile to show that they are interested, engaged, relational, and connected to the speaker. We practice mitigating intensities of joy and sorrow as a spiritual practice. If it feels a little wonky, artificial, or awkward, just remember how it feels when you first got on a bike! I invite you into just noticing that awkward feeling, and still practicing mindfulness if you can. I am not inviting you to suppress anything but rather to flow into a new channel of expression.

Try not to brighten the eyes, instead turn inward with a smile, inward with intoning such as "umm hmm" that you would normally communicate to your speaker. Let everything flow backward toward angelic wings behind us, providing nourishment to the spiritual world. Can we let that echo in us in a living way, with an inward smile or intonation?

We sink deeply into ourselves and see what is living for us in our relationship with our own angel and what wants to be shared with the group. After I finish my sharing there is no discussion. No piggybacking. No one begins speaking and says, "Based on what Edmund said..." We trust that there is an activity going on in the silence.

Paradox

Mindful conversation is analogous to a backward or backspace conversation, a countermovement conversation. The opposite of this backspace conversation would be a discussion, which flows back and forth on this side of the threshold. Try not to have a response to what is said. If we have a response we try to be empty and let it flow within us. We get out of our own way. Laughter is included in what we do not respond with. But let's be gentle with ourselves and nonjudging. Tears and chuckling will arise during these conversations. We develop awareness and practices around how to notice those responses without either moving toward them or away from them, just as I sit down with my client and I don't know what to do, but I trust that someone behind me does.

Practicing listening and speaking in this way does not blunt you to the gifts of the other, nor does it disconnect you. On the contrary, you are able to allow the speaker to hear her thoughts and words reflected back to her in a way never before experienced. And you are able to hear in a deeper way, particularly because eighty percent of communication is nonverbal. We know that attachment and bonding during our earliest years occurred nonverbally. As infants, our whole body was exquisitely attuned as a sense organ for tone, sight, sound, smell, and touch. At one moment we experienced our whole body like an ear. At other moments it was as if we were made of thousands of eyes. This right brain to right brain attunement, which cements relationships together in the healthiest of ways, is what mindful conversation adds to our current strength of left brain to left brain communication.

To Speak, or not to Speak?

How does our listening lead to our either speaking or not speaking? What are we listening for? Are we listening in order to speak? How do I judge that? The answers to these questions are discovered as one practices mindful conversation. Initially, some folks sense timing, which is a kind of "in the world," mechanistic listening. Others listen for a sense of breathing. Still others sense spatially when it is time to speak. Before you speak, ask yourself, "Does the thought that I feel called to voice feel germane to the present moment in the conversation?" And "Is this coming from me, or through me?" Just as Rumi asks himself, "Who speaks these words with my mouth?"

Ask yourself how: "How do I tend to contribute in the group? Do I tend to listen or speak, move forward or back? Do I just need to pipe in? Am I waiting for the other person to finish talking so I can talk? Am I thinking about what I am going to say next? Or am I remaining open, empty, and clear versus feeling tension or filling myself with sympathy or antipathy?" Some people feel moved inwardly, with a tingling neck or solar plexus;

another's heart begins to pound. A third person seems to see a word appear across her forehead. Sweaty palms, shifting breath patterns, or the person feels nervous, any of these may be somatic indications to share.

Challenge yourself to share the non-share, the thing that frightens you the most, the thing you do not want to say, the thing that someone might react to, or take the wrong way. Remember that you do not have to understand what you are about to say. Often it does not make sense or seems opposite to sense. Often it may make sense later or others will understand it right away. Speaking from the right brain intuitive center is a challenge.

Sensing Others

Other members in the group seem to sense when someone else is going to speak. This often occurs when you find yourself in the role of facilitator. Your body may find itself turning toward the participant who feels called to speak next. Some joke that a "disturbance in the force" occurs when a person in the group is moved to speak. A facilitator who is present to this often makes eye contact with that person, and that contact helps to test whether the speaker really feels the need to speak. When hearts and space are open, and willingness to be seen and felt as members occurs, it is easier for facilitators to sense impending speakers.

Facilitators practiced in these methods rightly fear sharing their process because they are concerned that speaking about it may result in a loss of it. It is wise when first practicing these skills to remain silent about them. Because one's ability is largely unformed, we cannot speak intelligently about what is occurring. And like any prenatal life form, our practice is highly vulnerable to teratogens, which in this case means the killing power that our intellect can have on budding capacities in subtle endeavors. Given this, if we are to speak about our development in the area of mindful conversation, it is suggested to cultivate a mood similar to that you feel when engaged in the actual practice. This state-specific quality forms a protective membrane around the otherwise intellected telling of the process. In addition, it is as important, if not more so, to discern in your listener if she has the capacity to hear this sensitive process without adding anything to it.

It is important to know that not every member will allow a facilitator to sense her, which requires vulnerability. Individuals who are unable or unwilling to be vulnerable will often surprise the facilitator when they speak. And even those members who consistently open themselves to being read may not do so every time. Thus it is incumbent on the facilitator not to lapse into predicting patterns of response based on past performance. She must remain awake and choose to erase all predilections of what she thinks she knows about the individuals before her. As far as possible, she must forget that she knows them, must seek to forget their faces, their voices. Again, far from the seeming inhumanity or counterintuitive nature presupposed, this practice of forgetting allows the facilitator to see anew, and allows the individuals to be seen anew. It leaves the speaker totally free to show up in this moment, unencumbered by previous iterations. This allows maximum space to grow, to be different, and to surprise oneself with one's expression in the world.

Mindful Dialog: Blending non-reaction with decision-making

Facilitators each find the practice that works for them. Once a group has practiced working in this way for some time, then they can begin to grow this practice into meetings where agenda items must be decided. This is a rarified time out of busy-ness to step into this special space and work through things and conduct business in this way. Ideally there is a threefold rhythm in place of introducing the item and taking clarifying questions during the first week, discussing the topic during week two, and deciding it during week three.

Mindful conversation marries traditional meeting conversation at this point, so at some times individuals respond to each other. During this time, participants listen mindfully and then respond directly to the point just made. Thus manifests something between discussion and mindful conversation, akin to a mindful dialog. The hope is that both practices will be practiced by all individuals as indicated by the need of the dialog.

During meetings with agendas such as these, I keep my body open, legs slightly parted, solar plexus and heart space open. I do not eat or drink before the meeting, simply because I find my digestive processes encumbering and distracting. The sounds of gastric juices and an occasional burp don't tend to facilitate my listening skills. I sit upright and still. I am the rock in the river. The water braids itself around me. In terms of process, when the group is working well, we do not need to raise hands or make a list on the chalkboard for who gets to speak next. These methods tend to inhibit listening and prevent flow of conversation, because the next person in line to speak is very often sharing from a place that occurred up to several minutes ago in the conversation. A living conversation is difficult to sustain in this way.

How can a facilitator facilitate during a hybrid blended meeting such as this "mindful dialog," when the group must make a decision, as opposed to a mindful conversation, where nothing needs to be decided during that conversation? Here is one possibility. During the flow of the meeting, all of a sudden I feel a ripple, sometimes from the head, other times the heart. Or I feel nervousness coming from a member who may be finding her way to speak. Someone else may move his or her body, itching to say something.

Someone's breathing will shallow or deepen. I take interest, which means I inhabit the space between ("inter," the space between, and "esse," to be—interest) myself and the group. Sometimes I feel two persons at the same time, and often the thought is the same thought... Two sensitive persons have picked it up. Which one needs to say it? Do I play a part in helping to figure this out? I give it over to the two people and trust that the one who is meant to speak will speak.

All these experiences occur in silence. And I am not always accurate in my turning and attunement. The same thought can be heard by the group more effectively from this person in this moment and from the other in the next moment. Other times I may feel the need to gently hold back a speaker that might ignite a feeling mood that would stand in strong contrast to the directional current of the conversation.

Can they let go of saying what they wanted to say? It no longer feels pertinent. It would have been helpful three comments ago, but no longer. Shall I request that they hold their thought for a moment and allow another person to speak first, in the hope that this will allow them the time to reflect and determine whether what they have to share will move the conversation forward? I feel all of this as a movement, as their ripple; their flow guides me. And the only times when it works and when it was totally not me. I was not thinking. I was thought through. The facilitator conducts by being conducted. If I have stuff going on, I cannot feel people. The opening verse helps me to drop in and be acted through as a vessel. Singing helps too, and a relationship to dance and movement. I love the movement of language and the language of movement. I am more than a rock. I am seeking too. Like stroking a lyre's strings, not plucking them: Who needs to give a voice to the score? The meeting is humming in a beautiful tone. If not, do we need to stretch, or sing, or snack?

Freedom is the ultimate goal of conversation. How do we leave one another free to contribute? How do we choose a theme that is living? Everyone can say their thoughts and no one judges.

E. Some Dangers of Meditation

by Edmund Knighton

I would like to invite you to be mindful that, both for yourself and for people you may guide in meditation, during some moments in a person's life, meditation can be counterproductive. These moments include active manifestation of trauma, depression, anxiety, substance abuse, and psychosis. If you are a clinician, please note that for specific challenges, specific mindfulness techniques may be helpful (e.g., MBCT for depression, DBT for BPD, ACT for OCD).[12] Persons who tend to move and

---

12　Dr. Knighton refers here to Mindfulness-Based Cognitive Therapy (MBCT), Dialectical Behavior Therapy (DBT), Bi-Polar Disorder (BPD), Acceptance and Commitment Therapy (ACT), Obsessive-Compulsive Disorder (OCD). The acronyms provide a kind of gate-keeping function – if you don't know what the letters mean, you likely don't know what they are describing – and an invitation to learn more about the various techniques used for these complexes.

think rapidly, and those who do not value silence and reflection are unlikely to benefit, as well as those who tend toward brooding and cognitive reactivity.

Meditation is contra-indicated in the above situations. Other possibilities exist also, such as if chronic pain increases, or panic attacks return or ensue. Research has also found that during some moments, meditators can also feel unmotivated, bored, confused, disoriented, vulnerable, grandiose, guilty, and dissociated. They may experience paradoxical increases in tension, relaxation-induced anxiety and panic, or uncomfortable kinesthetic sensations.

Meditation increases awareness of your life, both of positive and negative aspects. When mindful, one is less likely to avoid unpleasant emotions or interpersonal problems. This may require adjustment and integration before the person is able to remain attentive to whatever arises. Meditation leads one into deep exploration of inner space. Grief, tension, and judgmental thoughts may be experienced for the first time with full attention. Tolerance needs to develop for such unpleasant material. Practitioners are taught to reframe such thoughts and feelings as mind events, but the capacity for disidentification takes time to manifest.

I encourage you to rely on clinical experience to determine your own and your clients' ego strength or emotional resilience. Decompensation when cognitive controls are loosened is a contraindication for sitting meditation. Fragile personalities may benefit if you shorten the duration of practice. In such cases, begin to become mindful, for a few moments. Then titrate, gradually increasing the time as the faculties of tolerance and disidentification grow. Practice your ability to be with fear, pain, trauma, dissociation, reactivity, escape, panic, in yourself and others. Become comfortable tracking body signals through observing breath, gesture, posture, eye contact, voice tone, prosody, tempo, and pitch.

Assess the ability in yourself and in the client to: (1) experience, contain, and integrate affect; (2) listen and respond in the present; (3) follow instruction; (4) remain in the room bodily and

soulwise; (5) practice yoga or another body awareness movement; and (6) organize thoughts, manage logistics, and time
commitment. Provide resourcing strategies regarding how to respond when disconcerting emotions arise (e.g., techniques for
stabilizing the body and mind through breath awareness).

If you have worked with meditation for a number of years and
you are guiding and supporting others in meditation, be able to
provide referrals to therapists and community resources surrounding these practices. Be able to offer the required support
both during and after training by guiding participants towards
reputable resources or referring to qualified meditation teachers or communities (e.g., meditation centers or established practice groups) that could both guide and support an individual in
his or her process. Finally, remind participants that they know
best what they need and when a type of practice will or will not
work, e.g., yoga for rheumatoid arthritis. People are responsible
for their own well-being, both in the present moment and in the
long-term.

Invite the client to discern what may be harmful and counsel
him or her how not to engage in such activities. When in doubt,
invite the client to speak with you individually.

First off, screen prospective participants by asking a few questions. Ask them, "Have you taken workshops previously that involved groups? If yes, could you describe the experience?" One
of the biggest reasons for negative experiences or dropping out
of a group occurs if participants are uncomfortable in group situations, especially if they experience strong emotions. Second,
ask them, "Have you ever experienced trauma? (any intrusive
thoughts, avoidance, body arousal)? Alcohol/substance abuse?
A mental health problem?" If yes for any, inquire further and
then make a determination about what's the appropriate course
of action.

F. Aids to Meditation

by David Tresemer

In chapter 11, the authors have given some hints about their own
practices of self-care, including meditation. Look there for some

good ideas. As for poems or verses that stimulate a relaxation of consciousness and an expansion of imagination, there are hundreds of these—though, at times of dire need because of personal crisis, one can feel that these resources have all suddenly disappeared. Find a poem or verse that you memorize and keep it with you, in your personal tool kit, so to speak. In the anthroposophic psychology training, we emphasize not only the meaning of the words, but also how they are said, and sometimes how they are gestured with the hands and body.

Resources Mentioned in the Chapter
(in addition to the resources at the end of the book)

Germer, Christopher, and Ronald Siegel (2013). *Mindfulness and Psychotherapy*, second edition. Guilford Press. This includes a thorough review of the many studies done on the effectiveness of mindfulness training for a variety of ailments. Since we perceive mindfulness training in accord with anthroposophic psychology, these studies can be cited as support for an anthroposophic approach to psychological issues.

Goldstein, Joseph (2013). *Mindfulness: A Practical Guide to Awakening*. Boulder: Sounds True. This book offers a very clear outline of all of Buddhism—with sections on the four noble truths, the eight-fold path (referred to in chapter 11), the seven factors of awakening, and more.

Hughes, Gertrude Reif (2011). *More Radiant than the Sun: A Handbook for Working with Steiner's Meditations and Exercises*. Great Barrington, MA: SteinerBooks. This little book is a goldmine of meditations, and importantly, Gertrude Hughes' recommendations on how to use them.

Kabat-Zinn, Jon (2011). *Mindfulness for Beginners: Reclaiming the Present Moment—and Your Life*. Boulder: Sounds True. When a Buddhist says something is for beginners, it means everyone: Especially those who have lots of experience approach these matters with a fresh or "beginner's" mind.

Satprem (1999). *The Mind of the Cells*. Paris: Institut de Recherches Evolutives. This little book investigates the quality of consciousness of our trillion cells, as initially explored by Mirra Alfassa, to whom Satprem was student. It gives points of view far beyond the conventional, and a glimpse into vastly different modes of consciousness. If nothing else, it is expansive for one's meditation.

Tresemer, David, and Lila Sophia Tresemer (2014). *The Sophia Elements Meditations*. Boulder, Colorado: www.SophiaLineage.com. Here are specific meditation techniques for developing imagination and then inspiration.

Zajonc, Arthur (2009). *Meditation as Contemplative Inquiry: When Knowing Becomes Love.* Great Barrington, MA: Lindisfarne. Once the General Secretary of the Anthroposophical Society of the United States and a professor of physics at Amherst College, and now president of the Mind-Life Institute, Dr. Zajonc combines these fields of expertise to create a marvelous document on meditation.

CHAPTER 13

Seeing the Initiatory Process
in Pathologies
by William Bento, Ph.D.

Let's look at a phenomenon by which none of us is left untouched, whether through our own experiences or someone else's. I'm referring to the many varieties of addictions that tend to run people's lives. In the grip of addictions individuals tend to lose a sense of their "I."

In chapter 3, I introduced you to the salutogenic paradigm. I asked you to hold to that healthy, wholesome picture of the human being. Yet one must not turn a blind eye to pathology. We have to be conscientious enough to know that no one is really excused from having some kind of encounter with it. It is very important for us to know how pathology in our time actually indicates to us something of what humanity as a whole is undergoing as a kind of initiatory process into the future.

Rudolf Steiner was prophetic in addressing the fact that humanity would be crossing the threshold at the end of the 20th century. He warned that there would be tremendous consequences to this crossing if done unprepared, if done without some kind of navigational map such as he provided for us in spiritual science. With all of the best of his intentions, spiritual science is still one of the best-kept secrets in the world. It is not accessible. Anthroposophic esoteric schooling is not the only way one could navigate across the threshold of the spiritual world. In fact, Rudolf Steiner isn't the only one who pointed to this capacity of spiritual science to assist human beings. Many, many spiritual traditions have also described this phenomenon of crossing the threshold between our physical mundane world and the spiritual world.

Every night we make this crossing when going to sleep. However, when one moves from one dimension of awareness or experience to another without conscious intention and will, it's very jarring and it can disorient us. Part of this disorientation is the phenomenon that in our soul life, we naturally have a certain unity of thinking, feeling, and willing. Those three are always somewhat interrelated. If I go into a room and smell something rotten in it, I'm not only having a sense experience, I am also feeling disgust. I plan how to get out of the room as soon as possible, and then I leave because it's unbearable. You can see that thinking, feeling, and willing will always be interrelated as long as we have a healthy consciousness.

In crossing the threshold of the spiritual world, thinking, feeling and willing separate. They go their own way, so to speak, so it's very possible to actually confront something that is horrific and terrible in the spiritual world without all your faculties cooperating in your service. If your predominant faculty is merely thinking about it, there will be no feeling for this terror. You will miss what feeling used to tell you about a situation. It will appear simply as an object, a phenomenon, and you may be in a kind of trouble of which you aren't aware.

The consequence of the splitting of thinking from feeling from willing will lead to a kind of inhumanity. For the past thirteen years [since the year 2000], we have more and more frequently seen possibilities of crossing the threshold of the spiritual world. The events of 9/11 became a kind of global phenomenon in seeing the terror that actually does take place across the threshold. There we saw a tragic event, which set into motion a cloud of terror for everybody who observed it. It's not just the experience across the threshold in the spiritual world; it's an experience we're having on this side as well now.

This crossing of the threshold is not a one-dimensional crossing. With our sophistication and our capacity to understand the laws of nature, we're now creating a new world out of the forces of sub-nature, the realms of the forces that move invisibly below the surface of apparent phenomena. We don't only cross into the spiritual world, we can now cross into sub-nature. As we stand in the midst of both, they have tremendous influence on how humanity's consciousness can actually go forward.

Any psychology that doesn't really understand the situation of the time we're living in is bound to be ineffective. The situation is serious, for an immature or naïve psychology is more likely to harm than to help. The salutogenic approach, trying to keep the image of the whole human being, trying to keep the whole soul intact in every encounter, is absolutely essential. We know the human being as body, soul, and spirit, as a being who lives in a created social world. So if we take this term "humanity" as being all of us, then we must realize that the whole society is crossing the threshold of the spiritual world. Our whole society is encountering the creations wrought from forces of subnature. We are having to learn how to deal with a brand new set of elementals, those beings that animate the four elements as well as the living things that work within those elements. These influences or characters are ridiculed by a modern science that sees only the invisible that it wishes to see (as in X-rays and DNA codes). But we all have personal experience of their existence. I was just dealing with a set of elementals while I was trying to photocopy some papers, and I had a tremendous struggle to keep my center without feeling unduly frustrated. These things happen and they can affect our soul lives. We are creating more and more things, and having less and less being-ness, even within ourselves.

On the following page is an archetypal picture. On one hand this picture is about the human being, and we could say the human being has the capacity of soul to think (A), to feel (B), and to will (C). But what keeps this thinking, feeling and willing interwoven and harmonious within our being? It is the "I" (at G) that has this possibility of being a conduit to the higher spiritual world, and a conduit to that presence of self that we operate out of in our personalities. It is that sense which allows us to be ourselves, that sense of our temporal earthly biographies. The "I" connects the eternal and the temporal of our being.

Threefold Soul Capacities

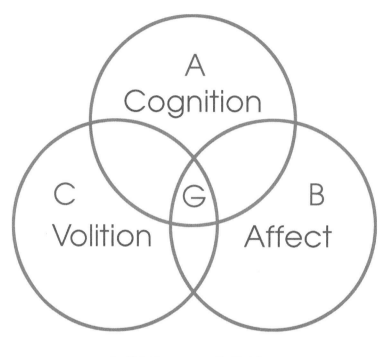

A=Thinking   E=Right
B=Feeling   F= Economic
C=Willing   G="I"
D=Cultural   H=Cosmology

To cross the threshold between this and the spiritual world, one can prepare by cultivating a well-developed "I," by sincerely focusing on and taking up the practices that are in spiritual science. Not merely the ideas which we find in spiritual science, but also the practice of it, wherein our feeling life relates fully both to the ideas and the practice. Those who have been able to survey the spiritual world as initiates, these individuals were able to keep their "I" intact at the same time their "I" was here, there, and everywhere. In other words, the "I" follows thinking, feeling and willing simultaneously, even though they may have split apart and exist in different regions of the spiritual world.

It's only through this sense of the "I" that we will be able to manage the kinds of eruptions that we've been discussing, eruptions in the behaviors of ourselves and our brothers and sisters, these unexpected and sometimes very unintended crossings of the threshold.

The aim of the cultural life is to assure that every individual is free to utilize his or her capacity of thinking. Each is free to exercise this spiritual activity of thinking in such a way that there is enrichment not only for one's self, but also for others.

We have also created a rights sphere in the realm of feeling so that we do not fall into just mere abnormality, but that we have an unconditional regard for each human being having the same rights as we do. The core needs (from chapter 3) are rights of every human being, and are presently not being honored in so many different ways. (See the drawing on the following page.)

We have with our willing capacity created an economic life where we can find a way to depend on one another to meet our bodily needs, an economic life that demands fraternity—working with brothers and sisters to create an economy that serves the whole. We can express our appreciation and gratitude for Sophia that gives us the substance to exist (chapter 6). We have festivals dedicated to the fact that we have been able to take in Sophia's gifts and exist on the earth.

This is Rudolf Steiner's idea of the threefold social order. He boldly opened up the possibility that human beings could take up what was emerging as psychology in an entirely different way. The 1910 Psychosophy lectures in Berlin were really his invitation to do so. In them we were told to look at the soul from the standpoint of its innate wisdom and not overlay too many intellectual concepts trying to figure out what it is, because we already know what it is, if we pay attention and fully experience the phenomena around and within us. That set of four lectures by Steiner is on phenomenal experiences, not concepts. We can extract concepts from them. From living with the experiences that the descriptions evoke, we can find a basis for comprehending these fundamental ideas that Steiner gives of the soul life.

In the 1910 Psychosophy lectures Steiner gave a living picture of the soul, and then seven years later he gave a vision of the three-fold social order. As you will recall, we looked at seven-year cycles (chapters 4 and 5) without necessarily giving it all its esoteric significance. Let it suffice to speak of the seven-year rhythm as an ordering principle that reveals development. So we have accentuated in the three-fold social order the soulful and practical outcome of a worldview that springs from Psychosophy, the Wisdom of the Soul.

Threefold Soul Order

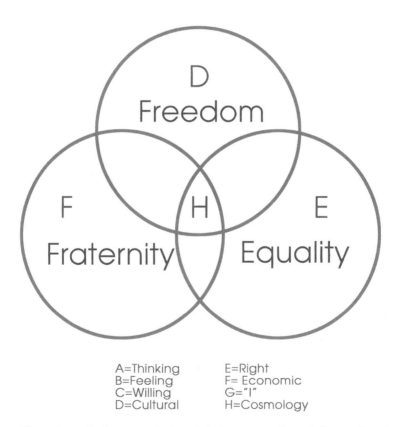

A=Thinking
B=Feeling
C=Willing
D=Cultural

E=Right
F= Economic
G="I"
H=Cosmology

There is an intimate relationship between the wisdom of soul life and that which we would call social life. Social life is nothing but the support for the soul life to exist in as free and creative a way as possible. And when that is hampered, we have problems. At the center of this three-fold social order, where all three are interwoven for us, the "I" stands. Moving through the I is the entire cosmos. Out of this center a cosmology needs to exist, for through it we gain a map that our "I" can use to navigate our soul's journey and to keep us in touch with the higher realities of the spiritual world.

At the center of these three circles (at G, and then at H) is a core need I have identified as "alignment." Because we in the western world have no consensus of cosmology any longer, we not only find ourselves lost and at times empty of meaning, we find filling this vacuum an increasingly strong drive: a drive for things and more things. Our western world is driven not by cosmology, where we are in relation to the stars and the stars' purpose for us, but by a fascinating drive to build and be merged into a world of technopoly. We are creating a very different world from that which our ancestors inhabited.

Just down the road in Palo Alto, we have an institute that is preparing to merge the fruits of scientific innovation (cultural sphere, labeled D) in its highest sophistication, with the driving force of capitalism (economic sphere, labeled F) with its highest sophistication. The emergence of singularity, of human beings actually being fused with machines, with computers, and robots, is at hand. There is no question now that technopoly reigns supreme. This isn't something that is just for curious science fiction enthusiasts. It is a riddle before us all. This is something real, something we must face in the next few decades. And it is prophetically what Rudolf Steiner pointed out, stating that humanity will one day be at a place where it may lose its humanity to machine or animal. This is a very serious situation.

Thus when we talk about anthroposophic psychology, it must also include understanding all the social and cultural influences that are impinging upon the human being. The human being does not live in a vacuum. Each human being who suffers with some form of pathology is really only mirroring something about the society we live in and the possibilities that will spring up due to our own particular weaknesses as a species. We have to draw strength from imaginations that will allow us to navigate these pressing dilemmas.

What happens in the crossing of the threshold of the spiritual world is a dissociation of our human personality, and we will all undergo that. For a period of time that is an important experience, but to be trapped in that dissociation would lead to a resigning of our humanity to something else. We would lose it.

In our society today, the basis for a lot of pathology can be seen as twofold in that we do not have spiritual alignment, and we are also experiencing forces in the world that are now trying to do their best to keep human beings isolated from one another. Each human being as an "I AM" being is being asked to create his or her own kingdom, and it's an exclusive kingdom. It's very tempting to have your own kingdom, but it excludes us from relationship, which is where we truly learn and grow.

For healthy psychological development, everything comes down to relations. Life is not all about one's personal self-development. Even taking up anthroposophy and finding the wonderful concepts within it will not translate into the moral fiber that gives the human soul its dignity. When you cross the threshold of the spiritual world, your attention will only be with your own thinking. That's a kind of cold, loveless wisdom. We have to integrate all aspects of our being here on this side before we get to the other side, because the other side will show you the terror of your errors.

Because of this particular crossing of the threshold of humanity, we are experiencing a number of things. In our personal "I" kingdom, our individual islands, we all are suffering under the weight of deep loneliness. It's a loneliness that comes out of a certain form of grief. We're grieving the loss of our connection, our connection to each other as spiritual beings when all of us had no physical boundaries. Nothing separated us from being with one another, from seeing that every thought was transparent, and every feeling could actually be experienced, every action was a kind of effect upon whether we felt uplifted or deflated. There was an immediacy of understanding that didn't take a whole lot of cognition. To some degree today, we all long to have this kind of experience. For this experience, people are crashing the gates of Heaven by whatever means they can find.

Addictions, as we presented in chapter 9, are another symptom of trying to escape from the utter despair of loneliness. Addictions betray a longing for finding some spiritual alignment that our society is not providing. Addictions show a longing for finding another human being who can recognize you. These qualities of loneliness are at the core of much of our pathology. We experience a deep existential despair. Looking at some of the drawings that Roberta has brought from clients, we saw people who are suffering from deep depressions and trying to escape, whether through alcohol, drugs or some form of abuse. But what did we see there? We saw people whose rights as Human Beings had not been honored, who were treated as objects. The 6-year-old child who had to become the mother and cook; the other one who had to be as far away from her father as possible to keep from being abused. How do we protect these rights? This is what our children are growing up into, a world in which the protection of rights is not safeguarded.

What arises out of this condition is a justified and righteous anger, a powerful indignation. No child should ever be wounded, hurt or exploited, and no adult should be either, and it's happening every day, even in the violence of how we talk to one another. One doesn't have to have a physical blow to experience being psychologically abused.

These worsening human conditions lead to a whole realm within our society wherein violence and the struggle for survival predominate. It is not the struggle that we should be focused on. The struggle should be in redeeming and reclaiming our humanity. We have a cultural life that no longer has the enlivening jubilation of festivals, the rites of passage, or the sacredness of rituals, which give us an opportunity to be spiritually grounded, which give us our alignment. Now we go to the theatre, we go to the show, as passive consumers, not as participants. We don't even have to go to the show, we can pick up our cellphone and watch a movie. Soon you can put on a pair of glasses and just be watching cinema as you go down the street.

We're surrounded with virtual realities. So many of these virtual realities reveal a longing gone awry. In the ancient civilization of Atlantis, we could have such vital imaginations that we could enter it together, one with another. There was a sense that we could actually see the spiritual beings in dance and play. The whole world was colorful, lively, and vital. The heavens were open to our perception. It isn't as accessible now. In a yearning for that ancient ease of communion, people, without developing the "I," are trying to find a way to create that kind of instant clairvoyant capacity.

All kinds of psychosis are being set loose. It becomes very difficult to know whose life you're living, what is reality, and what is fantasy. Because we're not really calling upon our culture to be innovative, imaginative and active, we're being lulled into a passive complacency. There is an inner emptiness, a lack of self-confidence, and a lack of capacity to be creative. This means we become all the more dependent on what is given to us rather than on what we can create from our own wellsprings of creativity. Thus we have deep insecurities in the capacity of the human being to maintain dignity. Many of us are simply losing faith in humanity, the world, the spiritual realms....

None of us are exempt from experiencing how the current global economic conditions are shaping our lives. We live in a world marked by competition, not cooperation. The ideal of fraternity will never arrive if that is the way we continue to look at our economic sphere. What does the dominance of the markets do for most of us? It puts us in a state of perpetual fear. Will I have bread on the table tomorrow? Will my house be taken from me? This worry is not just for those who have been traditionally called the disenfranchised. This is everyone from the middle class on down—anything can be taken away now just because of the way the economic system has been set up. It is bound to collapse, and has collapsed in places, bringing immeasurable suffering.

All of these outer social elements are actually catalysts for our rude awakening into the days of the apocalypse. If you fall asleep in this time, it's a dangerous sleep you take. If, however, we see that all of these are really symptoms of humanity crossing the threshold of the spiritual world, then these world events are asking us to re-evaluate who we are, how we are interacting with each other, and why we experience what we experience. That is the true value of experiencing a world in crisis. Although it is not something most of us like to entertain, these situations are just a way to invite us to wake up and be prepared for our own crossing of the threshold.

For every "I," the crises of the world act as a precursor to an initiatory path. Everybody who wishes to step on a path of initiation will realize that the more they take up esoteric knowledge in their days, the more the mystery will visit their nights. They will begin to feel a transformation deep within their souls, and they will no longer sleep in numbness without awareness. One's sleep can then become super-conscious. One starts to have conscious dialogues in the night. This calling, this "night school" that we have invoked every evening of our time together, is closer to us than it ever was. One of the big issues on the part of the adversaries is to make sure that you do not prepare yourselves to go to sleep. With awareness, we can overcome that resistance, and tread the path of initiation into greater and greater realizations of what it means to be a balanced healthy human being.

But what are the usual facts? You can't sleep; you've got 1001 undigested images; you have been stimulated to the nth degree; you are restless. In short, you don't create the sacred space of crossing the threshold. Over 50% of Americans have sleep problems in one form or another, so if you don't sleep, you're not only not going to get the forces of regeneration that your physical, vital body needs, you're also going to deprive yourself of having a meeting with your own angel, and others of the divine realms waiting there to work with you. If you keep abandoning that nightly appointment with your angel, don't be surprised if that angel lets you down one day. If this occurs then you may well find yourself in agony and despair pleading, "Why me?"...and the aloneness and the isolation become even deeper.

[Edmund Knighton:] Here is a verse that may assist you in the task of constructive sleep:

I go to sleep.
Till I awaken
My soul will be in the spiritual world,
And will there meet the higher being
Who guides me through this earthly life—
Him who is ever in the spiritual world,
Who hovers about my head.
My soul will meet him,
Even the guiding genius of my life.
And when I waken again,
This meeting will have been.
I shall have felt the wafting of his wings.
The wings of my genius
Will have touched my soul.

[William Bento:]

Yes, I still live today with tremendous gratitude for my mother and father for the nine years of my life that they were together. During those years I never went to bed without being on my knees in front of my bed praying with my mother on my left side and my father on my right. I don't know how many still have this experience, and it was about my soul—the prayer was "Now I lay me down to sleep; I pray the Lord my soul to keep..."

There was still an innate folk wisdom, in the middle of the last century, on how to live life. Today it seems rather odd to ask someone, "Are you saying prayers with your child at night?" Or, "Are you lighting the candle?" Many of us here live in the Waldorf School world where that is common, but you might be surprised at how uncommon those things are generally in today's world. This quality of preparing yourself for sleep is being wrested away from us. This preparation to practice what you need to do in order to navigate and be consciously in communion with the spiritual world is under threat.

What is the main principle involved in meeting your angel? Homelessness. On a path of initiation one has to experience homelessness. All attachments to place, to persons, to customs, and to values must be let go of. One must surrender everything with which one has been familiar. There is no shelter to be found other than the interior of your soul. In there, it's not loneliness. There it is really being at one with oneself. And it allows one to then have perceptions and experiences of the world that can be seen anew. "Behold I make all things new." That is a matter of perception, that is, the ability to perceive what the truth is, even if unseen.

Homelessness has the qualities of grieving in saying, "I won't be the person I was yesterday, with all the pleasures that there may have been, because I have to become something other now." Homelessness is not just a sociological phenomenon; it is a psychological phenomenon of great importance.

We have spoken about Soul, and we've even touched upon the Sentient Soul, the Comprehension Soul, and the Consciousness Soul. In the sacred temple of the body, there are boundaries. I have my skin that allows me a pervasive sense of touch, of knowing this is me and everything outside is not me. In the soul we also have a boundary; we have a skin of the soul that Rudolf Steiner called the "sentient body."

Like the skin, the sentient body has a kind of porousness that can breathe. The sentient body has sense organs where the sense organs are unified, so that I can hear something at the same time that I can see something. Our whole system of twelve senses actually works through the sentient body. The world now is full of stimulation and sensations. We take in far more than we realize every day. When a sense perception grabs something in the outer world and brings it in, the first things that I experience are sensations. I say, "That's the color red," or, "That was the smell of a rose." All of these become alive in me. They stir, they move, they now become a part of my soul. We're taking in more and more sensations than we can even process. With that sensation we then try to create a visualization. What is it that is now living in me?

Just think of the onslaught of sense perceptions that we're all taking in every day. Each one of these sense perceptions actually brings some quality of sensation within you. It stirs something within you. There is constant activity taking place even if it's below the threshold of your consciousness. You try to make some sense of it. You create a visualization of that which you just experienced in your sense perception outside/inside. That visualization is a representation; it's a mental picture of what you just experienced.

Step one is the sense perception; step two is the sensation; step three, the visualization. Then, Steiner explains, you have the judgment, the activity of judging. You inwardly ask yourself, "Is this something that is meaningful? Is this something I can relate to something else within myself? Can I integrate it?"

This judging is a decision. This judging comes from the activity of the "I." But our sense organs are a vital part of our unconscious wills—to sense and see the world is the will to grasp it, whether it's my eyes going out and grasping an image or my sense of smell bringing in the essence of something. As human beings we have come to the earth because we love the earth. We want to unite with the earth. We unite with this earth, this abundance and plenty of Sophia, through the pathways of our senses. But it's an unconscious will that interacts. I can't shut my ears off. I might be able to close my eyes, but I don't want to shut the sense organs off unless I wish to go to sleep. We are just naturally sensing all the time.

Sensations tell us something, but only if you pay attention to them. All that we've been doing in these days of psychosomatic work, of embodiment, is remembering the physical body as the wise elder, and remembering that every sensation is the beginning of feeling. If I really do not bring my attention to what I just took in, I can't have a genuine relationship to it. And yet it may have a relationship to us that we don't want. Thus the "I" needs to be attentive to paying attention to the sensations. Then the birth of feeling as a sense is born. The visualization is the birth of a pre-thinking, a thinking, that helps us organize our experiences.

The way I have a mental picture of this computer before me is through my own perception, my own coloring. The way you have it will be different because we think differently, we organize our sense experiences differently. We are all of us having more and more challenges to sustain attention. If you do not sustain attention, then it's very difficult to process your experiences. Your experiences begin processing you. If you do not take hold of an idea and make it your ideal, you will be a slave to the idea. That's a form of compulsion. Thus ideas and notions and undigested impressions can become a form of addiction.

All these situations are challenging us to be awake and aware of what is really entering into our souls. Is it something we are saying yes to? With our sense perception of attention, are we focusing on what it is that we feel is important to us? Are we taking it in and forming a relationship to what we have just experienced? And can we visualize it, bring a mental picture of its value and meaning to us? Can we judge how we as human beings can use this experience for our development? Can we do this, rather than being arrested or skipping what that opportunity brings to us out of the experience?

We're in the Consciousness Soul Age, which asks us to be aware of Spirit; this is the mandate of our time. One of the most critical issues of the Consciousness Soul Age is to discern good from evil. It's a very difficult task, yet we not only need to discern good from evil, we must realize that in this time you have only two choices—either be good or evil will be you. There is not a whole lot of gray in this. We're being asked to choose what path of development the human being should go, so these questions are big questions. The human being should see the world as good, should see the world as beautiful, should see the world as true. But it's not a common experience, nor is it one that we actually have available to us at all times. We have to be with the good, be beautiful and be true. And that's the task with anyone in anthroposophic counseling—it's not something you do, it's something you ARE, it's this quality of Being.

So how do we do something that will be an antidote to protect our souls from so much that wants to wreak havoc within them? You have to be guardian of your own soul before you can attempt to stand by another and help that soul find its way. You can learn to be a guardian of your own soul through some of the practices shared in chapters 11 and 12, for example, through the basic six exercises of the meditative life.

What does the sentient body need most? The sentient body needs peace. It's very difficult to find yourself at peace with all the stimulation that surrounds you.

In the gnostic gospel called *Pistis Sophia,* Mary Magdalene had asked the Christ how one could actually confront these demons of the underworld. We might paraphrase, "How can we in the modern sense confront evils?" The Christ said, "What you need is to cultivate peace and within this peace you must find the power of righteousness. Within the power of righteousness, you must stand for the truth. And in standing for the truth grace will be yours." Basically he was talking to Mary Magdalene about the need for protection.

The quality of peace belongs to the sentient body. The quality of righteousness belongs to the sentient soul. In fact, there are other occasions where Rudolf Steiner named the theme of the sentient soul phase of life from age 21 to 28 as the acquisition of righteous anger. The world is not what it should be. Anyone in their 20s who doesn't have a streak of anger about not finding the world a better place than it is, is not tuly living, is not awake. This righteousness can act by standing up against all the complacency that may surround one—because complacency is an invitation to sleep. And we know if you go to sleep unawake, it's dangerous.

The quality of standing for the truth is the quality of the Comprehension Soul. The whole task is to discern what is true from what is false. Discern what is true and what is a lie, what is true within yourself and what is not so you can get to work on developing yourself. In the *Pistis Sophia*, Christ tells Mary Magdalene that if she finds her peace and stands for righteousness, in the fullness of truth then grace can occur. In the Consciousness Soul period we have to rely on grace, and that means we have to create spaces for Angels, Archangels, and Archai. These Spirits of Beauty, Truth, and Goodness can actually accompany us in life. In these times, the individual alone cannot face the evil that is unleashed upon the world. It's pure grace to have a friend to walk with.

Here is the situation. Peace is established by the practices you were doing this morning (meditative practices as given in chapters 11 and 12). If you're going to be an anthroposophic counselor working with people who are very distressed, severely damaged, hurt and wounded, you need to be sure that you are creating the space for spirit—for spirit to inhabit you, and for spirit to really take interest in the work that you are doing with another. You cultivate what comes out of this place of the inner meditative life so that you can continue it while awake with your client, so you can continue that quality of presence and mindfulness, of not being distracted, of being able to take in every perception. This practice Rudolf Steiner referred to as the new yoga: with each sense perception I have, I must learn how to unite with it in my soul, to breathe it in; I must become it; with each gesture I see my client doing, I must accompany them and do the gesture to find out what's in the gesture. This is developing a quality of righteousness.

The quality of righteousness takes a great degree of courage. And courage comes out of the still voice of the heart. When the heart is open, the voice of conscience speaks and guides what is right. But this element of knowing what is right, what is good and what should be good, is not something we can ever think about. We have to do it. We can't think it through, as it would always be late in the deed. This is the courage to risk going somewhere you may not know, somewhere that exists in that threshold between you and your client. You do this in order to be with them and be able to meet whatever wounds are there. Know that your client's wound isn't a singular wound, but is also shared by you and others. The courage of the wounded healer is not just a well-known phrase; it's a real experience. It takes a risk to leave your self. If I have practiced being homeless, then it gets easier and easier because I can experience not having an attachment to myself, which leaves me open to have an interest in the other.

The sense of truth: One has to be faithful to all that you have prepared yourself to know and to share, because in the truth we can free ourselves from the attachments to our wounds. The truth is being able to have some understanding that evil exists in the world, and at times it is not all that particular as to who or what situation it visits. Truth is in understanding that there is always a hidden reason for evil to exist. There is greater good to emerge from any wound. This truth, although it may not always be apparent, is something we have to stand for. It is a faithfulness in the human being. From Edmund we heard what faithfulness really is: It is never losing sight of that divine spark that still exists within the other human being. This kind of faithfulness is the source of healing; it's an activity that invites a healing process.

And lastly, grace. The grace has to be prepared. It's prepared by actually being willing to be engaged in the sacrament of humanness. Conversation is one of the most precious sacraments that human beings can share. We create a space, a chalice for something higher to exist. For me, the consultation room is where I practice this. That is the altar, that it is where it must be taken, into the Light and lifted up.

Why? Not all Spiritual Beings can understand a child being abused by a father. They can only understand such a phenomenon through us. We have to offer it up. For the spiritual beings to be as fully engaged in helping us, they need our eyes, they need our pain, our tears, our struggles. That feeds them; that gives them a sense of knowing how to help the human being at that being's crisis hour. If we do this, then grace falls upon us. It doesn't come as if it was some lucky fortune. It takes a lot of preparation to create the space for a Spiritual Being to come down into our experiences. Probably more than other places, these grand beings can enter when you are present with somebody who's been devastated and wounded, and your whole conversation is a prayer. You perhaps say inwardly, "Allow this being to be whole because I behold him or her as whole." My beholding is then joined by other higher Spiritual Beings.

What is this work that an anthroposophic counselor is doing? If they're actually aware of this larger dimension that we're living in, this time of consciousness soul, this time of a kind of rehearsal of the apocalypse, an anthroposophic counselor must see himself or herself as clearing the etheric world from the debris that gets in the way of others' ability to see the true healer, who is the Christ in the etheric world. We clear space for something much greater. Rudolf Steiner often said that if someone was meditating in a town, that light could be seen from miles and miles away. If you are working with somebody in your counseling room, this effort is generating a light that clears the darkness of the etheric world and it may become more and more apparent who is coming towards us as help, as the great friend, as the great healing spirit.

Everybody is on a path of initiation now. This is not something we need reserve for just a few initiates. This is something that we're doing together. But we're doing it in the context of the Grail. You'll recall Parzival was not allowed to go to the Grail on his own; he had to take his brother, that magpie black-and-white guy Feirefiz. And before long, everyone in the Grail Castle found out they were related. What a remarkable story that is, a wonder! In the same way, you have a task of attempting to accompany. Accompaniment is a central word here. You are on a path of initiation and so is the one who is suffering. The one who is suffering is actually your teacher.

If you start regarding the clients as your teachers on your path of initiation, you will have tremendous gratitude for them, gratitude that they have suffered as deeply as they did in order to bring you something of an opportunity to take your next step of development. When you take your next step of development, out of grace they do too. It can't help but work that way. Why? Because in the etheric plane, we are still all related. This longing we have in our astral body, this longing to be united with each other, is a very important motive. If we only identify with our physical body, we don't experience these steps as a reality.

I have tried to open our eyes a little bit to the social and cultural dimensions that pertain to our crossing the threshold of the spiritual world. Through this process you will have an experience of, "I am homeless, and yet at the same time I am longing to unite with everyone that I can. I will still have this experience of homelessness until I reach the Grail Castle, until I have actually come to the feast and the great sacrament of everybody being healed."

We don't stop the work; it never stops; we continue. As you journey on this path of initiation, you will come to know the way from homelessness to aloneness. When you begin to do this, there's an experience you'll have in homelessness that Rudolf Steiner and Valentin Tomberg described quite well. You will have experiences as if water is washing your feet. It's the first stage in the Christian initiation, the washing of the feet. This is really an etheric phenomenon. This is a feeling of "my feet carry me through my destiny." There you have an experience, the strength to know your destiny even in the state of homelessness.

As we bring more of this approach to the world, you will encounter the second stage of initiation: People will laugh in your face! They will mock you for these strange and quirky ideas. You're not out to change the world in one swift go, but you're out to make the world better one by one each day, and you have to stand for that truth. Too long those of us in anthroposophy have suffered the stigma of being a cult by being involved in spiritual science. The day is going to come when we can stand shoulder to shoulder with any clinician, because some will have listened to us and understood the depth that lives in this approach.

In the third stage of this Christian path of initiation we will be crowned with thorns; that's where we judge ourselves. Have we followed our ideals? Have we been listening to the breakthroughs that have come from the other side of the threshold? It's one thing to fail on this side; it's a very different thing to make a commitment to another and not mean it. We must have the strength to go forward and carry the cross of brotherly and sisterly responsibility for each other. We can and must carry this movement for an anthroposophic psychology into the world. It will have its ups and downs; it will be a burden at times; you will feel alone. But you'll learn to carry your cross. And if you fall, all you need do is just call one of us, your colleagues in this endeavor.

I'm overwhelmed with the fact that I can call on others when I fall. I don't know how many others can. But I can. I have others in my life who will pick up the receiver and be there. None of us are going to do this alone. We'll have to do this as a community, and then we can carry the cross, and we can undergo the transformation that we have been talking about. We undergo a transformation where I no longer live my life only as "I," but out of my spirit life I live my life as "We." This is the secret to the emergence of Spirit Self.

This kind of fellowship is a homeopathic dose to that disordering that's going on around us. In that we will have our realignment to find out truly who we are willing to become. In that longing to become that which is our ideal, we can then enjoy and celebrate the resurrection of Anthropos.

Suggested References for Further Study
(in addition to the resources at the end of the book)

Steiner, Rudolf (1921). "Anthroposophy's Contribution to the Most Urgent Needs of Our Time," Stuttgart, September 5, 1921, GA 78. A single lecture, available on the web from rsarchive.org.

Steiner, Rudolf (1979). *The Challenge of the Times*. Spring Valley, NY: Anthroposophic Press.

Steiner, Rudolf (1919). "Cosmogony, Freedom, Altruism," Dornach, October 10, 1919, GA 191. A single lecture, available on the web from rsarchive.org.

Steiner, Rudolf. "The Crossing of the Threshold and the Social Organism: Spiritual Life, Economic Life, Juridical Life," GA 193. A single lecture, available on the web from rsarchive.org.

Steiner, Rudolf (1980). *Initiation, Eternity and the Passing Moment*. Spring Valley, NY: Anthroposophic Press.

Steiner, Rudolf (1990). *Psychoanalysis in the Light of Anthroposophy*. Hudson, NY: Anthroposophic Press.

CHAPTER 14

Finding the Healing Spirit
by David Tresemer, Ph.D.

In the presentations at our seminar, and now in this book, we shared a picture of the human being much grander than what materialistic science offers. We saw how anthroposophic psychology comprehends a human being in all of its greatness. We tackled many challenges to human development in the personality disorders and the more serious psychological problems that humans experience.

Throughout the encounters with dysfunction and disturbance, a counselor is supported by the spirit of healing. A counselor can call upon that spirit whenever needed, and it comes.

In chapter 6, I spoke about Anthropos-Sophia. Anthropos connects with Sophia, working through the human "I" in the middle. It's as intimate as a marriage. In the Lineage of Sophia work, there is a growing awareness of Sophia as a living, intelligent being, not just conceptually, but somatically experienced, with whom one can have a living relationship. The divine feminine works through capacities of soul and capacities of spirit— and through the individuality of the human being, the "I."

Perhaps more important than the conceptual frameworks that guide an anthroposophic psychologist has been your encounter with those who practice it. Either in person or through these pages, in the beings of Roberta Nelson, Edmund Knighton, and William Bento, you can feel something extraordinary, a deep spring of power, warm and bright, and without fear. Each one is someone whom you could trust to understand and assist with the soul struggles in your life—someone who has accessed the possible human being, Anthropos, and brings that wisdom to others.

In my final comments, I will bring in some new perspectives on what we have already encountered, as a way of integrating them.

Journey through the Elements

What characterizes this process of Anthropos-Sophia working through the "I" of the human being? Trauma. That may sound strange, yet let's explore this more closely. Trauma is a factor of human life—shocks to the system, small and large. The threat of surviving or not surviving occurs on many occasions in one's life. We can speak about trauma in terms of the elements, warmth, air, water, and earth. In anthroposophy, we speak of the evolution of the whole world, first an entire creation characterized by warmth or fire, then eons later a creation that adds the element of air, then much later the addition of water, and finally our Earth evolution which adds the density of the mineral. Let's go through those elements in relation to trauma.

In the realm of warmth or fire, any sudden change in temperature can be felt as traumatizing, the sense of being unprotected in the cold or unprotected also in excessive warmth. If you are naked in the sun for even an hour or two, you feel it. Several hours and you might be testing the edge of survival. Exposure to the cold can likewise swiftly lead to hypothermia. The time that you can survive naked in freezing water is one minute. Any change in temperature or even anything above or below our comfort zone can be experienced as traumatic. We hold the memories of those encounters in our bodies. In an air-conditioned building, it's really remarkable the small number of degrees in which we feel comfortable. Anything above or below that range, and especially a sudden change in warmth, can be experienced as a trauma, either small or large.

The element of air is the carrier of light; the light of interrogation is a traumatic event. The flash of explosions can be a traumatizing event. In air itself, any brush with asphyxiation through being smothered, even for a minute, leaves the traces of trauma. Again it is remarkable how swiftly one reaches the limits of one's tolerance. Anything beyond that is remembered as trauma.

In the element of water, the realm of sound, one can experience trauma in, for example, heavy metal music. Some people actually enjoy it for that purpose; they try to traumatize themselves more than they've already been traumatized as a way of reducing the previous trauma in proportion. Intoxication with the waters of alcohol means pouring in something toxic. Young people are increasingly binge drinking, taking their bodies to the limits of tolerance, and sometimes over that limit into unconsciousness. These traumas are remembered in the physical, etheric, and astral bodies.

Water-boarding is a form of induced trauma. The interrogators strap someone to a board and put them under water until technically they are drowned. Then the interrogators pull them out and resuscitate them. They threaten the victim with another drowning unless he or she answers questions.

When the Inquisition prepared to question someone about whether he was a heretic in the eyes of the church, they tied his arms behind his back and lifted him up from the wrists so that his shoulders threatened to dislocate, a position called strappado. They hung him up for half an hour before they asked him a question about his beliefs. The accused would ask, "Why did you do that before we had even conversed?!" They answered it's just our policy. Just as water-boarding, this was a threat, via trauma to the body, of greater trauma. These experiences go deeply into the physical, etheric, and astral bodies.

The punishments meted out by the Inquisition were experiences of trauma in the earth element. Gravity can be traumatizing. Whenever a child falls or gets knocked over, that's a kind of trauma, small or large. Gravity clunks us to the earth.

The four elements were cited in chapter 3 in relation to many different psychological categories, for health and for dysfunction. The four elements also relate to trauma.

One characteristic of trauma is that you cannot remember;

another is that you cannot forget. In your biography and in that of your client, these experiences become extraordinarily important.

The Greatest Trauma—Shared by All

The greatest trauma that each of us has undergone is birth. In a very short time, we each moved from warmth to cold, a rapid and large temperature change. We emerged from darkness into bright light. We reversed the process of drowning—we were happy in our water-soaked lungs and then suddenly we took in our first breath of air. It burned, that first breath. From the watery realm where sound was muffled and we had the rhythmic sense of heartbeat, we experienced loud arrhythmic sounds for the first time. There are few sounds that can match a surgical instrument being thrown into a metal pan. That jarring noise to a newborn extends far beyond the pain threshold in hearing.

At birth, we experienced the gravity of the earth element in a new way. From a place where we had been buoyed and floating, we were knocked down flat. We couldn't get up. As infants all we could do was wiggle. Perhaps this is why adults are willing to spend many thousands of dollars to go up in an airplane to experience thirty seconds of weightlessness. They can get back that feeling from before birth.

We are all trauma survivors of the large trauma of birth. How did we survive that? We've had to call on the spirit of healing. Astrology is based on the idea that you can't forget the birth experience. It has been seared into your being, a kind of branding of every cell in your body. You live the rest of your life, certainly the first half of your life, conditioned by that branding. This suggests that, if you know the time that some large traumatic event occurred, you can treat it like a new birth. A new biography begins then.

The only way you can survive your birth, or survive the many other traumatic experiences that you may have had, is to contact the healing spirit.

Healing means whole, but it's better than whole, because healing is a verb. Whole suggests that there is a state of wholeness that you can attain. There's some activity that you could perform or diet you could eat, after which you could say: "I am now whole. My homework is done. I don't have anything else to do and from now on I'll just party." That finality never occurs. Healing, realizing wholeness, is an ongoing process, where you move between Sophia and Anthropos, move through the cosmos amongst all the characters that we've mentioned, become increasingly aware of them, increasingly interact with them. Healing means moving freely in realms of soul and spirit.

Through the Elements to the Spirit of Healing

During a morning meditation, you can go through the sequence of the elements.

Paralleling the process of creation of the world, you first feel your relationship to warmth. Yes, I was warmer in the womb, but I've taken on the challenge of this cooler world and am generating my own warmth. I feel comfort and safety in my own generation of warmth. Are you warm enough right now? Have you managed the warmth element?

I feel my relationship to air and light. Yes, I'm breathing, breathing air. I've gotten quite used to that. In each breath I bring in light.

I feel my relationship to water, feeling the watery nature of my own body. This water is good water.

Finally, I feel my relationship to earth, to bones and substance, all borrowed from Sophia. Indeed, all the elements come from Sophia, and I borrow them for expression through this body.

This sequence reminds me that I am safely imbued with the elements, living with the elements.

Recall the meditation with the sun, that we can relate to the three planes of frontal, sagittal, and horizontal (from chapter 7). Above a sun, below a sun, working the horizontal plane. Before the sun, behind the sun, working the frontal plane. To the right a sun, to the left a sun, working the sagittal plane. The sun in every direction. I am safely supported by the sun's power in every direction.

And in the center of these six directions, what do we discover? The verse tells us it's something more radiant than the sun. *More radiant than the sun! Purer than snow, finer than ether, is the Self, the spirit of my heart.* At the center of all these suns, my true "I" is more radiant than the sun, the spirit of the heart. *I am this Self.* I am this Self, capital "S," for the self that knows the realms of soul and spirit. *This Self am I.* Speak it aloud:

> More radiant than the sun,
> purer than snow,
> finer than ether,
> is the Self,
> the spirit of my heart.
> I am this Self.
> This Self am I.

These words deserve repetition and pauses to experience them fully. *I am this Self. This Self am I.* They form an entry for the spirit of healing.

Group Trauma

I'd like to describe an event with a musician offering a sound meditation with gongs. His central brass cymbal was huge, about four feet in diameter, hanging on a frame. He sat before it cross-legged on a bench with many different implements on right and left. I came forty minutes early. Already there was a line of thirty people out front, all with cushions and sleeping bags. I had none of this as I was attending for the first time. When they entered they began to place themselves with their heads toward the center lying down on their cushions and sleeping bags. Each made a little campsite. I wouldn't have been surprised if someone had set up a little burner and started making tea. They packed in very closely, heads to the center, one circle, then another circle further out, and so on. He was to play for an hour.

The musician talked about the sacredness of sound. He said this vibration will come through your head and it will loosen up some toxins, but they'll go out through your feet and into the earth. Then you will feel healed. That was all he said. I thought immediately, that's not an adequate introduction if anything of what he says is true, either negative or positive.

I had heard gong performances before. I was concerned from the beginning because he said it will get loud at a certain point, but don't worry, it won't affect your hearing. He didn't mention that it's not your hearing that's most at risk from loud noises. It's your otoliths: Inside the balancing organs of your ears, there are tiny little hairs with crusty calcium deposits on the tops, little stones. Oto means hearing; lith means stone. If you tilt to the side, gravity pulls the stones down through the viscous medium of the inner ear. Nerves in the hairs feel that movement and your brain tells you that your head is tilted. When you bring your head back up to vertical, the stones spring upright, and your brain says that you're upright. With loud sound, the calcium deposits on the otoliths can pulverize. They turn to dust which falls down to the floor of the balance organ. This is something that can't be fixed. I'm normally optimistic about the body's ability to heal, but some things can't be fixed.

I was concerned about the loudness. I started out lying in the third circle from the center because I didn't want to get in the way of the people who ardently desired to be close. Soon I got up and sat down on the outer bench to observe. The musician was a master at drawing interesting sounds from his gong. Most of the time he was tapping the gong rhythmically with one hand. For his tools he had rubber balls on sticks, and whisks, and large, white, fluffy balls on sticks. From his tapping he excited a wide range of sounds from his gong, especially a long low standing-wave roar.

At the beginning it was delightful, stimulating for me a wide range of imaginations. Then it started to get loud, so intense that I could see it blasting people's etheric structure. People have structures around them, etheric and astral bodies. The waves of sound were blasting the structures away. At a certain point I heard the words very clearly in my mind: "Leave this room immediately!" I would have done that, as the words were so strong. Those who look after my welfare were speaking out on my behalf. I paused; I asked, "Is there an alternative?" Because I wanted to stay if possible, to see it through. "If you shield yourself thoroughly and immediately." I did so, something anyone can do. I created a shield, a kind of cylinder of light around me. I also held my hands over my ears. There were only two other people in the room with their hands over their ears. The inner voice instructed, "Wait and watch closely." The sound grew louder.

I observed that out of the torsos of the people lying with their heads toward the center there began to rise little bits of stuff, a kind of crud. The room began to fill up with these smidgens of rejected junk, fragments of old habits, broken parts of bad memories. First it was hundreds and then it was thousands of specks of stuff floating in the room, and I could only think, "This is going to be a very big cleanup job." And I heard, "Wait."

Some people's heads were only two feet away from the cymbal. I was very concerned about that. I noted that the musician inserted earplugs into his own ears. No one was watching except for me, because everybody else was there because they enjoyed this kind of catharsis. The decibels climaxed and then slowly receded, going back through the realms that had stimulated my imaginations. At the end the musician spoke about sacred sound and temples and Tibetan traditions in which he had trained. The clouds of etheric junk continued to float about.

The audience began to get up, to pack up their campsites, and to say to those lying near them, "Wow, wasn't that amazing?" I observed many, dazed by the experience, begin to rebuild their energetic structures from within. These etheric structures are necessary for us to function in the world. Knowing how to walk is a kind of structure; patterns of behavior are structures; language is structure. These people began to restructure themselves. Then the most amazing thing happened—this was why I was instructed to "watch." The little bits of crud began to be absorbed to the people nearest—phhtt, phhttt, phhttt. By the time everybody left, there were only some bits of crud still floating in the room. In the midst of this affair, there had been a flurry of crud in the atmosphere, but then it all went out the door again attached to people. Sadly, many went out the door with stuff that wasn't theirs originally. I realized that catharsis should always include two aspects—transformation and replacement.

First, transformation: you may have observed a hands-on

healer who works on someone; you may have seen them make a flicking gesture off to the side, ostensibly to get rid of the crud that they had just removed from the client. Whenever you observe such a phenomenon, you need to ask interiorly that you be shown what's happening with the flick. Some of the time the healer has made an arrangement with divine beings who take what's been flicked off and transform it. This is a miracle, and worth observing. Some of the time, the healer flicks it off and it's moved but not transformed. It started as crud and ends up as crud, floating around and sticky, waiting to stick on to something else. The client gets up and says, "whoa, that was an amazing experience," and as they move toward the door, the crud comes back into them—phhtt, phhtt—because it's familiar. Not transforming the rejected energy is in my view irresponsible. You have to learn how to do that with your clients. The spirit of healing can assist you in that process.

Second, replacement: When you flush all that crud, you create space that you must with awareness and intention replace with something else. You need to fill the spaces with something different, something full of light, something strong. This fills the vacuum and the crud is much less likely to come back in. Again, your guide is the spirit of healing, drawing from realms whose existence materialistic psychology denies, yet everyone knows is real and true.

I speak this story because it has a little moral about how to work with energy and also because it illustrates capacities that counselors—and all human beings—deserve to have. There are expanded forms of seeing, new forms of sensing, available to all. Recall when I talked about the senses (in chapter 6), that we have a conventional view of senses that is small, whereas actually each and every sense can move deeper into matter and also deeper into cosmic refinement. We each deserve that expansion in both directions of our senses. When you go beyond the narrow range of consensual sense reality, you are far more likely to feel and perhaps to meet the spirit of healing.

For me there was an additional lesson from this experience: Some people, including the clients that walk through the door of the counselor's office, may carry stuff that didn't originate with them personally. It can better be worked with when understood as the crud arising in the journey of Anthropos toward Sophia through human beings. The client has taken it on, perhaps not deservedly, but perhaps as a service to the one from whom it originated. Permitting this possibility, we can tackle the aberrations and sufferings that we've been studying—without taking too much time to assign the dysfunction to a particular cause, and without blame.

Finally, this story relates to the question, "Where is the spirit of healing in this experience?" The spirit worked through me, from within my own being, permitting me to see what was happening in the room. That is often how the spirit of healing can be experienced, not as a being exterior to myself, but from within myself. This is where the counselor can find the spirit of healing, from within.

Capacities

Inspired by our study of anthroposophic psychology, we seek to develop greater awareness and more sensitive perception. These are capacities that we must develop. There is a responsibility that one takes on by learning about these expanded capacities of human beings. You now have the challenge and the ability to respond to your own development in relation to your Self (chapters 11 through 14 on Inner Development) and in relation to those who have needs of your expertise (chapters 7 through 10 on Clinical Issues).

You must continue to develop all that you've learned in this study and apply it, either professionally or simply in your relationships to yourself and others. We're all odd and eccentric and have strange personality patterns and physical imperfections, but that kind of variety merely announces the human growth process. It's our willingness to work on those things that makes the difference, working with the assistance of the spirit of healing, the spirit engaged in our ongoing growth. When we seek the spirit of healing, look no further than your heart—spirit of healing... *spirit of my heart... I am this Self. This Self am I.*

APPENDIX

References for
Anthroposophic Psychology

*[A more thorough list of resources and references for anthroposophic psychology is available at www.APANA-services.org. Specific references related to the topics of chapters are cited by the individual authors at the ends of chapters. Double asterisks ** here indicate books, resources, and authors that are particularly helpful.]*

ANTHROPOSOPHY as it relates to anthroposophic psychology

Baur, A. (1993). *Healing Sounds: Fundamentals of Chirophonetics.* Fair Oaks, CA: Rudolf Steiner College Press.

**Bamford, Christopher. He has edited a great portion of Steiner's work, with introductions that open up anthroposophy in a completely new way. Watch for any of the books that he has edited.

**Ben-Aharon's work brings anthroposophy into the cutting edge of trends in modern science, philosophy, and art. Each of these have exceeded the bounds of consensus reality, and demonstrates how that anthroposophy is the best way to apprehend these changing times.

Ben-Aharon, J. (1995). *The New Experience of the Supersensible.* East Sussex, England: Temple Lodge Publishing.

Ben-Aharon, J. (2011). *The Event in Science, Philosophy, History, and Art.* VirtualBookWorm.com.

**Bento's work can be accessed through his thesis (citation at chapter 5), and the following book, as well as through a host of articles and lectures given all over the world:

Bento, W. (2004). *Lifting the Veil of Mental Illness: An Approach to Anthroposophical Psychology.* Great Barrington, MA: Steiner Books.

**Star Wisdom forms an important part of anthroposophic psychology in its connections beyond the social realm to the heavens and their impacts on consciousness and behavior. This book traces the crossing of two comets in relation to modern social phenomena.

Bento, W., R. Schiappacasse, and D. Tresemer (2001). *Signs in the Heavens: A Message for Our Time.* Boulder: www.StarWisdom.org.

Buhler, W. (1958, 1962,1967, 1973, 1980). *How to Overcome Sleeplessness.* Sussex, England: New Knowledge Books.

**Ad Dekkers and Henriette Dekkers-Appel are leading the development of anthroposophic psychology internationally.

Dekkers-Appel, H. & Dekkers, A. & Meuss, A. (2001). *Psychotherapy and Humanity's Struggle to Endure: Anthroposophical Approaches.* Goetheanum, Dornach: Medical Section of the School of Spiritual Science.

Dekkers, Ad, with H. Dekkers-Appel (in publication) *A Psychology of Human Dignity*, Great Barrington, MA: SteinerBooks.

**Dunselman, R. (1993, 1995). *In Place of the Self: How Drugs Work.* Gloucestershire, U.K.: Hawthorn Press. This is the best description of the energetic, psychic, and spiritual effects of many different substances, showing how they displace the "I" of the human being.

**Glöckler, M. (1997). *Medicine at the Threshold of a New Consciousness.* London, England: Temple Lodge Publishing. Michaela Glöckler has given speeches and papers that can be found in several places. Here is a major statement of her work.

Goldberg, R. (2012). *Addictive Behaviour In Children and Young Adults: The Struggle for Freedom.* Edinburgh, England: Floris Books.

Kaine, K. (2007). *I Connecting: The Soul's Quest.* Canada: Goldenstone Press.

**Klocek, Dennis. Any of Klocek's writings, even on apparently unrelated topics such as climate and agriculture, are full of insights that pertain to anthroposophic psychology.

**Karl König has written the most accessible pathways into anthroposophic psychology. *The Human Soul* is a fundamental text for his approach. *A Living Physiology* deals with the twelve senses and the four organ systems introduced in chapter 3.

König, K. (1973). *The Human Soul.* Spring Valley, NY: Anthroposophic Press.

König, K. (1989). *Being Human: Diagnosis in Curative Education.* Hudson, NY: Anthroposophic Press.

König, K. (1999). *A Living Physiology.* Camphill Books.

**Georg Kuhlewind has given many books on working with consciousness. More at APANA-services.org

Kuhlewind, G. (1976, 1984). *Stages of Consciousness: Meditations on the Boundaries of the Soul.* West Stockbridge, MA: Lindisfarne Press.

Kuhlewind, G. (1983, 1988). *From Normal to Healthy: Paths to the Liberation of Consciousness.* Hudson, NY: Lindisfarne Press.

**Bernard Lievegoed's work on the development through life stages is pure anthroposophical psychology.

Lievegoed, B. (1979). *Phases: Crisis and Development in the Individual.* London, England: Rudolf Steiner Press.

Lowndes, F. (1996). *Enlivening the Chakra of the Heart.* London, England: Sophia Books, Rudolf Steiner Press. Lowndes analyzes and amplifies some of Steiner's recommended meditations in great detail.

**Though mostly known for his work with the living soil, Pfeiffer was a Renaissance man that contributed in many fields.

Pfeiffer, Ehrenfried. (1982). *Heart Lectures.* Spring Valley, NY: Mercury Press.

Pietzner, C. (1993). *Inner Development and the Landscape of the Ego.* Glenmoore, PA: Camphill Publications.

**Romero, Lisa (2014). *The Inner Work Path: A Foundation for Meditative Practice in the Light of Anthroposophy.* Great Barrington, MA: SteinerBooks. We use this book to introduce students to personal practices, which Romero introduces thoroughly.

**Robert and Cheryl Sardello continue to write and to offer workshops on anthroposophy and anthroposophical psychology made practical. Note his important editorial remarks in Steiner's *A Psychology of Body, Soul, & Spirit.* Here are two samples of his work:

Sardello, R. (1999). *Freeing the Soul From Fear.* New York, NY: Riverhead Books.

Sardello, R. (2002). *The Power of Soul.* Charlottesville, VA: Hampton Roads Publishing Company.

Schwarzkopf, F. (1997). *Beholding the Nature of Reality: Possibility of Spiritual Community.* Fair Oaks, CA: Rudolf Steiner College Press.

**Virginia Sease, a member of the Board of Directors (Vorstand) of the Anthroposophic Society in Dornach for many years, has written helpful pieces that show anthroposophy applied to the world. This is one example:

Sease, V. & Schmidt-Brabant, M. (2005). *The New Mysteries: And the Wisdom of Christ.* East Sussex, England: Temple Lodge Publishing.

Seddon, Richard, and Jean Brown (2012). *The Wonders of Sleep: An Anthroposophical Study.* Stourbridge: Wynstones. In several books, Richard Seddon has given us detailed and technical anthroposophical analyses of a third of our lives.

Smit, J. (1987). *Spiritual Development: Meditation in Daily Life*. Edinburgh, England: Floris Books.

Steele, R. (2011). *Psychophonetics: Holistic Counseling and Psychotherapy*. Great Barrington, MA: Steiner Books/Anthroposophic Press, Inc.

Steffen, A. (1984). *The Determination of Evil*. Dornach, Switzerland: Verlag Fur Schone Wissenschaften Publisher.

**Rudolf Steiner's every lecture (over 6000 of them) and every book (he wrote a dozen of them) assists you to understand part of anthroposophy. Here is a short list that may be helpful as a beginning. You may wish to begin with those marked with **, though, honestly, any way you can dip into Steiner's work can assist you to understand the larger view of the human being:

Steiner, R. (1944, 1968). *The Four Temperaments*. Spring Valley, NY: Anthroposophic Press.

Steiner, R. (1946, 1967, 1984). *Therapeutic Insights, Earthly and Cosmic Laws*. Spring Valley, NY: Mercury Press.

Steiner, R. (1947, 1960, 1966). *Study of Man*. London, England: Rudolf Steiner Press.

Steiner, R. (1958, 1981). *Man as a Being of Sense and Perception*. Vancouver, Canada: Steiner Book Centre.

Steiner, R. (1964). *The Philosophy of Freedom*. London, England: Rudolf Steiner Press. **The Philosophy of Freedom* (or *Philosophy of Spiritual Activity*) is the foundational work that works into the very psychological issues of percept and concept, memory and forgetting.

Steiner, R. (1969). *Esoteric Science: An Outline*. London, England: Rudolf Steiner Press. **Most of Steiner's work comes back to the Esoteric Science/Outline that he wrote, rather than spoke, about the genesis of our world—because this genesis is relived in every moment, and Steiner explains how this freshness of genesis is here and now. Once one understands this development of whole worlds, one can understand psychology much more intimately.

Steiner, R. (1971). *Theosophy: An Introduction to the Supersensible Knowledge of the World and the Destination of Man*. Hudson, NY: Anthroposophic Press, Inc.

Steiner, R. (1972, 1977, 1994). *Guidance in Esoteric Training: From the Esoteric School*. London, England: Anthroposophic Press.

**Steiner, R. (1980, 1999, edited by Robert Sardello). *A Psychology of*

Body, Soul, & Spirit: Anthroposophy, Psychosophy, & Pneumatosophy. Hudson, NY: Anthroposophic Press. Sardello's editorial comments in this book are very valuable. These are the lectures given in Berlin that form the basis for practical psychology from anthroposophy.

Steiner, R. (1980). *The Origin of Suffering: The Origin of Evil, Illness and Death.* Vancouver, Canada: Steiner Book Center.

Steiner, R. (1990). *Psychoanalysis and Spiritual Psychology.* Hudson, NY: Anthroposophic Press.

**Steiner, R. (1994). *How to Know Higher Worlds: A Modern Path of Initiation.* Hudson, NY: Anthroposophic Press. Often thought of as an introductory work to anthroposophy, and originally a collection of essays that he wrote early in his career, the chapters of *How to Know Higher Worlds* nonetheless offer terrific support for an anthroposophic counselor.

Steiner, R. (2001). *Freud, Jung, & Spiritual Psychology.* Hudson, NY: Anthroposophic Press.

**Steiner, R. & Scala, P. (2008). *Weekly Meditations: Calendar of the Soul.* Great Barrington, MA: Steiner Books. Some find The Calendar of the Soul helpful in their daily meditations.

**Steiner, R. & Wegman, I. (1983). *Fundamentals of Therapy.* London, England: Rudolf Steiner Press. Ita Wegman worked together with Steiner to develop anthroposophic medicine, which overlaps closely with anthroposophic psychology.

**Valentin Tomberg, though the subject of controversy amongst anthroposophists, has to be appraised through experiencing his many contributions, of which this is one:

Tomberg, V. (1985). *Group Work.* Spring Valley: Candeur Manuscripts.

**Perhaps the best overview of anthroposophic psychology:

Treichler, R. (1989). *Soulways: Development, Crises, and Illnesses of the Soul.* Stroud, UK: Hawthorn Press.

**Two examples of star wisdom used in relation to anthroposophy and psychology:

Tresemer, David, with Robert Schiappacasse (2007). *Star Wisdom & Rudolf Steiner: A Life Seen Through the Oracle of the Solar Cross.* Great Barrington: SteinerBooks.

Tresemer, David (2011). *The Venus Eclipse of the Sun.* Brooklyn: Lantern.

Tresemer, David (2012-2015). "A Drinking Problem," in six parts, from *Lilipoh Magazine,* or also at www.Apana-services.org

**Relationships, first with one another, then with Sophia—these books seldom mention anthroposophy yet are completely inspired by it.

Tresemer, Lila, and David Tresemer (2015). *The Conscious Wedding Handbook.* Boulder, CO: Sounds True (formerly One-*Two*-ONE: *A Guidebook to Conscious Partnerships, Weddings, and Rededication Ceremonies.* Brooklyn: Lantern.)

Tresemer, Lila, and David Tresemer, two DVDs showing energy dynamics within the single human being—*Brain Illumination*—and between two humans in relationship - *Couple's Illumination.*

Tresemer, David, and Lila Sophia Tresemer (2014). *The Sophia Elements Meditations,* from www.SophiaLineage.com.

Van den Brink, M. (2004). *Transforming People and Organizations: The Seven Steps of Spiritual Development.* East Sussex, England: Temple Lodge Publishing.

Van den Brink, M. & Stolp, H. (2008). *Time for Transformation: Through Darkness to the Light.* East Sussex, England: Sophia Books.

Van Emmichoven, F.W. (1982). *The Anthroposophical Understanding of the Soul.* Spring Valley, NY: Anthroposophic Press.

Van Emmichoven, F.W. (date unknown). *The Human Soul: In Sleeping, Dreaming and Waking.* Sussex, England: New Knowledge Books.

** Some of Van Houten's Other works are cited in chapter 2.

Van Houten, C. (2011). *Creative Spiritual Research: Awakening the Individual Human Spirit.* London, England: Temple Lodge Publishing.

Vogt, F. (2000, 2002). *Addiction's Many Faces: Tackling Drug Dependency Amongst Young People: Causes, Effects and Prevention.* Gloucestershire, U.K.: Hawthorne Press.

Wehr, G. (1990, 2002). *Jung & Steiner: The Birth of a New Psychology.* Great Barrington, MA: Anthroposophic Press.

Wolff, O. (1990). *The Etheric Body.* Spring Valley, NY: Mercury Press.

Transpersonal Psychology

**Roberto Assagioli's teachings about the will, about disidentification, about sub-personalities, and many other topics—complement anthroposophical psychological approaches.

Assagioli, R. (1965). *Psychosynthesis.* New York, NY: Penguin Books.

Assagioli, R. (1973). *The Act of Will.* New York, NY: The Viking Press.

Clay, P. (2000, 2002). *Reflections on the Will, Part I and II.* Amherst, MA: Association for the Advancement of Psychosynthesis.

Daniels, M. (2005). *Shadow, Self, Spirit: Essays in Transpersonal Psychology*. Charlottesville, VA: Imprint Academic Philosophy Documentation Center, and Imprint Academic in England.

Davis, J. (1999). *The Diamond Approach: An Introduction to the Teachings of A. H. Almaas*. Boston, MA: Shambhala Publications.

De Quincey, C. (2005). *Radical Knowing: Understanding Consciousness Through Relationship*. Rochester, Vermont: Park Street Press.

Edinger, E. (1972). *Ego and Archetype*. Baltimore, MD:Penguin Books.

Ferrucci, P. (1982). *What We May Be: Techniques for Psychological and Spiritual Growth Through Psychosynthesis*. New York, NY: Jeremy P. Tarcher/Putnam.

**Firman and Gila's books each stand on their own, and are all essential to understand how psychosynthesis brings anthroposophic psychology into the modern day.

Firman, John, & Gila, A. (1997). *The Primal Wound: A Transpersonal View of Trauma, Addiction, and Growth*. Albany, NY: State University of New York Press.

Firman, John, & Gila, A. (2002). *Psychosynthesis: The Psychology of the Spirit*. Albany, NY: State University of New York Press.

Firman, John, & Gila, A. (2010). *A Psychotherapy of Love: Psychosynthesis in Practice*. Albany, NY: State University of New York Press.

**Frankl's power of insight comes from his surviving of a concentration camp in World War II, and his observations of humans coping with extreme situations.

Frankl, V. (1971). *The Doctor and the Soul: From Psychotherapy to Logotherapy*. New York, NY: Bantam Books.

Frankl, V. (1985). *Man's Search For Meaning*. Boston, MA: Beacon Press.

**Stanislav Grof is a major force in the re-vision of psychology. We mention here two of his works:

Grof, S. (2000). *Psychology of the Future: Lessons From Modern Consciousness Research*. Albany, NY: State University of New York Press.

Grof, S. & Grof, C. (1989). *Spiritual Emergency: When Personal Transformation Becomes a Crisis*. Los Angeles, CA: Jeremy P. Tarcher, Inc.

Guggenbuhl-Craig, Adolf (1998). *Power in the Helping Professions*. Dallas, TX: Spring Publications. This book challenges the one called to help—to understand the shadow sides of this urge. These insights can be very challenging.

Jacobi, J. (1973). *The Psychology of CG Jung*. London: Routledge & Kegan Paul Ltd.

James, William. (1892). *Psychology: The Briefer Course.* New York, NY: Harper Torchbooks.

**Carl Jung's approaches to the spiritual world complement those of anthroposophy. You can begin anywhere with Jung, including the more popularized versions of his ideas.

Jung, C.G. (1954). *The Collected Works of C.G. Jung.* New York, NY: Bollingen Foundation, Inc. Publishers. Twenty volumes.

Lowen, A. (1990). *The Spirituality of the Body.* New York, NY: Macmillan Publishing.

**Abraham Maslow has written many books and articles, and you can even see him lecture in You-Tube archives. This grandfather of humanistic psychology still sounds fresh and relevant in his approach.

Maslow, A. (1968, 1999). *Toward a Psychology of Being.* New York, NY: John Wiley & Sons.

Mindell, Arnold & Mindell, Amy (1992). *Riding the Horse Backwards: Process Work in Theory and Practice.* London, UK: Penquin Books.

Pierrakos, John C. (1987). *Core Energetics: Developing the Capacity to Love and Heal.* Mendocino, CA: LifeRhythm.

**Carl Rogers's *On Becoming a Person* and his *Client-Centered Therapy* are classics, important historically, and also important to be re-read and learned from today. His *Counseling and Psychotherapy,* published first in 1942, created a huge stir, and set the stage for the discipline of counseling psychology.

Rogers, Carl (1961). *On Becoming a Person: A Distinguished Psychologist's Guide to Personal Growth and Creativity.* Boston, MA: Houghton Mifflin Company.

**Marie-Louise von Franz is a pillar of Jungian psychology. Fairy tales, dreams, and other imaginations are also the province of a psychology informed by anthroposophy.

Von Franz, M. (1974). *Shadow and Evil in Fairytales.* Dallas, TX: Spring Publications.

Von Franz, M. (1977). *Individuation in Fairy Tales.* Dallas, TX: Spring Publications.

Walsh, R. & Vaughan, F. (1993). *Paths Beyond Ego: The Transpersonal Vision.* New York, NY: Jeremy P. Tarcher/Putnam.

**Michael Washburn has written extensively on transpersonal psychology. Here is a sampling:

Washburn, M. (1995). *The Ego and the Dynamic Ground: A Transpersonal*

Theory of Human Development. Albany, NY: State University of New York Press.

Washburn, M. (2003). *Embodied Spirituality in a Sacred World*. Albany, NY: State University of New York Press.

Weiser, J. & Yeomans, T. (1988). *Readings in Psychosynthesis: Theory, Process, & Practice*. Toronto, Ontario, Canada: The Department of Applied Psychology/The Ontario Institute for Studies in Education.

**Not only has Ken Wilber included psychology in his theories of everything—they are fundamental to an understanding of the integral approach to all of reality.

Wilber, K. (2000). *Integral Psychology: Consciousness, Spirit, Psychology, Therapy*. Boston, MA: Shambhala Publications.

OTHER PSYCHOLOGY REFERENCES

Of the many hundreds of books on psychology, these have been especially useful for *The Counselor*. Other one-time references come at the ends of the chapters.

Cashwell, C. & Young, J. (2005). *Integrating Spirituality and Religion Into Counseling: A Guide to Competent Practice*. Alexandria, VA: American Counseling Association.

Childre, D. & Wilson, B. (2006). *The HeartMath Approach to Managing Hypertension: the Proven, Natural Way to Lower Your Blood Pressure*. Oakland, CA: New Harbinger Publications.

Frances, Allen (2013). *Essentials of Psychiatric Diagnosis: Responding to the Challenge of DSM-5*. New York: Guilford Press. And, Frances, Allen (2013). *Saving Normal*. New York: William Morrow.

Allen Frances was head of the team that created the DSM-IV, the version just before the present one. In these recent books, he argues against the trends found in DSM-5. All of his points go in a direction consonant with anthroposophic psychology, though we take the critiques further.

Lederman, Leon, and Christopher Hill (2011). *Quantum Physics for Poets*. Amherst, NY: Prometheus. This has been especially helpful for understanding how mainstream psychology is decades behind the new thinking in physics.

Penrose, Roger (2002). *The Emperor's New Mind: Concerning Computers, Minds, and the Laws of Physics*. New York: Oxford University Press. Penrose's ideas about consciousness as multiple inter-penetrating wave functions are very helpful to wean us from the idea that we are ever a single point present in a single place at a single time, and that we are defined by MRI pictures of physical brain structures.

Ray, P. & Anderson, S. (2000). *The Cultural Creatives: How 50 Million People Are Changing the World.* New York, NY: Three Rivers Press. This sociological study demonstrates the rise in our world of what we call the consciousness soul.

Robert, Tracey, and Virginia Kelly (2015). *Critical Incidents in Integrating Spirituality into Counseling.* Alexandria, VA: American Counseling Association

Rosenberg, M.B. (2003). *Nonviolent Communication: A Language of Life.* Encinitas, CA: PuddleDancer Press.

**Van der Kolk, Bessel (2014). *The Body Keeps the Score: Brain, Mind, and Body in the Healing of Trauma.* New York: Viking. Van der Kolk has been called a "traumatologist." His insights prepare one for the approaches of anthroposophic psychology, as begun in *The Counselor*, by relating trauma to the will, the physical body, and the etheric body.

Whitaker, Robert (2010). *Anatomy of an Epidemic: Magic Bullets, Psychiatric Drugs, and the Astonishing Rise of Mental Illness in America.* New York: Broadway Books. This important study (supplementing his other immense study *Mad in America*) shines a light on the notion of one-pill-fixes-all and finds it wanting. It opens the question of where mental illness comes from, and how we label it and treat it, the very questions that anthroposophic psychology addresses. In its laying open of the too-close connection of pharmaceutical companies and psychiatry, including the framing of the DSM, and the documentation of the creation of an epidemic of mental illness, it sets up the possibility of re-inclusion of soul and spirit.

ABOUT THE AUTHORS

William Bento, Ph.D.

 An active member of the Anthroposophical Society for over 36 years, William Bento has lectured on subjects of cosmology, inner development, community building, and adult education. He has published over 50 articles in Anthroposophical journals in the USA, Canada, England, Germany, and Switzerland. William Bento wrote a column in the LILIPOH magazine entitled, "Meditative Moments." He has co-authored the book, *Signs in the Heavens: A Message for Our Time,* and has written the book, *Lifting the Veil of Mental Illness.* William Bento, along with Dr. James Dyson, has pioneered a seminar on the research and development of an anthroposophic psychology. He has also published books on *The Eightfold Path* and *The Holy Nights Journal* on a yearly basis. He has advanced the ideas of Rudolf Steiner about the human soul under the title of *Psychosophy: A Wisdom of the Soul.* He is currently a clinical psychologist at Folsom State Prison, a consultant and educator for Camphill Curative Communities in North America and the Executive Director of APANA (Anthroposophic Psychology Associates of North America; see APANA-Services.org for further details.)

William enjoys training those working in the helping professions. His capacity to think both in systems and in phenomenological modalities allows him to meet a broad spectrum of needs. He is an avid researcher in the fields of human development and is eager to make a contribution in the area of Transpersonal Psychology. His dissertation topic demonstrated his innovative approach—*A Transpersonal Approach to Somatic Psycho-diagnostics of Personality: A Contribution to its Development, Disorders, and Embodied Transcendence.* The contents of this dissertation have been published by the Vancouver Medical Association in a three lecture series, entitled *You Are How You Move: An Anthroposophical Somatic Approach to Psycho-diagnosis.* William's compassionate and contemplative orientation to working with others is one of his key attributes. His attitude as a seeker and life-long learner is also a noteworthy quality, particularly for working in collegial settings. His goal to research, publish, teach, and practice Anthroposophical approaches in the fields of Adult Education & Transpersonal Psychology are paramount to his professional calling.

Roberta R. Nelson, Ph.D., LPCC, LAC

Born amidst the warmth-conducting copper fields of Montana, raised under the expansive skies of the Minnesota prairie, maturing on a North Dakota organic farm, Roberta brings the fruits of her heart, thought, and will forces to conversations with others. Schooling in counseling, human development, psychosynthesis, and anthroposophy have contributed to her aspirations. She has a doctorate degree in Counselor Education from North Dakota State University where her dissertation focused on incorporating anthroposophy and psychosynthesis in counselor education and training. A doctorate in Counselor Education qualifies her to supervise, educate, and counsel. In addition, Roberta is dual licensed as a Licensed Practical Clinical Counselor (LPCC) as well as a Licensed Addiction Counselor (LAC). Specializing in trauma therapy, Dr. Nelson is employed at a residential treatment facility journeying alongside men and women who have co-occurring diagnoses. In 1997 she founded *ReConnect: A Center for Schooling and Counseling* dedicated to bridging the gap between mainstream mental health, psychosynthesis, and spiritual science. Roberta strives to enliven concepts through a variety of experiential learning activities, designed for the non-artist, fostering a heart-centered approach to psychology. A recent affiliation with APANA (Anthroposophic Psychology Associates of North America) is a continuation of her life-long goal to establish a professional training that would connect contemporary education with the wellspring that lives in esoteric traditions.

Roberta's ongoing commitment to healing and renewal is most recently demonstrated in her founding role in a biodynamic land-based therapeutic initiative arising on her 750-acre family farm.

Edmund Knighton, Ph.D.

Associate Professor and Department Chair, Clinical Psychology PhD/MA programs, and for Marriage and Family Therapy, Somatic, Pre/Perinatal Psychology Concentrations, through The Chicago School of Professional Psychology. Department Chair and Professor, MA in Education for Public Charter School Teachers, Rudolf Steiner College. Organizational Development consultant. Founding Member: Anthroposophic Psychology Associates of North America (APANA). Research: brain development and spatial perception. Faculty and administration of nine graduate institutes and four Waldorf Schools. Currently working on a book on mindfulness in education. PAST: Postdoctorate: Family Systems, Hakomi Body Centered Psychotherapy. Certifications: Conflict Management, Yoga, Spacial Dynamics Movement Therapist, Ropes Course Instructor. Educator for 25 years at early childhood, primary, secondary, graduate levels. Trained in circus arts and drama. K-12 PE teacher for 20 years. High School Humanities/Science Teacher. Created SES 4th-12th grade programs using Kessler's Mysteries Curriculum. Neuropsychological assessment at UC-Davis Med-Center Department of Physical Medicine and Rehabilitation specializing in traumatic brain injury, multidisciplinary medical team biopsychosocialspiritual model.

David Tresemer, Ph.D.

With a doctorate in psychology from Harvard University, Dr. Tresemer has followed many paths of research into the transpersonal realms of consciousness, including the Diamond Heart method of A.H. Almaas, Psychosynthesis with David and Judy Bach, Jungian analysis, Star Wisdom (enlightened astrology), Barbara Brennan Hands of Light training, University of the Seven Rays training, Psychomotor Therapy with Al Pesso, and other techniques attuned to Anthroposophia (the angel mediating the possible human being—anthropos—and wisdom—divine Sophia). He co-founded the StarHouse in Boulder, Colorado, for community gatherings and workshops of various kinds—from music to personal development—in 1989 (complete in 1990), www.TheStarHouse.org. He has led numerous workshops there over the years. He has written in many areas, ranging widely, including purely psychological works (such as *Fear of Success*, and several articles in psychological journals), "spiritual horticulture" (as in *The Scythe Book: Mowing Hay, Cutting Weeds, and Harvesting Small Grains with Hand Tools)*, and star wisdom (as in *War in Heaven: Accessing Myth Through Drama* and the astro-biography of Rudolf Steiner in *Star Wisdom & Rudolf Steiner: A Life Seen Through the Oracle of the Solar Cross)*. Recently he wrote *The Venus Eclipse of the Sun 2012*, concerning the social-psychological impact of a rare celestial event that is still with us. With his wife, Lila, Dr. Tresemer has co-authored the DVD *Couple's Illumination* on energy dynamics in relationship, the DVD *Brain Illumination*, the book *One-Two-ONE: A Guidebook for Conscious Partnerships, Weddings, and Rededication Ceremonies* (to be reissued as *The Conscious Wedding Handbook*), and a trilogy of theatre scripts (which have all been performed in various places). More recently they have pioneered the initiative of the Mountain Seas Arts and Wilderness Community in remote Australia (MountainSeas.com.au), and *The Sophia Elements Meditations* (SophiaLineage.com, with a serialized workbook on that process available from the website). He has also founded the Star Wisdom website (www.StarWisdom.org), and conceived of and wrote the Oracle of the Solar Cross, relating to the heavenly imprint received on a person's day of birth and its consequences for personal development. He has written several articles for the *Journal for Star Wisdom* making the connection between celestial phenomena and social-psychological events on the earth. He has recently written a series on the anthroposophic understanding of the alcoholic for *Lilipoh Magazine,* as well as several articles for APANA (Anthroposophic Psychology Associates of North America, www.APANA-services.org.)

ANTHROPOSOPHIC
PSYCHOLOGY
ASSOCIATES OF

ANTHROPOSOPHIC PSYCHOLOGY ASSOCIATES OF NORTH AMERICA (APANA) is a collaborative research and networking association, which seeks to foster the insights of Rudolf Steiner's views on "Psychosophy," the "wisdom of the soul." Through bringing clarity to the essential principles shaping Anthroposophic Psychology, we are committed to formulating an approach to psychotherapy and counseling that embraces the best practices of the major streams of psychology.

Rather than emphasizing psychopathology as our starting point, we emphasize Salutogenesis, the view of the healthy, developing human soul. We offer embodied practices of mindfulness and *presencing*, and paradigms to guide the counselor in therapeutic processes with a client.

As an association of mental health professionals, APANA is dedicated to:

- o offering workshops, seminars and programs on Anthroposophic Psychology;
- o fostering research into the many dimensions of human consciousness;
- o supporting the emergence of a culture of universality;
- o cultivating enhanced states of consciousness on the part of practitioners;
- o creating a language of soul phenomena for the interested public, students, and professionals alike;
- o promoting a style of education that is experiential, not merely conceptual (to convey the values of Anthroposophic Psychology—a style that relies on integration of artistic mediums, including movement and color).

The APANA-services.org website holds information about courses, events, articles, books, and research projects relevant to advancing Anthroposophic Psychology. There are also Forums, open conversations amongst members who are dedicated to exploring the riddles of the soul in the 21st century. The Forums also provide opportunities for individuals practicing Anthroposophic Psychotherapy and Counseling, to collaborate, network and communicate with one another, sharing research topics, resource materials, and engaging in fruitful dialogues.

To access APANA, please go to www.APANA-services.org.

Mission Statement for APANA

Anthroposophic Psychology:
To guide the becoming human being—Anthropos—through all stages of development and to realize in each person and in community the full potential of freedom of thought, power in action, and warmth of heart.

Inspired by the Spirit of the Time and grounded in the Way of Anthroposophy.

APANA: Anthroposophic Psychology Associates of North America:
To guide those in mental health and other caring professions, educators, and laypersons in discovering together an Anthroposophic Psychology and provide them with a schooling for interpersonal soul-spiritual practise.

Vision & Values:
We live in a very conflicted yet potentially progressive time, a time of chaos, transformation and challenges. To move forward and strive for a healthy present and dynamic future, our healing modalities need to address the Whole Human Being in Body, Soul, and Spirit.